The Sociological Worldview

For my teachers, mentors, and educators

The Sociological Worldview

SAL RESTIVO

Basil Blackwell

First published 1991
First published in USA 1991

Basil Blackwell, Inc.
3 Cambridge Center
Cambridge, Massachusetts 02142, USA

Basil Blackwell Ltd
108 Cowley Road, Oxford, OX4 1JF, UK

Library of Congress Cataloging in Publication Data

Restivo, Sal P.
The sociological worldview / Sal Restivo.
p. cm.
ISBN 0-631-17779-5 — ISBN 0-631-17781-7 (pbk.)
1. Sociology. I. Title. II. Title: Sociological worldview.
HM51.R42   1991
301 — dc20   90-34916
7/8323   CIP

British Library Cataloguing in Publication Data

A CIP catalogue record for this book is available from the British Library.

Typeset in 10 on 12 pt Palatino
by Graphicraft Typesetters Ltd, Hong Kong.
Printed in Great Britain by Billing & Sons Ltd, Worcester

Contents

Acknowledgments

This book is, first of all, for my teachers, mentors, and educators. They encouraged me to ask: "What is *really* going on here?" about everything; to seek explanations in the material world, but never to trust them implicitly; to keep education from deteriorating into training; and to value the ideals of the good person in the good society even when everything around me called for pessimism and cynicism. Most importantly, they showed me the importance of a marginal social role for developing and sustaining a critical perspective on self, society, and world.

This book is also for all my friends who, over the years, have forced me into the "real world" against my better judgment and natural inclinations, and helped me add flesh and bone to the abstractions that guide me through the chaos and labyrinths of everyday life. I owe a very special thank you to my cousin Emily and our rocking chair; without them, this book might never have been written.

And finally, this book is for my parents, May and Phil, who taught me (sometimes unwittingly, to be sure, and always with the assistance of my sisters, Nancy and Emily) the dangers of Authority and the virtues of Disobedience.

Given the subject of this book, this is the appropriate time and place for me to thank my sociology educators: Aaron Noland, Bernard Rosenberg, and Burt Aginsky at the City College of New York; John Useem, Ruth Hill Useem, Jim McKee, Jay Artis, Frank Camilleri, Bill Form, Vince Salvo, and Herb Karp at Michigan State, along with my graduate student friends and colleagues, especially Chris Vanderpool and Frances McCarthy. Many of my students at Michigan State, Wellesley College, and Rensselaer have been my educators as well, especially Marilynn Jones Hildebrandt, Leslie Ehrmann, Pete Bellomo,

Inez Pagnotta MD, Diana Pardew Sandberg MD, and Judy Cusick; and Dr Gil Peach, of whose NYU doctoral committee I was a member. I have learned too from my sons David and Daniel; they have, in an important sense, been my greatest educators.

I have had some very special school teachers, and I would like to remember them here: Mrs DeLio, Mr Rosoff, Mr Lincoln, Mr Quinn, and Mr Sanders.

The preparation and publication of this book have benefited from the advice and encouragement of Julia Loughlin, Randall Collins, Gil Peach, Valerie Alia, and Barry Glassner. I also want to thank Daryl Chubin, Karin Knorr-Cetina, Sharon Traweek, Leigh Star, and Susan Cozzens for continuing to educate me about the nature of society, culture, and human relationships.

My editor at Basil Blackwell, Simon Prosser, appreciated my objectives and my orientation in writing this book, and he has been in all respects supportive of this project from the very beginning. I also want to express my appreciation for Valerie Shepard's copyediting, which was thorough and thoughtful. My friends and colleagues at Rensselaer have provided a truly collegial environment for me to work in for nearly 20 years. Dave Ellison was especially supportive and sensitive as my chair during my years in the Sociology and Anthropology Department, and Shirley Gorenstein, my chair in the Department of Science and Technology Studies which was organized in 1982, has provided constant and consistent support and encouragement for my research. My intellectual life has been profoundly influenced by my friendships with John Schumacher, an STS colleague, and Mike Zenzen of RPI's philosophy department. And staff members Sandy Charette (now with another department), Cathy Burniche, Carol Halder, Marge McLeod, and Therese Landry all helped in one way or another and at one time or another to see this project through to completion.

Finally, it is a great pleasure for me to thank my friend Arlene Sklar-Weinstein for allowing us to use one of her paintings in the cover design for this book.

Introduction:

The Cautious Inquirer

There is a low tradition in sociology that is represented by the motley collection of titles in the sociology sections of shopping mall bookstores. That tradition is also expressed in images of sociology as a "soft science," a form of socialism or social work, and a pretentious jargon that disguises commonsense in the trappings of science. Even the idea that sociology is a "hard science," to the extent that it entails a sexist and scientistic view of the field and stresses formal and methodological concerns over substantive social ones, is part of the low tradition. The uses and abuses of sociology in the interest of the privileged classes, though they can be grounded in a sophisticated appreciation and manipulation of sociological knowledge, are features of the same tradition. And many introductory textbooks, through errors of commission and omission, cater to it. In contrast, this book is an introduction to the high tradition in sociology.

The high tradition in sociology traces its roots to the revolutionary discoveries about society made by Karl Marx, Max Weber, Emile Durkheim, and others between 1850 and 1920. Many readers, even professional sociologists, may find the idea that sociologists and sociological thinkers have made discoveries pretentious at best. But in fact there are many findings in sociology that qualify as discoveries. The works of Weber and Durkheim, for example, include discoveries about the social roots of religion. (It is helpful on this matter to learn from sociologists of science that discovery is not a simple matter of finding something new in the world. It is actually a rather complex social process that involves, among other factors, techniques of communication, and crystallization of the discovery over time.)

The discoverers of society carried out a Copernican revolution that transformed our understanding of self and society. They identified the group as the center of the human universe. This achievement does not subordinate the individual to the collectivity. Rather, it reveals how varieties of individual growth and development, and the formation of different types of persons, are dependent on forms of social organization and culture. Through its influence on the sociology of science and knowledge, the Copernican sociological revolution has also had an impact on our understanding of natural and physical realities. We are, in fact, in the midst of a second sociological revolution that is changing our conception of the nature of knowledge. The seeds of this revolution were planted during the earlier revolution. It is only recently, however, that sociologists have developed the appropriate tools, concepts, and orientations to pursue Emile Durkheim's conjectures on the social nature of logical concepts, and Oswald Spengler's ideas on mathematics and culture.

A new sociology of science has developed during the past 20 years. Sustained empirical research on scientific practice has revealed that dichotomies such as fact and value, theory and practice, and objectivity and subjectivity grossly oversimplify reality. They are not, indeed, separable in any of the usual ways which many people, including intellectuals and scholars, take for granted. The idea that scientists can be value-free or value-neutral has been discredited. All of this does not entail the relativistic conclusions that all modes of knowing are equal, or that we can never really know anything. It does mean that we need to be more sophisticated about evaluating what and how we know. We have to attend to sociological factors that enhance or inhibit our ability to understand and explain our experiences in ways that can appropriately be called objective. Objectivity, however, is not something we can achieve in any final, absolute, or pure sense. We can, nonetheless, improve the degree of objectivity in our knowledge by reducing the number of factors that make it likely we will experience the world in terms of hopes, wishes, illusions, delusions, or hallucinations. We also need to be alert to the extent to which we seek knowledge primarily to temper our fears and calm the terrors that assail us; it is unrealistic to think we can eliminate such factors, but their impact can certainly be reduced. That is one of the functions of education.

We have to constantly be on guard against relying on faith, authority, tradition, narrow self-interest, and implicit assumptions about the reality of some thing or event ("a fact is a fact," "facts speak for themselves"). All or some of these factors will, again to be realistic, play a role in our arguments and explanations, but we should strive to become aware of and to control them. We can do this by orienting ourselves to a critical, explanatory mode of inquiry; evidence should be sought from multiple sources and evaluated in an open-ended, expanding, and reflexive (self-critical) framework, and conclusions accepted cautiously and tentatively. Explanations should be experienced as arising within ourselves. We should never have absolute faith, belief, or trust in anything we feel, do, or think. Everything should be open to criticism and change, including our convictions about sociology. Our aim in inquiry should be a cautious conviction about conjectures based on well-founded evidence. One way to achieve this is to sustain a sense of humor about even our most serious concerns and convictions. A detailed discussion of the sociology of objectivity is outside the scope of this book, but I do address this matter to some extent in chapters 3 and 8.

THE HUMANISTIC IMPULSE

There is a strong humanistic impulse in the high tradition that alerts us to the perils of unbridled authority and unconditional obedience. This impulse can even show up in the works of the more socially and politically conservative thinkers as an unintended consequence of their sociological analyses. That impulse compels us to reveal, resist, and root out all forms of oppression and exploitation of humans by humans, and commits us to improving the conditions under which people live. One of the distinctive features of this book is the extent to which the humanistic impulse pervades my analyses and interpretations. It is not something I merely tack on as an afterthought or separate out as a distinct task or goal. I draw attention to this dimension of sociological inquiry in chapter 3.

SOCIOLOGY AS WORLDVIEW

Sociology can be variously described and experienced as, or in terms of, a discipline, profession, course, textbook, lecture, or statements on a blackboard. I wrote this book because I did not find anything in this variety, or in the public, private, and professional images of the field, that expressed my experience of sociology as a way of seeing and organizing reality as a whole – a worldview. Nor was I satisfied that the best of these presentations and images conveyed the complexities of sociological reality, or the challenges and difficulties of sociological understanding. I have tried to express these complexities and difficulties directly and with a view to recreating in the text the same sorts of challenges we face in the world as we go about trying to make sociological sense of our experiences.

This book can stand alone as an introduction to the sociological perspective, and especially to sociology as a field of inquiry simultaneously concerned with understanding, explaining, criticizing, and improving the human condition. It is not, however, designed to stand alone as a defense of the idea of sociology as a Copernican revolution. I expect that teachers and students, for example, will work on the materials in this book together, criticizing, discussing, expanding, deepening, affirming, disconfirming, and reformulating ideas and concepts in an encounter with sociology in action. I also expect that the book will be read alongside the works of other sociologists, especially those who share my view that sociologists have made revolutionary discoveries about society. Two things should be kept in mind in reading this book: (1) it is *not* created as a recipe for sociological understanding; readers will have to actively work with it to tap its full potential; (2) it *is* designed to appeal to the more general, theoretical, and conceptual aspects of readers' orientations to learning; and to provide resources for sociological thinking and research. But the book is not simply a string of abstractions. It provides opportunities to place experiences in conceptual spaces as well as opportunities to test individual experiences against the experiences depicted in the text.

TOPICS

The topics chosen for this book, especially in the last four chapters, reflect my interests and values, and my reading history. But they all have a role to play in the defense of the thesis of a Copernican revolution.

The first chapter outlines the historical development of the sociological perspective. In chapter 2, key sociological ideas and concepts are introduced in the process of describing the contributions of key figures in the classical period, 1850–1920. Chapter 3 focuses on the value dimensions of sociology, and of science and inquiry in general. This chapter reflects, to a certain degree, a sociological understanding of science and inquiry. The nature and implications of the sociology of science are brought out more clearly in chapter 8. There is a real danger in using the term "science" in a positive sense because of its institutional history since the West's scientific revolution. When I use "science" in a positive sense, I mean the sort of critical inquiry I argue for in this book, and not "science" as a magic formula, an emblem of professional authority, or a tool of ruling-class interests.

The classical sociologists discovered society as a level of reality and an object of inquiry. Chapter 4 provides some of the basic conceptual resources needed to develop a mental picture of, and to understand, that discovery. In chapter 5, I explore the idea of the self as a social structure. This begins our introduction to sociology in action. In chapters 5 to 9, the focus is on illustrating – in different ways and styles, and with varying degrees of difficulty – the sociological perspective.

The chapter on the self illustrates a core concept of sociology as a Copernican revolution; the self is not a single entity manifested in a body, but a set of social relationships. Love is not simply an emotional state, or a property relationship; it is a key to the cooperative imperative in social life. Religion is not just an institution with certain functions; the sociological analysis of religion challenges the assumptions and beliefs of millions of people, believers and unbelievers, atheists and agnostics, about the origins, nature, and functions of the gods. To paraphrase Karl Marx, who said that the critique of religion is the beginning of all criticism, the sociology of religion is in a similar sense the beginning of all sociology. If we cannot understand the profound transformation in our understanding of religion wrought by Marx, Weber, Nietzsche, Durkheim, and others, and the challenge it poses to all sorts of transcendental and supernatural beliefs, we cannot understand or realize the full power of sociology, and our full power as human beings.

The chapter on mathematics explores the power of sociology from another angle. Until relatively recently, even sociologists of science were convinced that scientific and mathematical knowledge was outside their jurisdiction. Mathematical knowledge (along with logic) was the arbiter of the limits of the sociology of knowledge. This was true in spite of Durkheim's speculations on the sociology of logical concepts and Spengler's pioneering analysis of mathematics and culture. Chapter 8 is an introduction to some of the basic ideas in contemporary sociology of mathematics.

The final chapter is designed to draw attention to the global context of everyday life. We are all aware of various external forces that affect us. For some of us, our awareness of the nature and range of these forces does not extend very far beyond our own noses. For others, these forces may extend to friends, communities, regions, and even the international social or political and economic scene. But few of us carry on everyday life with an awareness of the realities of the global and evolutionary contexts of our being. Part of the power of sociology is its capacity to help us see that we are creatures of evolutionary and devolutionary forces that play themselves out over millions of years, and on a global scale. That this way of seeing ourselves is more than just a mental exercise is illustrated in chapter 9.

In each chapter, my objective is to simultaneously (1) analyze, explain, and put in perspective; (2) criticize and evaluate; and (3) suggest pathways to constructive social change. There is no question that pursuing these goals simultaneously complicates the text. Even sociologists who recognize that these three tasks are interrelated try to separate them for the sake of focus, clarity, and simplicity. But this conveys a view of social life and of inquiry that is at best misleading and at worst dangerous (because it can prompt people to behave as if, for example, facts and values are completely independent).

Self, love, religion, mathematics, and ecumene – all may seem beyond the grasp of sociology; the self because of notions of free will and soul; love because it is viewed in terms of spiritual and emotional qualities; religion and mathematics because they are transcendental, pure, or cognitive; and the world because it is beyond our capacity as individuals to relate to it as a context for everyday life. But these are just the reasons why these topics provide crucial tests of and evidence for the power of sociology. Inevitably, in examining these topics sociologically, we will find that our ideas about such notions as free will, emotions, the transcendental, and pure thought will not escape unscathed.

I have dealt with a very small part of the human condition. There are many other aspects of social life that sociologists have studied or will eventually study and bring into critical, analytical focus – death and dying, for example, and the various activities carried out, literally and metaphorically, behind closed doors and in the dark (that part of social life that is loosely analogous to the unconscious). As we continue to carry forward the Copernican sociological revolution, it will become increasingly clear that we must stand on our own without transcendental or supernatural supports, individually and collectively, and rely on ourselves and each other to construct whatever meaning we can for our lives. In the end, we will be able only to turn to ourselves as human beings with our feet on the ground for the resources to survive, and to survive with a reason.

I have drawn heavily on the ideas of Abraham Maslow and other humanistic social theorists to help bring into sociology a positive, secular view of human beings and human potentials. I introduce the idea of self-actualization to counter neutral and bleak views of humans, and to counter the cynicism one can meet when encouraging people to improve the conditions under which they live – their selves, their communities, their world. Some intellectuals and scholars, especially those who claim to view the world objectively, are especially cynical about and distrustful of humanistic programs. Clearly, the humanistic impulse has its dangers and shortcomings. It can be part of a strategy to make the world seem or feel better than it really is or can be. It can be a defense against the terrors, the horrors, the violence of the everyday world. It can be elitist, discarding or denigrating those people who cannot afford the pseudo-self-actualized lifestyles of the rich, famous, and powerful, And it can be part of a strategy used by some people to gain power over and to manipulate others, especially people who have fared badly in our highly competitive society, or who have not developed the strong egos needed to defend against cultism and charlatanism. I do not want to defend, reinforce, or encourage these sorts of distortions. Defending ideas about actualizing human potential is difficult in a world such as the one we live in today, but I do not adopt it as a naive, rosy-colored glasses strategy, nor as a spiritual quest, an alternative religion, or an alternative to religion. When I join Maslow and others in writing about the Good Person in the Good Society, I do so with the understanding that there are many types of self-actualization, many types of good persons, and many forms of good societies. The humanistic impulse is a tool to help us stop taking the social worlds around us for granted, and to learn about them, criticize them, propose alternatives to them, and to create new ways of living and thinking.

In keeping with the global, historical, and cross-cultural orientation of the sociological worldview, I have used the minus sign or BCE instead of BC for dates "before the common era" (while the plus sign, CE, or no sign at all replaces AD to refer to the "common era"). Notations such as − and + and BCE and CE are not common, but are used by globally oriented intellectuals and scholars. I first learned this notation alternative from Joseph Needham, author of the monumental series on *Science and Civilization in China*.

CODA

The high tradition in sociology is not an end in itself. I can imagine, for example, that sociology as a discipline might disappear (compare the way that "natural philosophy" disappeared); and even that new modes and levels of knowing would so transform our understanding of the "social" that sociology as we know it today would vanish (just as Aristotelian physics vanished). Sociology today is a critical part of the intellectual apparatus we need to understand ourselves and the world we live in, and to solve the personal, societal, and ecological problems with which we are faced. But it is also just one path in the high tradition, just one way to pursue and protect the freedom to think and the freedom to control our own everyday lives without the interference of authorities. Everyone engaged in the high tradition is in one way or another busy demystifying, unveiling, revealing, demythifying what lies behind the public images and facades of knowledge and belief. This is not a tradition in which people are awed by or worship mysteries. Things may be mysterious because we do not understand them, or cannot in principle understand them, or because some people have veiled something understandable to protect their own interests. In all cases, uncompromising inquiry is our only choice.

There are some things we are virtually certain never to understand in any meaningful sense. But in the high tradition we do not respond to this by erecting barriers to inquiry; rather, we press forward even where the task seems hopeless. There is nothing else for thinkers in this tradition to do but think – and even to try to think about the "unthinkable."

Because intellectuals and scholars in the high tradition value thinking, questioning, criticism, evaluation, and revaluation they have always been and always will be (certainly for the foreseeable future) at the mercy of thugs and barbarians. And they will always live and work under the dark and oppressive shadow of cosmic indifference to human life and values. How long and how successfully the high tradition can continue to provide a defense of ways of being human cannot be answered. All that can be said is that the high tradition challenges us to do something worthwhile in the world without dominating or hurting others or ourselves, and without being dominated or hurt by others. It provokes us to be accountable to ourselves, to past, present, and future generations, to our communities, and to our planet. To be human: to think well, to think differently – to think at all.[1]

NOTES

1 This concluding reference to *thinking* is borrowed from R. J. Hollingshead's "Introduction" to Friedrich Nietzsche, *Twilight of the Idols/The Anti-Christ* (New York: Penguin, 1968), p. 8.

Part I
Discovering Society

1

Thinking about Society

The sociological perspective is rooted in the fact that we live in societies and within historical periods. This way of looking at ourselves has its origins in that prehistory when people first began to ask questions about the social organization of their lives. In this chapter, I sketch the emergence and development of social thought, and its crystallization into sociology. My objectives are to provide some sense of the way in which we have historically become conscious of the sociological level of reality; and to introduce the sociological perspective by exploring central issues, problems, and ideas in the works of selected social philosophers and the nineteenth- and early twentieth-century founders of sociology. I emphasize definitions and conceptions of the nature and subject matter of sociology in order to illustrate the struggle to establish sociology as a distinct field of inquiry, and to help identify that aspect of reality that is the special province of sociology.

Chapters 1 and 2 are designed to stimulate an initial "feel" for the sociological way of looking at the world. They should not be read as an in-depth history, or a detailed analysis of social and sociological theories. They are an introduction to the historical emergence of the sociological perspective. History is not merely a plaything for antiquarians. Besides being inherently interesting, history is related to the present in several ways: (1) it increases the range of our effective experience; (2) it sensitizes us to the epochs and trends into which we have been born; (3) it is a source of data on long-term patterns (e.g., linear sequences, cycles, and evolutionary and devolutionary patterns which may be historically specific or widely, if not universally, invariant); (4) it opens up pathways to ideas which may have a direct (immediately applicable) or indirect (stimulating) impact on contemporary problem-solving. The last point is important because, even though there may be long-term linear developmental or evolutionary tendencies or directions in human history, short-term and local experiences are clearly not always linear. As a society changes, problems may crop up that are best dealt with, initially at least, using "old" approaches. In the face of the energy crisis, for example, alternative technologies from windmills to aquaculture are drawing on the experiences of human beings in a variety of times and places, including the Chinese of two to four thousand years ago. History is an enlivening and humanizing part of human living; it is also a resource for survival.

PHILOSOPHICAL FOUNDATIONS

The ancient philosophers who flourished between 2,000 and 3,000 years ago were heirs to complex and sophisticated traditions of social inquiry. Their analyses of the nature of the individual, society, and history represent a consciousness of social reality that is at the root of sociology. They developed ideas about social change, drafted programs to deal with social problems, and examined the impact of factors such as the physical environment and the long period of human infant dependency on society. Documents such as the Bible, the Hindu Laws of Manu, Hammurabi's Code, and the Five Books of ancient China are among many codified descriptions, prescriptions, and proscriptions concerning human behavior which manifest consciousness of social reality.

Plato and Aristotle were astute social analysts. They were not sociologists; but they observed human behavior, tried to understand it, developed ideas about the nature of social reality, and proposed ways of improving the human condition. In *The Republic*, Plato discusses the ideal state. A wise person rules this state, and citizens accept and perform their subordinate roles in the interest of creating and maintaining a good community. Plato argues that such a state would tend to degenerate. He identifies the first degenerate state as "timocracy." It arises as a consequence of the usurpation of "rule by reason" by ambition and the love of honor. He goes on to discuss, in turn, the passage of power into the hands of an oligarchy, democracy (of the limited Athenian variety), and despotism. From the standpoint of sociological theory, this attempt to identify types of political systems and processes was premature, and it served conservative political interests; but it represents a type of proto-sociological inquiry based on systematic observations and critical thought.

Aristotle analyzed society in terms of the relationships between parts and wholes. For example, he identified the relationships between a husband and a wife, and between parents and children, as parts of the household. The household, in turn, is part of the *polis*; and "the goodness of the *polis*" is related to "the goodness of children and women." Aristotle's theory of the household is based on conclusions drawn from his observations of political associations. In general, Aristotle is important because he applied an analytic method to the study of the individual and society. He also showed a concern for identifying types of social phenomena, and for defining social and political terms.

In ancient China, Confucius analyzed society in terms of five elemental relationships: ruler-subject, husband-wife, father-son, elder brother and younger brothers, and friends. He also identified five factors which, he contended, explained why the ancient kings provided good government: they honored the virtuous, the noble, and the old; they revered the elders and they were kind to the young. Like Plato, Confucius had a conservative political agenda.

Aristotle, Confucius, and the other ancient philosophers were not sociologists in the modern sense. (They were not philosophers in the modern sense either; terms like "philosopher-merchants" and "philosopher-politicians" would be more accurate). But sociology could not have developed without an awareness of social reality, and of the social patterns that make it possible to theorize about human behavior. The ancient philosophers exhibited this awareness. The continuity between ancient philosophy and modern sociology can be illustrated by examining the question, "Who gets what and why?" Many social scientists consider social inequalities to be universal, that is, present in all human societies. The presence of social inequalities has elicited two types of responses from ancient times to the present: support for the system of social inequalities on the basis that it is just, equitable, and/or inevitable; or criticism and denunciation of the system as unjust and unnecessary. These two viewpoints are often labeled "conservative" and "radical," respectively. In modern sociology, the conservative view has been associated with functionalist or consensus theories, and the radical view with conflict theories. These two modern theoretical orientations in sociology are mirrored in ancient ideas about social stratification.[1]

Among the Hebrew prophets Micah denounced the injustices of the house of Jacob and the house of Israel. The Hindu Laws of Manu the lawgiver (ca. −200) defended caste inequalities. Manu is said to have assigned caste duties to the Brahmans (teaching and studying the sacred Veda), the Kshatriya (military activities), the Vaisya (tending cattle), and the Sudra (serving the other castes). Then, as now, there were disagreements about inequality. The Hebrew prophets had their critics; the Laws of Manu were attacked by Jainists and Buddhists. Aristotle defended private property and slavery, while Plato and Phaleas of Chalcedon advocated forms of "communalism" or "communism." Plato objected to the social inequalities he found in Greece, but not to the idea of social inequality. Phaleas was more radical; he objected to all forms of social inequality.

Jesus is said to have preached a form of communalism that at least implicitly (and perhaps unintentionally) brought into question existing social inequalities. Later, St Peter claimed that slavery was sanctioned by God. In China, a similar conflict emerged between Confucianists and Taoists. Confucianists adopted an ethic of social reform based on prevailing inequalities; Taoists denounced the existing social order, and glorified society as it existed before the decay of the "Great Way."

The beginnings of the sociological perspective are clearly outlined in the concepts, definitions, generalizations, typologies, and ideal social systems conceived by ancient philosophers such as Plato, Aristotle, Confucius, and the Taoist Chuang Tzu. At the same time, two basic modes of inquiry were established. One mode is the root of modern analytic, rational, experimental, mathematical, empirical, hypothesis-testing science; this mode is developed in a variety of classical Greek studies by Hippocrates, Pythagoras, Democritus, Archimedes, Aristotle and others. Aristotle approached politics, ethics, logic, poetry, and oratory in the same way as he approached the study of "natural things" in physics, medicine, and biology. In the East, *ko wu chih chih* ("the attainment of knowledge lies in the investigation of things") has been the watchword of Chinese naturalists and scientific thinkers in all ages. This phrase appeared in The Book of Great Learning (*Ta Hsueh*) about -260.[2]

The second mode of inquiry, widely but erroneously considered an exclusive product and possession of Eastern culture, is passive, wholistic, and directed toward appreciation and wisdom. Tao sage-knowledge, or no-knowledge, is oriented to *Wu*, "non-being" that transcends events, qualities, shapes, and time. In contrast to the analytic scientist, a detached, disinterested, objective spectator who explores by breaking wholes down into analyzable elements, the Taoist participates in the oneness, the wholeness of all things. Sage- or no-knowledge has not been a salient feature of Western intellectual history; but there is a Tao-like mode in Western thought, just as the analytic mode is present in Eastern thought. In the West, the Tao mode is evident in Plato's conception of wisdom: the dialogues settle nothing but clarify and enhance everything; treatises are very detailed but leave the essential wisdom untouched. In Epistle VII, Plato writes that he does not, and never will, have a treatise on philosophy because the subject cannot be treated through exposition.

Summary

The biography of the sociological way of looking at things begins in prehistory when people translated their dependence on other people, and their responses to group sanctions and social rituals, into a consciousness of the group. By the time human civilization had advanced to the point we know as ancient history, priests, philosophers, and artists were capable of systematically observing social interaction, and constructing complex explanations for what they observed. At the same time, they carried out their observations and constructed their explanations in terms of two basic modes of inquiry: one way was analytical and elemental (it is considered the prototype of modern scientific method); the other was synthetic and wholistic (it is usually associated with artistic and irrational or nonrational approaches to reality). In some cases, inquiry was used to defend the social status quo; in other cases, it was used to oppose the prevailing social order.

TOWARD A SCIENCE OF SOCIETY

Plato, Aristotle, Confucius, and the other ancients were unsurpassed social observers and analysts for centuries. Important contributions to social thought were, nonetheless, made between −1 and +1300.[3] Between 1300 and 1600, however, major developments in the biography of the sociological perspective occurred. These developments paralleled, to some extent, developments leading to the scientific revolution which began in sixteenth – century Europe. The roots of the idea that there could be a science of society began to take hold. It was during this period that Machiavelli's *The Prince* was published. *The Prince* was published in the sixteenth century and provided a proto-sociological study of leadership. There was more than a hint of the sociological perspective in Machiavelli's works; but they were more political handbooks than examples of systematic sociology. In the same century, Jean Bodin traced the origin and development of society from a primeval family, describing the process of societal evolution with a comprehensiveness unmatched since Aristotle. But the central figure during this period was Ibn Khaldun (1332–1406). His studies of Arab society have been ranked with the anthropological studies of later scholars such as Lewis Henry Morgan. Ibn Khaldun's work is a milestone in the biography of sociology, and his contributions are worth reviewing in some detail.[4]

Ibn Khaldun outlined a science of culture whose subject matter was human association, whose problems were approached through demonstration, and whose goal was to distinguish truth from falsehood in history. This new science was conceived to reflect on and explain history, to be combined with the art of history in order to provide the historian with some knowledge and understanding of the nature and causes of the external events he or she studies.

The three basic principles of this new science were: human existence is dependent on society; the individual and society are related to the physical environment; and the individual and society are related to a spiritual world beyond the perceptible world. The major problem areas in Ibn Khaldun's science of culture were the transition from primitive to civilized culture; the state; the city; economic life; and the sciences.

Ibn Khaldun distinguished humans from other living things by their desires or instincts, and their habits. He viewed culture as a product of human activity, experience, and changes in "primitive" human nature. Culture arises as habitual activities become stabilized and "conventionalized" in social institutions and art. Ibn Khaldun was among the first students of human behavior, if not the first, to try to distinguish between society and culture. At one point in his writings, he defines culture as "human association." But he did not choose society as the core concept for his new science, perhaps because society refers simply to the fact of human association, whereas culture refers to a complex set of habits, organizations, and technologies that are created and destroyed, transmitted and lost over time.

Ibn Khaldun clearly recognized the relationship between basic human needs, the fact of association (society) as a mode of adaptation, and culture as a product of the association of human beings trying to satisfy basic and then higher level needs; but we are still a long way from translating this form of consciousness into an organized field of study.

At about the same time that Ibn Khaldun was carrying out his studies of Arab societies and developing his new science of culture, Ma Tuan-Lin, a Chinese scholar, was developing a sociological history which represented a radical departure from the traditional Chinese historiography of dynasties and military adventures. His comprehensive history of civilization (*Wen Hsien Thung Khao*), notable for its emphasis on causality in history, had much in common with Ibn Khaldun's science of culture.

Summary

During the period 1300–1800, the consciousness of social reality characteristic of the ancient philosophers was developed further. The budding scientific revolution was already having an impact on scholarship, and the idea of a science of society began to take root. The most important figure in the biography of sociological perspective during this period, Ibn Khaldun, outlined a science of culture.

THE SOURCES OF MODERN SOCIOLOGICAL PERSPECTIVE

During the period 1400–1900, a variety of social philosophies developed, some elements of which ultimately converged in the crystallization of sociology as a distinct field of study and profession. One stimulus for the development of sociological thinking was the idea of the social contract. Proponents of the social contract sought to establish the conditions under which human beings achieved the transition from pre-social existence to society.

In the sixteenth century, Richard Hooker argued that society was a product of a deliberate attempt by human beings to change the conditions of their pre-social lives. This idea had been proposed more than a century earlier by Aeneas Sylvius. The classic statement of this idea was given in the seventeenth century by Thomas Hobbes, who posited a pre-social state of nature characterized by a war of everyone against everyone. Hobbes probably did not believe in this pre-social state literally; rather, his imagery reflects his understanding of human psychology in relation to social conditions. Hobbes, sometimes referred to as the father of social psychology, believed that the agreement among people to unite for their mutual benefit took the form of an irrevocable assignment of their individual powers to an all-powerful sovereign. Without such sovereignty, supported by contract, human life would degenerate into its pre-social state of brutality. Hobbes' theory, while an important contribution to the evolution of sociological consciousness, was basically an explanation and justification of royal absolutism.

A second source of modern sociological consciousness was the idea or theory of progress. This idea was developed in the works of a number of seventeenth and eighteenth century scholars.[5] It played an important part in the works of Saint-Simon and Auguste Comte, two major figures in the nineteenth – century crystallization of sociology. In its simplest form, the idea of progress reflects the belief that modern society has progressed (evolved, or developed) from ancient and more primitive stages, and is destined to continue to evolve to higher stages. Some scholars viewed this process as a cycle; some, like Vico, conceived it as a spiral. Progress was sometimes viewed in terms of the cumulative nature of science and industry. Kant discussed moral progress, Herder formulated laws of progress based on the relationship between nature and God, and Godwin defined progress as a consequence of abolishing private property and promoting rationality in human affairs. The keynote of the idea of progress was an optimism about human and societal perfectability.

A third source for sociological thinking was utopian literature. Plato's *Republic* is sometimes referred to as the first utopia in Western literature. Plato, like the utopians who followed him, combined intuition, imagination, empirical facts, and logic to construct his republic. Over the centuries, this combination contributed to the development of increasingly systematic ideas about society. Among the more interesting of the utopias was Tommaso Campanella's *The City of the Sun* (1623). His idea of a society based on principles of power, love and intelligence anticipated contemporary ideas in humanistic social science.[6]

In the eighteenth century, the transition from social speculation and philosophy to sociology began with such contributions as Vico's theory of progress and his approach to the study of "primitive" society, and the contributions of Berkeley and the social reformers who were influenced by Newton's papers. In *The Principles of Moral Attraction*, Berkeley tried to apply Newtonian mechanics to the study of social processes. Some of the key contributions to sociological consciousness during this period are sketched in box I.

There were other contributions to the increasing systematization of ideas about society and its elements. The Physiocratic doctrine of laissez-faire individualism, and the Cameralist thesis that the good society requires general state controls, focused attention on economic factors.[9] In political theory, Romanticists developed a conservative, even reactionary, politics.[10] But they focused attention on the "natural-

I THE WORKS OF MONTESQUIEU, MALTHUS, HUME,
AND FERGUSON

Montesquieu's *Spirit of Laws*, published in 1748, has been called "the first great, objective and descriptive treatise on sociology."[7] Malthus published his *Essay on Population* in 1798. He proposed two basic hypotheses in this influential volume: (1) population tends to increase geometrically, and food supply arithmetically; and (2) population tends always to put pressure on the capacity of the basic means of subsistence to provide sustenance. He identified positive (war, pestilence, and starvation) and negative (postponement of marriage, and moral restraint) checks on population. Hume made some progress toward a psychological sociology in his critique of the social contract doctrine. He argued that society has its origins in the sexual instinct, not in deliberate self-interest; that it develops under the influence of emotions and feelings; and that it eventually becomes directed by intellect. Adam Ferguson brought together high – level descriptive and analytical powers in his attempt to study society "as it is," and argued that the basic social fact is human sociability based on instinct and utility. He has been referred to as the "first real historical sociologist."[8]

ness" of social institutions, and their sociocultural foundations. Legal theory, comparative law, historical jurisprudence, and legal rationalism provided a background for Cesare di Beccaria's *Essay on Crimes and Punishment* (1764), a milestone in the history of criminal law reform.

Western colonial explorations and expansionism were also a factor in the development of the social sciences. European contact with different cultures stimulated comparative studies in ethnology, religion, ethics, and politics. Much of this work reflected administrative and not intellectual needs. But the work nonetheless was a foundation for the later emergence of anthropology, as well as sociology.

The commercial revolution of the age of exploration and colonization waned, giving way to an even more far-reaching transformation of Western society, the industrial revolution. Sociology was born out of the turmoil of this transformation. The misery and suffering that accompanied changes in the political and economic structure of European society stimulated a wide variety of proposals for social reform.

These proposals were linked to arguments for a social science to guide reform. Sociology was established as a distinct field of inquiry in nine-teenth – century France. The concept of society as a unit of analysis and an independent entity was outlined by Saint-Simon in his pro-gram for a social physics, or social physiology. The symbolic if not the literal birth of the discipline came when Auguste Comte coined the term *sociologie* in 1838.

One of the unheralded sources of the sociological perspective is working-class culture. From the late eighteenth century on, workers responded to intolerable social conditions by joining together in a variety of activities ranging from food riots to highly organized trade unionism. The workers' viewpoint often rested on a sociological found-ation. A supporter of Luddite machine-breaking, for example, wrote a pamphlet defending the idea that it is social conditions and not indi-vidual character that determine our lives. E. P. Thompson's *The Making of the English Working Class* may give workers too much credit for their role in social change, but it illustrates the sociological features of work-ing – class consciousness.[11] The anarchists (Michael Bakunin, Peter Kropotkin, Pierre Proudhon, and others) were also busy during the nineteenth century formulating and practising sociology. Their version of sociology reflected their activism in defense of liberty and in opposi-tion to authority. This is a much needed antidote for the widely held notion that sociological perspective emerges amidst the industrialists and their apologists.

The role of women in the history of sociology has yet to be documented. When that history is written, we will have a better appre-ciation and understanding of women's achievements in this field. Har-riet Martineau (1802–1876) will be a prominent part of that history. Graduate students in sociology are likely to hear about her sooner or later even if they do not actually read any of her writings, or at least learn about the scope of her interests through the titles of her various articles and books. Her book *Society in America* (1837) included an ex-tended analysis of the position of women in society. She argued that, "If a test of civilization be sought, none can be so sure as the condition of that half of society over which the other half has power – from the exercise of the right of the strongest."

Women have certainly played a greater role in the development of sociology and the other social sciences than is generally acknowledged (although the situation is improving for the history of the physical and natural sciences). But it was women who, like Martineau, were con-cerned with "the woman question," women's rights, and feminism who played a central role in formulating the sort of sociology I argue for in this book. Martineau's ideas on the position of women in society were the basis of her understanding of society. "It could be said," Dale Spender argues, "that at the dawn of sociology, a woman was there, helping to shape the discipline and helping to establish the visibility and centrality of women in any analysis of society."

> Had Martineau's thesis on women been taken up, explored and refined within the social sciences – as many of her other theses have been appropriated but without due recognition as to their origin – over the last 140 years, we would not today be required to confront exclusively male-controlled and defined disciplines which are passed off as pertaining to the human condition.[12]

Summary

From the Renaissance onwards, Western society underwent a series of large-scale transformations: the Reformation, the commercial revolution, the scientific revolution, and the industrial revolution. The rise of science was interpreted by many Europeans as a promise of a general methodology for identifying and solving problems. At the same time, rapid and large-scale social changes stimulated an increased awareness of the problematic nature of social reality. The industrial revolution meant radical increases in the productive capacities of machines and people, and the promise of vastly improved living conditions among all social classes. But this promise made the human costs of the industrial revolution highly visible and, for some humanitarians, intolerable. Programs of social reform were proposed to deal with the problems of human misery and suffering that accompanied the rapid industrialization of Europe. Given the rate and scale of scientific and technological successes during this period, it is not surprising that the calls for social reform became linked with the calls for a science of society. It was in this atmosphere that the crystallization of sociology began.

THE CRYSTALLIZATION OF SOCIOLOGY

The emergence of sociology as a distinct field of inquiry reflects the distinctiveness of the social level of reality. In order to appreciate this distinctiveness, it is useful to follow the founders of sociology and observe how they struggled to define and clarify the nature of their new discipline. The emphasis throughout this book is on sociological

---

II   SAINT-SIMON'S SCIENCE OF SOCIETY

1. Science is distinct from art in all types of knowledge;

2. The sciences can be arranged in a hierarchy of increasing complexity; the science of society (variously referred to as *la science politique, la physique sociale, and la physiologie sociale*) is the newest and most complex of the sciences;

3. The science of society must be derived from an inductive history and observations, and must be conceived in terms of development and progress in society;

4. The law of progress, formulated by Turgot and Bourdin, expresses the psychological evolution of the human race through three stages: conjectural, miconjectural, and positive. This idea was later stated by Comte as the Law of the Three Stages: theological, metaphysical, and scientific (or positive). This law became the basis of some sociological theories of progress;

5. A new morality must be based on the realities of social life, not on supernatural sanctions; human happiness must be achieved through a transformation of social conditions on earth, not in heaven;

6. The transformation of society requires a new social, political and economic system, and the unification of Europe in a new Christian fraternity, *le nouveau christianisme*.

---

perspective – the sociological way of looking at things. In this section, I outline some of the basic characteristics of this perspective, and sketch its development from Saint-Simon's proposals for a social physics to the debate in sociology and anthropology about the "reality" of society and culture.

Saint-Simon

Saint-Simon (1760–1825) expressed the intellectual impact of the industrial revolution and the emergence of social science movements. His ideas about the science of society are summarized in box II.

Saint-Simon's "new society" was to be controlled by industrial experts under the direction of a social scientific elite. It is of more than passing significance to note how many great social thinkers, up to and including the founders of sociology, have expressed concern about social disorder and sought in their philosophies and sciences to prepare a plan for achieving social stability; and to note further how invariably the rulers of the new order were created in the image of the person or persons who conceived the plans. In his *Republic*, Plato attempted to create an orderly society free from the turmoil that had led to the collapse of Athens in the Peloponnesian War. The rulers of the Republic were philosopher-kings. Confucius outlined a system of social order in response to what he perceived as intolerable conditions of conflict and oppression in 5th-century BCE China. The Confucian order was to be ruled by men of character and wisdom.

Saint-Simon and Comte were concerned with reconstructing the social order that was emerging out of the revolutionary turmoil of the late eighteenth and early nineteenth centuries, particularly the French Revolution and its aftermath. They envisioned a society ruled by sociologist-priests. Durkheim, too, was concerned with ascertaining the conditions for social order. Critics have correctly pointed out the generally conservative bias in this orientation; but this orientation also anticipates attempts to apply social science to the problem of organizing human beings in ways that will facilitate survival and evolution.

Saint-Simon believed that science, as developed and practised by physical scientists, could be applied to the study and improvement of society. This belief was based on a conception of society as an entity amenable to scientific control. Saint-Simon argued that society is an "organized machine." His formulation of the concept of society had the virtue of drawing attention to society as an object of systematic inquiry; but the emphasis on its existence apart from real people led to many difficulties in expressing and interpreting the nature of society. Was society a collective mind, a supra-individual, a super-organic entity, a mental construct, or an abstraction from the activities of living individuals? We will follow this controversy as we explore in this and the following chapter the early attempts to establish sociology.

It now remained for Comte, greatly indebted to Saint-Simon and his followers, to systematize the ideas of sociology as a separate science in his positive philosophy.

Auguste Comte

Auguste Comte (1798–1857) is widely referred to as the founder of sociology. There are other claimants to this title, including Ibn Khaldun. Saint-Simon, himself more an organizer than a creator of ideas, formulated the theses that Comte systematically organized – or, as one sociologist has put it, "ungraciously plagiarized."[13] Durkheim credits Saint-Simon with the ideas, words, and outline of the positive philosophy Comte began publishing in 1817; the positive philosophy was the foundation of sociology. On this view, Comte is sometimes referred to as the "godfather" rather than the "father" of sociology.

Saint-Simon had originally called for a new social science based on the conception of society as a separate and distinct entity and unit of analysis, outside the province of physical, natural, and psychological sciences. Comte was his employee, colleague, and friend from 1817 until a publication dispute severed their friendship in 1824. Comte's intellectual debt to Saint-Simon is clear. His claim to the title "father of sociology" rests on his attempt to develop a coherent and comprehensive sociology, and not incidentally on his introduction of the word "sociology" (*la sociologie*) in 1838 to replace "social physics." From that point, the development of sociology as an autonomous field of inquiry proceeded rapidly. The University of Chicago established the first American department of sociology in 1893; three years later, Chicago began publishing the *American Journal of Sociology*. In 1898, Durkheim began publishing *L'Année Sociologique* at Bordeaux; in 1913, the first French university chair in sociology was established for Durkheim at the Sorbonne. He was named Professor of the Science of Education and Sociology. The American Sociological Society (later the American Sociological Association) was founded in 1905.

Comte was an important link between utopian socialism and the emergence of academic sociology. He grew up in the midst of widespread revolutionary turmoil, and conceived a new type of social order emerging out of this turmoil based on his understanding of the laws of historical change. The function of sociology, Comte maintained, was to contribute to this understanding; sociology was not merely another science. First, its development coincided with what Comte (following Saint-Simon and others) viewed as an evolutionary progression of all forms of knowledge through three stages: the theological, or fictitious; the metaphysical, or abstract; and the scientific, or positive. In the theological stage, causality is conceived in terms of the immediate actions of supernatural entities. In the metaphysical stage, abstract forces are substituted for supernatural ones. And in the positive stage, the search for absolutes is abandoned, and the laws of nature are uncovered through the application of scientific methods.

The positive philosophy Comte developed was viewed in terms of the evolutionary development of a "physics of nature." Celestial physics, terrestrial physics (mechanics, chemistry), and organic physics (biology, zoology) had already been established. One more "physics" was needed to logically complete this system: social physics, or sociology.

Comte followed the model of physics in distinguishing social statics (the analysis of the structure of society at some given point in time) from social dynamics (the discovery of the laws of human, mental, and societal evolution). He visualized a social system composed of social elements. Following Leibniz's dictum, "the present is big with the future," Comte conceived the history of society as a series of states, each necessarily following the prior state, and inevitably developing toward the next. In nature, social phenomena are the most complex; within the social world, each of the three classes of subject matter in sociology – the individual, the family, and the society – represents a new level of complexity.

Comte classified the methods of sociology as indirect (those that apply to all sciences) and direct (those peculiar to sociology). He argued that social phenomena are not amenable to direct experimentation; but "spontaneous alterations" allowed the possibility of indirect experimentation. In biology, Comte argued, pathological cases can be substituted for "pure experimentation." Pathological cases in the social world (e.g., criminal behavior) are the functional equivalent of experiments which cannot, because of such factors as size, complexity, and values, be designed and carried out by the sociologist. Comte argued that all living things must be studied using the comparative method; the higher the organism in the hierarchy of living things, the more important comparative method becomes.

Comte conceived sociology as the objective (scientific, positive) attempt to discover the basic laws of social structure and social evolution. Sociology was at the top of the hierarchy of the sciences; mathematics, the simplest and least inclusive science, according to Comte, was placed at the bottom of this hierarchy; next, in order of increasing complexity, came astronomy, physics, chemistry, biology, and finally sociology, the most complex and inclusive science. Sociology was a predictive science, intimately associated with the goal of reconstructing society. It is necessary to know in order to predict, Comte wrote, and necessary to predict in order to control (*Savoir pour prévoir, et prévoir pour pouvoir*). Other salient aspects of Comte's sociology were (1) an argument against social contract; (2) a view of egoism and altruism as opposite sides of the coin of human nature; (3) a postulate on the universality and immutability of social laws, a necessary condition for predicting the general direction of social evolution, rates of social evolution, and the nature of social order; and (4) the postulate of inequality: human beings are neither equal nor equivalent.

In the latter part of his life Comte devoted more and more energy to establishing the identity between sociology (the science of humanity), and the religion of humanity which was to become the moral basis for the new social order (an echo of Saint-Simon's "new Christianity"). This development in Comte's sociology may have been stimulated by his brief, tragic, and Platonic relationship with Clotilde de Vaux, who died in 1846.[14] In any event, this turn of events led an otherwise admiring J. S. Mill to describe Comte as "morality intoxicated." The triumph of science and the emergence of exaggerated versions of science such as positivism, had become associated with removing questions of ethics, morality, and human values from inquiry. Comte's moralism underscored the assertion that the founder of positivism was the least positive of scholars. But, in a sense, Comte anticipated critics of value-free science who have argued that science and values are inseparable, and further that science should be tied to understanding and improving the human condition. In his later years, Comte placed ethics above sociology at the top of his hierarchy of the sciences.

Two aspects of Comte's thinking must be emphasized because of their profound consequences for the early and later history of sociology. One was his positivistic perspective. The positivists argued for the adoption of the methods of physical science in the study of social phenomena. They:

1 believed in a universe ordered by invariable and discoverable natural laws;
2 focused on the phenomenal world, the world immediately accessible to our basic senses;
3 ignored the supernatural;
4 believed in the mutability of the social (more generally, the external) order;
5 exhibited optimism in their theories of social progress, but ignored the theological roots of optimism;
6 subordinated material to intellectual power;
7 were concerned with organic truth, useful knowledge, facts, precise knowledge; and
8 believed that their approach must lead to universal acceptance of their discoveries and plans for social action.

Their idea that society could and should be studied scientifically was basically sound. But they often applied this idea rigidly, uncritically forcing social phenomena into the conceptual and methodological frameworks of physical science.

The second aspect of Comte's thinking that needs to be emphasized is his sociologism (or, negatively, his anti-psychologism). The word "sociologism" refers to a synthesis of positive method with the conception of society as a reality *sui generis*. The social philosophers DeBonald and DeMaistre are credited with introducing this idea into French social thought. They argued for the primacy of the social over the individual: the individual is constituted of the social group. Culture and the "higher values" are group products; and social statics and dynamics are collective processes which are not and cannot be produced, affected, or modified by individual wills. They viewed society (with Saint-Simon and Comte) as a "Great Being," amenable to a strictly conceived scientific inquiry.

In part, the exaggerated emphasis on the primacy of the group was related to the more reasonable enterprise of establishing the validity of a sociological perspective against the rival claims of philosophy, psychology, economics, history, theology, and other human studies. No social scientist was more vigorous in his attempt to establish the validity of sociological inquiry – especially in opposition to psychological explanations of social phenomena – or more successful in giving witness through research to the power of sociological analysis, than Emile Durkheim. We will see that Durkheim, the sociologist's sociologist, was, like Saint-Simon and Comte, caught up in the moral questions of establishing and maintaining social order, with the result that his sociology too became tied to religion.

Whatever claims Saint-Simon and Comte, and other thinkers I have discussed or mentioned in this chapter, have on our attention as founders of modern sociological thinking, the people discussed in the following chapter were among those who established the foundation for the sociology discussed at today's professional meetings, written about in today's textbooks, and taught in today's universities. Some, like Durkheim and Weber, are universally recognized for their roles in this development. Others, like Morgan, are somewhat marginal in terms of their actual influence on what modern sociologists do. I have focused on those social theorists more or less within the mainstream history of sociology who I think made the most important contributions to sociology as a perspective.

NOTES

1 G. Lenski, *Power and Privilege* (New York: McGraw-Hill, 1966), chapter I.
2 J. Needham, *The Grand Titration* (Toronto: University of Toronto Press, 1969), p. 282.

3 The following thinkers and schools of thought would figure prominently in a detailed history of social thought in this period: Cicero, Seneca, Plotinus, Christian leaders from Paul to Augustine and Aquinas, Dante, and the neo-Confucianists. For more information on these thinkers and others discussed in this chapter, see H. E. Barnes (ed.), *An Introduction to the History of Sociology* (Chicago: University of Chicago Press, 1966).

4 For an introduction to Ibn Khaldun's ideas, see Muhsin Mahdi, *Ibn Khaldun's Philosophy of History* (Chicago: University of Chicago Press, 1964).

5 For example, Bernard de Fontenelle, Perrault, Helvetius, Vico, and the Abbé de Saint-Pierre.

6 See the critical discussion of this work by William J. Gilstrap, and the translated excerpt in chapter 19 of G. Negley and J. M. Patrick (eds), *The Quest for Utopia* (New York: Anchor Books, 1962).

7 H. E. Barnes, "Social Thought in Early Modern Times," in H. E. Barnes (ed.), *An Introduction to the History of Sociology* (Chicago: University of Chicago Press, 1966), p. 46.

8 Barnes, 1966, p. 57.

9 The Physiocrats were an eighteenth-century school of political economists founded in France. They believed land was the source of all wealth. The Cameralists were eighteenth-century German public administrators who promoted mercantile policies that strengthened the powers of the ruler.

10 Burke, DeBonald, DeMaistre and others.

11 *The Luddites, Three Pamphlets, 1812–1839* (New York: Arno Press, 1972); E. P. Thompson, *The Making of the English Working Class* (New York: Vintage, 1966).

12 Dale Spender, *Women of Ideas and What Men Have Done to Them* (London: Ark Paperbacks, 1983), pp. 175–6; Gayle Graham Yates (ed.), *Harriet Martineau on Women* (New Brunswick, NJ: Rutgers University Press, 1985).

13 I. Zeitlin, *Ideology and the Development of Sociological Theory* (Englewood Cliffs, NJ: Prentice-Hall, 1968), p. 57.

14 R. Aron, *Main Currents in Sociological Thought*, vol. I (New York: Double day-Anchor, 1968), p. 79.

2

A Biography of Sociological Perspective

Emile Durkheim

Emile Durkheim (1858–1917) has been referred to as "the second inventor of sociology."[1] Comte first invented sociology by naming it and systematizing its scientific (positivistic) program; Durkheim invented sociology as an autonomous academic discipline. His research illustrated the power of sociological reasoning; he founded *L'Année Sociologique*, an outlet for sociological reports; he gave the first sociology course in a French university (at Bordeaux in 1887); and he held the first French university chair in sociology (at the Sorbonne in 1913). Durkheim was rigorous, diligent, and often polemical in his presentation and defense of sociology as a level of analysis in its own right, irreducible to other (especially psychological) levels. Like Comte, Durkheim emphasized the need for consensus in society, stressed the moral nature of social order and harmony, and viewed society as a supra-individual, quasi-religious order.

In *The Rules of Sociological Method* (1895), Durkheim outlined the science of social phenomena. The social level of reality, he argued, is made up of "social facts;" and social facts are things just as physical facts are things. This does not mean that social facts are material things. Durkheim conceived things in general to be objects of knowledge, and sources of observational and experimental data.

Society, according to Durkheim, is different from and external to individuals in the same way that the living being is different from the material substances of which he or she is composed. Social facts are qualitatively different from psychological, or individual, facts; they have their own laws.

One of Durkheim's major contributions to sociological thinking was his conception of statistical averages (e.g., rates of suicide, or marriage) as expressions of "l'âme collective," the "collective consciousness." The French Phrase, "conscience collective" connotes common *consciousness* and common *conscience*; Durkheim viewed the social order as a moral order.

Individual phenomena, according to Durkheim, are determined by social phenomena. For example, Durkheim illustrated the existence of social forces which determine the rates and types of what superficially appears to be a random, individualistic phenomenon, suicide. Suicide rates, he argued, are a function of the degree to which individuals are integrated into social groups: free thinkers have the highest rate; Protestants the next highest; Catholics a lower rate; and Jews the lowest rate. "Egoistic suicide" is the result of a social situation in which the individual is poorly integrated into the activities of a group. "Altruistic suicide" occurs when the individual is so tightly integrated into a group that he or she can give up his or her life for some collective "cause." Finally, Durkheim identified a third type of suicide, "anomic," which results from the deregulation, or "normlessness" characteristic of periods of social disequilibrium (e.g., a sharp, sudden increase or decrease in economic fortunes).

Durkheim argued that certain social forces create suicidogenetic currents. Variations in psychological constitution among individuals make some of them more, and some less, susceptible to these currents. Every society includes individuals whose "nervous degeneration" establishes them as potential suicides. Only a certain number of these individuals will actually commit suicide. The ones who do, according to Durkheim, will be those who have been nearer society's "pessimistic currents" and who have therefore felt their influence more strongly. He also considered the problem of why individuals who will commit suicide at some future date are "provisionally spared." The suicidogenetic currents in society penetrate individuals gradually. The tendency toward suicide varies directly with age; Durkheim estimated that this tendency increases ten-fold between birth and old age. He hypothesized, for example, that repeated experiences are needed for an egoist to recognize the emptiness of his or her life.

According to Durkheim, the determination of suicide rates by social forces leaves the free will issue open. Social forces do not affect the suicide of this or that individual. There are various outside forces that must be taken into account when examining a particular suicide. Durkheim conceived of social forces as one of a set of forces that act upon people, the others being physical, chemical, biological, and psychological forces. He pointed out that the individual is born into a situation in which ways of thinking and acting already exist. The individual must reckon with this social reality. Social facts can be modified by individuals, though not easily; and new social facts are generalized by individuals. But each new social fact is the product of the actions of at least several individuals; this joint activity makes the social fact established independent of the unique will of each individual.

Individuals have a sense of acting in accordance with external constraints; certain subjective feelings indicate the existence of group phenomena. Acting out traditional roles, for example, means adhering to established laws and customs which existed before the individual was born. Even if there is no conflict experienced between the roles and the individual's sentiments, the roles still represent an objective reality. The individual does not create the role of mother, father, brother, or sister, but rather inherits them in the process of socialization.

The preceding arguments are the basis for Durkheim's definition of a social fact as "every way of acting, fixed or not, capable of exercising on the individual an external constraint; or again, every way of acting which is general throughout a given society, while at the same time existing in its own right independent of its individual manifestations."[2]

In spite of Durkheim's reference to the significance of psychological and sociopsychological facts, and to the fact that individuals could influence social forces, his sociology has often been labeled "sociologism." The suffix "ism" denotes an overemphasis on social forces to the virtual exclusion of other forces. In his later years, Durkheim placed increased emphasis on the autonomy and reality of "collective representations." Collective representations reflect the history of a social group. The ideas in language are such representations; and their meaning transcends the knowledge of words that any individual can have. The problem with concepts such as "collective representations" or "collective consciousness" in Durkheimian sociology is that they suggest to some people the existence of a "group mind." This issue has been raised periodically in sociology and anthropology with respect to the reality of society and culture. For the moment, I will resolve the issue by considering society and culture as abstract concepts which we use to organize our thoughts about the activities of human beings in groups or collectivities. I will return to this question later.

Durkheim's sociologism has been criticized by some sociologists for its anti-individual bias. While Durkheim was concerned with the liberation of the individual, he tended to see liberation as a matter of understanding and accepting social necessities. This approach subordinated the individual to the state, or society. In a way, Durkheim "religionized" society the way Comte did; society was the sociologist's name for God, the source of morality. Later, I will discuss Durkheim's insight that God is a symbol for society.

Max Weber

Many students of the history of sociology consider Max Weber (1864–1920) the pre-eminent sociologist of the classical period. Weber's most famous thesis, set forth in *The Protestant Ethic and the Spirit of Capitalism* (1904–5), is that the Calvinist ethic in Protestantism was favorable to, and helps explain, the emergence of modern capitalism in the West. Among Weber's other contributions are an outline of the nature and characteristics of bureaucracy and the identification of types of authority. Two of the important methodological bases of Weber's sociology are ideal types, and Verstehen sociology.

The ideal type is an analytical construct which identifies what is typical of a given phenomenon, and stylizes the phenomenon to some extent in order to make the typicalities more distinct. Weber does not use the term "ideal" in an ethical sense; nor does he use it in the sense of an ideal model (as in "ideal gas"), though there is some overlap here. A Weberian ideal type can be variously constructed in terms of varying frames of reference: the ideal type of "liberalism," for example, can be constructed from the point of view of liberals, opponents of liberalism, political scientists, or other interested parties. Briefly, the ideal type is an abstraction that lends conceptual purity to unclear realities. It is, according to Weber, a conceptual construct (*Gedankenbild*). It is neither an historical nor a true reality. Real situations are compared to the ideal type as a limiting concept. Such comparisons allow us to explicate the significant aspects of the situation under consideration, and to identify the objective possibilities inherent in it. An example of an ideal type is given in box III.

Weber conceived *verstehende soziologie* as a sociology designed to let sociologists see social phenomena from the perspective of the social actors studied. This view emphasized the facts that people have minds, and that their actions have meaning. Weber noted the ambiguity of the

III BUREAUCRACY

Weber's ideal type bureaucracy is one of the most influential models of the classical period. According to Weber, a bureaucracy has the following characteristics:

1. Fixed and official jurisdictions, order by laws or administrative rules;

2. A hierarchy of offices and authority; in its fullest development, this hierarchy is monocratically organized (that is, with one overall governor or ruler);

3. A tendency for an office, once established, to continue in existence, even after the task it was established for is accomplished;

4. Management based upon written documents — "the files;"

5. A highly specialized division of labor based on thorough and expert training;

6. A tendency of work demands on officials to expand beyond the time limits established for their positions in the organization;

7. Management based on a more or less exhaustive set of general rules which can be learned;

8. The official, and the office:
   (a) office-holding is a vocation;
   (b) the official enjoys social esteem;
   (c) the official is appointed by a superior authority;
   (d) tenure for life is presupposed;
   (e) the official normally receives a fixed salary, and the security of an old age pension;
   (f) salary is a function of status and length of service;
   (g) the official moves through the stages of a career from low-status, low-salary positions to higher positions;
   (h) the conditions of entry and promotion tend to be fixed in terms of seniority or grades achieved in examinations;
   (i) higher political offices tend to be filled without reference to educational certification because of the importance of considering general personal and intellectual qualities.

term sociology; but he went on to define it as "a science which attempts the interpretive understanding of social action in order thereby to arrive at a causal explanation of its course and effects." Insofar as an individual gives subjective meaning to his or her behavior, that behavior is action. Action can be overt behavior or inward, subjective behavior; with regard to any given situation, action may involve actively intervening, choosing not to intervene, or passively acquiescing. In-so-far as the subjective meaning attached to action takes into account the behaviour of others and is oriented to them, the action is social. Social action may be past, present, or future oriented with respect to the expected behavior of others. It may, for example, be motivated by revenge, defense against aggression, or defense against possible aggression. The "others" may be individuals known to the actor, or an unknown and indefinite collectivity. Money, for example, is accepted in payment because of the actor's expectation that people he or she does not necessarily know will accept it in exchange for goods or services on some future occasion.

Weber identified four types of social action: (1) rational orientation to discrete individual ends (*zweckrational*); (2) rational orientation to an absolute value (*wertrational*); (3) affectual (especially emotional) orientation; and (4) traditional orientation based on habitual behavior. Social relationship is defined as "the behaviour of a plurality of actors in so far as, in its meaningful content, the action of each takes account of that of the others, and is oriented in these terms; it *consists* entirely and exclusively in the existence of a *probability* that there will be, in some meaningfully understandable sense, a course of social action."

Weber goes on to define two types of social relationships, "communal" and "associative," and two types of participation patterns in social relationships, "open" and "closed." The subjective feeling of belonging together is the basis for a communal relationship; a relationship is associative "if and in so far as the orientation of social action within it rests on a rationally motivated adjustment of interests of a similarly motivated agreement." A relationship is open "if and in so far as participation in the mutually oriented social action relevant to its subjective meaning is, according to the system of order, not denied to anyone who wishes to participate and who is actually in a position to do so." Where similar participation is excluded, limited or conditional, the relationship is closed.

A conflictful social relationship, in Weber's *schema*, is one in which a person is oriented to intentionally carrying out his or her will against an other's resistance. "Peaceful conflict" refers to a conflictful relationship free from the actual use of physical violence. "Competition" refers to a peaceful conflict in which actors compete for control over opportunities and advantages. "Regulated competition" implies competition in which ends and means are oriented to a set of rules, or order. Weber also distinguished between "social selection" (struggles for advantages and survival outside of a meaningful mutual conflict orientation) and "biological selection" (differential chances for the survival of inherited characteristics).

Another major area of interest for Weber was the problem of legitimacy and authority, and the conditions of obedience. He identified three pure types of legitimate authority: rational, based on belief in the legality of norms of authority and the right of those in authority to command (legal authority); traditional, based on belief in the sanctity of traditions; and charismatic, based on devotion to the heroic or exemplary character of an individual, and of the normative order he or she reveals or ordains.

Weber emphasized rationality as the defining characteristic of modern capitalism. He defined the spirit of capitalism as an ethic that combined earning more and more money with the strict avoidance of spontaneous and joyful activities. There is, Weber argued, a connection between this ethic and the Calvinist imperative to work hard. Why should people be so devoted to work and money? Weber finds the answer to this question in Benjamin Franklin's autobiographical reference to a Biblical quotation drummed into him by his strict Calvinist father: "Seest thou a man diligent in his business? He shall stand before Kings." (*Prov. xxii, 29*). Weber went on to conclude that the religious view of hard work in a worldly calling as the best path to asceticism and the surest proof of faith was the most powerful lever conceivable for expanding the spirit of capitalism.

Weber speculated on the outcome of the increasing rationalization of economic structures, and indeed of modern culture as a whole, in the closing paragraphs of *The Protestant Ethic and the Spirit of Capitalism*:

No one knows who will live in this cage in the future, or whether at the end of this tremendous development entirely new prophets will arise, or there will be a great rebirth of old ideas and ideals, or, if neither, mechanized petrification, embellished with a sort of convulsive self-importance. For of the last state of their culture development it might truly be said: specialists without spirit, sensualists without heart; this nullity imagines that it has attained a level of civilization never before achieved.[3]

Weber felt obliged to apologize for the intrusion of values in this passage. It is only in these final pages that he refers to the "inexorable power [of material goods] over the lives of men," and to the "iron cage" that care for material goods had become. Weber's values and faith become more obvious as we increasingly encompass the full range of his scholarship. We discover first a common theme, the problem of the uniquely rational characteristics of the modern West, and second an analysis and defense of reason and freedom in Western culture.

Science, as Weber conceived it, could not guide human beings to ends, or true values; it offered, instead, the narrower possibility of gaining insight into our ways of life, and their consequences. This is a conservative view of science and its potential; Weber, unlike Comte and Durkheim in so many ways, exhibited similar strains of political conservatism. He was a strong defender of German national interests, and glorified World War I. Weber has often been described as the "bourgeois Marx." His life's work has been referred to as a debate with Marx. He did not reject the Marxian position, but rather accepted the basic principles of Marx's methodology, clarified and elaborated these principles, and repudiated vulgar and dogmatic versions of Marx's approach.[4]

Weber argued that a theory of stratification must take into account politics and culture as well as economics. In particular, Weber drew attention to the role of cultural hierarchies, especially those based on religion. But a careful reading of his analysis of class (economic stratification), status (cultural stratification), and power (political stratification), and of Marx's analysis of the economic determinants of social life shows that their views of stratification were not very different. This is especially clear when it comes to analyzing capitalism, the virtually exclusive focus of Marx's analysis. Neither Marx nor Weber was an economic determinist in any vulgar sense; and Marx was no more one than Weber. The latter point is often missed by students of Marx and Weber. To see the convergence between Marx and Weber, one has to recognize the broad conception Marx had of "economic determinants" (factors involved in the full range of producing, distributing, and consuming goods and services), and the privileged place of class in Weber's analysis of modern industrial society.

The humanistic ethos is stronger in Marx than in Weber. It is to Marx rather than Weber or any other mainstream sociologist of the classical period that we must trace the roots of a sociology concerned with individual self-actualization and the creation of the good society. Marx's contributions to the sociological way of looking at things will be reviewed later in this chapter.

Georg Simmel

Georg Simmel (1858–1918), like Weber, commented on the chaotic, contradictory, and confusing opinions about the nature of sociology.[5] Simmel tried to cut through the disarray by focusing on the forms of human interaction. He affirmed the relativistic principle that things, including individuals, can be viewed in a wide variety of ways, each justified in its way. In sociology, we increase our distance from individuals to the point where single individuals disappear and society – with its particular characteristics – appears. Society, according to Simmel, is an event (rather than a thing or substance) that involves implicating individuals in each other's lives. Sociology is based on abstracting the concept of society from our observations of concrete reality. It poses the question: What is the effect of groups on what happens to individuals and on the rules that guide their behavior?

Simmel identified two basic problem areas in sociology. One involves studying history insofar as it is formed by society. He refers here to conceptions of historical development beginning in an undifferentiated unity, and proceeding to differentiated manifoldness, and then differential unity (or, as in Durkheim, development from "organic commonness" to "mechancial simultaneousness"). Other questions that arise in this problem area involve the effect of group power on individuals, and value relations between the collectitvity and the individual. The second probelm area, and the one Simmel is generally identified with, is the study of societal forms. Simmel labeled this problem area "pure sociology" (sometimes referred to as "formal sociology"). His discussion of sociability and the significance of numbers in social life illustrates this perspective. Pure sociology involves identifying and independently analyzing form and content in social interaction (even though form and content are inseparable in reality). A third (and peripheral) problem area, "philosophical sociology," involves studying the epistemology and metaphysics of society. General sociology is exemplified by the study of differences between social and individual reality, pure sociology by the study of sociability and society. Simmel's work in formal or pure sociology helped to establish the independence of sociological studies from other approaches to human behavior.

Simmel's sociology rests on two assumptions: that it is possible to distinguish form and content in any society; and drives (e.g., sex) and purposes (e.g., economic gain) are the basis for human interaction; this interaction *is* society. Sociation includes all those things that lead to reciprocity between and among individuals, such as drives, purposes, interests, inclinations, psychic states, and movements.

One of the significant effects of social life is the institutionalization of forms. For example, certain types of behavioral rules and regulation emerge and are followed because social existence depends on them. But these rules and regulations eventually become institutionalized into laws; they are then followed because they are laws and not because of their original ties to social existence.

According to Simmel, all forms of interaction or sociation are rooted in serious reality; but all have a "game" aspect he referred to as "sociability." This concept is illustrated by conversation. People will talk seriously when there is some content they want to communicate or reach mutual understanding about; but under some conditions, people talk for the sake of talking. Sociability is based on the art of conversation, not mere chatter:

> Talk presupposes two parties, it is two-way. In fact, among all sociological phenomena whatever, with the possible exception of looking at one another, talk is the purest and most sublimated form of two-way-ness. It thus is the fulfillment of a relation that wants to be nothing but relation – in which, that is, what usually is the mere form of interaction becomes its self-sufficient content. Hence even the telling of stories, jokes, and anecdotes, though often only a pastime if not a testimonial of intellectual poverty, can show all the subtle tact that reflects the elements of sociability. It keeps the conversation away from individual intimacy and from all purely personal elements that cannot be adapted to sociable requirements. And yet, objectively it is cultivated not for the sake of any particular content but only in the interest of sociability itself.[6]

On the surface, sociability is an escape and cannot offer serious persons anything that is in any sense "liberating, relieving, or serene"; in fact, Simmel says, sociability *is* liberating for the serious person because it gives him or her a chance to experience the seriousness of life in a sublimated and diluted manner.

Simmel also considered the effects of the forms of social life. He

IV DYADS AND TRIADS

In contrasting dyads and triads, Simmel makes the following points:[8]

1. In a dyad, there is no majority to outvote the individual;
2. The dyad cannot be separated from immediate interaction;
3. Intimacy is a function of the degree to which people interact directly without seeing a structure that transcends their relationship;
4. Delegation of duties and responsibilities to an impersonal group structure is possible in all groups except the dyad;
5. With three people in a group, each operates as an intermediary between the other two; if A, B and C constitute a group, there is a direct relationship between, for example, A and B, and an indirect relationship based on their common tie to C;
6. The sociological nature of the dyad is dictated by the absence of a third element and reciprocity free from disturbance and distraction.

argued, for example, that socialist, or near-socialist forms have always failed in large groups, but have had some success in relatively small groups. Just distribution of products and rewards, he argued, is more easily realized in small groups. He also explored the idea that radicalism and decisiveness vary inversely with group size. Simmel qualified this generalization for large political, social, or religious groups. He argued that the ideas that activate large groups must be simple in order to be accessible to "the lowest and most primitive" group members; and simple ideas, he said, must always be "one-sided, ruthless, and radical."[7]

Another example of the social effect of number is given by comparing a parliamentary party of twenty members containing four rebels, and a party of fifty with ten rebels. The ratio of rebels to others is the same; but, Simmel argues, ten rebels in a group of fifty have more power than four rebels in a group of twenty. The isolated individual, dyad, and triad are the best exhibits of the significance of numbers in social life (see box IV).

One of Simmel's major critics, H. Freyer, noted the danger of applying "sociological geometry" to phenomena that were historical processes and not static structures. But he also described Simmel's sociology as "excellent" because it was appropriately applied to "timeless" social phenomena.[9]

V SOCIETAL TYPES

Gemeinschaft	Gesellschaft
common will	individual will
no individuality of members	individuality of members
domination of community interests	domination of individual interests
belief	doctrine
religion	public opinion
mores and customs	fashion, fads, mode
natural solidarity	contractual solidarity – commerce and exchange
common property	private property

Ferdinand Tonnies

Ferdinand Tonnies (1855–1936) preceded Simmel in the formulation of a formal sociology.[10] In a book published in 1887, he identified two basic societal forms, or social relationships: *Gemeinschaft* and *Gesellschaft*. The Gemeinschaft society is characterized by a strong attachment between the individual and the group, and predates Gesellschaft society. Historically, people have become increasingly involved in more and larger groups; history progresses inevitably from Gemeinschaft to Gesellschaft social relationships, though every society has elements of these two ideal types of society. Gesellschaft relationships are, Tonnies argued, becoming predominant in modern society.

Gemeinschaft societies (e.g., primitive groups, families, and tribes) are bound by organic solidarity; community will prevails over individual will. Later, Durkheim referred to this type of society as one with "mechanical solidarity." Gesellschaft society is artificial; individuals enter into relationships according to their own wills and goals. In Durkheim's terms, such a society is bound together by "organic solidarity." Some of the basic differences between these two types of societies are given in box V.[11]

Tonnies' distinction between these two types of societies was not novel. He was influenced by Maine's concept of status versus contract societies or relationships. Durkheim's concepts of mechanical and organic solidarity have so much in common with Tonnies' types that Sorokin was moved to comment, "One cannot help thinking that

Durkheim intentionally gave to his social types names which were opposite to those given by Tonnies."[12] Sociologists have constructed similar dichotomies throughout the history of sociology: primary and secondary groups; traditional and modern societies; folk, or rural and urban societies. These distinctions generally reflect a tendency on the part of sociologists to value Gemeinschaft relations more highly than Gesellschaft relations, and to bemoan the increasing impersonality of industralized, bureaucratized, secularized society. As for Tonnies, he was called both a pessimist and a romantic. There is no doubt that Tonnies condemned many features of industrial, capitalistic society. But the transition from Gemeinschaft to Gesellschaft society was, Tonnies argued, akin to growing old; and while being young has its advantages, so does old age. Whatever the mixture of positive and negative verdicts in Tonnies' sociology, he was concerned with the function of sociology in improving the conditions of human life. The justification for sociology, he believed, lay in its capacity to increase the number of "friends of the people and of humanity at large," and to strengthen and deepen their knowledge.

Herbert Spencer

Herbert Spencer (1820–1903) conceived of sociology as the study of the evolution of society. His *Principles of Sociology* (1877) in three volumes was the first major effort to provide a systematic outline of sociology as an independent discipline. His sociology had much in common with Comte's. Both argued that social phenomena must be viewed wholistically, that knowledge is relative and based on experience, and that all phenomena in the universe are characterized by discoverable uniformities and invariable natural laws. Both viewed evolution as a slow, continuous process, characterized by progress through successive stages of development. For Comte the culmination was the emergence of a worldwide culture based on Consensus (Humanity); for Spencer, the ideal society was, by contrast, "anarchistic" and individualistic. Comte transformed conventional religion into a positivist Religion of Humanity; Spencer relegated religion to the realm of the "Infinite Unknowable." Spencer rejected Comte's law of the three stages, and his hierarchy of the sciences; but he did not consider Comte's point that certain periods in history are dominated by certain patterns of thought. His own sociology was constructed on the foundations of physics, biology, and psychology.

Comte was more strictly empiricist in abolishing the concern for ultimate causes; he conceived laws more as intellectual constructs than as manifestations of necessary and immutable relationships. For Spencer, sociology was more than a search for co-existences and sequences. Thus Spencer sought to subsume all phenomena under one law, the law of evolution. Here he was ahead of Comte in not believing that species were fixed and immutable. But Comte was more firmly committed to social phenomena as realities *sui generis*, not reducible to any other realities but subject to the methods of science. Spencer's sociology was not based on the possibility of experimental investigation. His approach has been described as "a physical philosophy of society."[13]

Spencer, like many other observers past and present, was intrigued by what he perceived as analogies between societies and organisms. Society, Spencer argued, is an entity "because though formed of discrete units a certain concreteness in the aggregate of them is implied by the general persistence of arrangements among them throughout the area occupied; this is also true of organisms." A society and an organism, he noted, have the following in common:

1 Both commence as small aggregations and insensibly augment in mass, becoming in due course thousands of times their original size.
2 Both are at first simple in structure ... but assume in the course of their growth a continually increasing complexity of structure, which is accompanied by a progressive differentiation of functions...
3 In their undeveloped states both manifest scarcely any mutual dependence of parts, and with the passage of time their parts gradually acquire a mutual dependence, which finally becomes so great that the life and activity of each part are made possible only by the life and activity of the rest ...
4 The life of both wholes becomes independent of and far more prolonged than the life of the component units.[14]

In the late 1930s, social scientists, notably Crane Brinton and Talcott Parsons, were claiming that "Spencer is dead." Certain aspects of Spencer's social evolutionism – especially his biological analogies, and the "iron law of evolution" which promised the gradual, unilineal evolutionary perfection of human society – have been discarded by sociologists. But as a more sophisticated conception of social evolution has developed in recent years, Spencer's work has earned a new appreciation as a pioneering effort. Evolution aside, Spencer's conceptualization of society in terms of structure and function, and his emphasis on the interrelatedness and interdependence of the various "parts" of society, pervade contemporary sociology.

Lewis Henry Morgan

Lewis Henry Morgan's (1818–1881) *Ancient Society* offered a systematic account of human society opposed to biblical dogmas. Morgan, like Spencer, was considered passé by social scientists in the decades immediately following his death. Two reasons for this were a tide of anti-evolutionism, and misrepresentations and misunderstandings of Morgan's work by critics. Marx and Engels, by contrast, were much impressed by Morgan's *Ancient Society*; Engel's *The Origin of the Family, Private Property, and the State* (1884) is about Morgan's book.

One of Morgan's contributions was yet another version of the Gemeinschaft-Gesellschaft dichotomy. Morgan divided human history into two societal types, ancient society and modern society, or in his terms, *societas* and *civitas*. Societas, the Gemeinschaft society, is based on persons and personal relationships; civitas (Gesellschaft) is based on territory and property. This distinction is elaborated in Morgan's view of the emergence of the idea of property as the major force in civilization:

> Since the advent of civilization, the outgrowth of property has been so immense, its forms so diversified, its uses so expanding and its management so intelligent in the interests of its owners, that it has become, on the part of the people, an unmanageable power.[15]

A "mere property career" is not, Morgan argued, humankind's final destiny. He saw in democratic government, social equality, and universal education the seeds of a new and higher plane of society. Experience, intelligence, and knowledge, he claimed, are the tools of a progressive evolution which will eventually revive, in a higher form, "the liberty, equality, and fraternity of the ancient gentes."

Morgan's theory of sociocultural evolution rested on the idea that tools and weapons allow humans to increase their control over nature and enlarge their source of subsistence. He traces cultural evolution through the invention of the bow and arrow, the discovery of metals, the domestication of animals, and the invention of the iron pointed plow, iron spades and axes. Building on these developments and horticulture, field agriculture provided "unlimited subsistence" and "unlimited" culture building potential. Social institutions changed with advances in technology. Civil society followed tribal society; the political state replaced the clan and tribe.

My own perspective as a sociologist has been strongly influenced by Leslie White's imperative that we "return," not merely "go back" to Morgan in order to "again go forward along the broad highway that he laid out for us long ago."[16]

Alfred Kroeber

One of the most important controversies in the modern development of the social sciences has centered on the issue of whether or not society and culture are "real." In 1952, Kroeber (1876–1960), by then an eminent anthropologist, noted that biologists had argued for at least a partial autonomy of the organic level since the time of Lloyd Morgan. Spencer, Tarde, and Durkheim had "asserted, adumbrated, or implied" a superorganic or superindividual level, society; Spencer discussed culture as a supra-societal level of reality.[17] But the distinction between society and culture in discussions of the superorganic level was not always clear. In 1917, Kroeber published a paper on "The Superorganic" in which he used the term synonymously with "social;" he did not use the term with reference to culture, which was the entity he referred to, in order not to be misunderstood by non-anthropolgists. He later defined culture as "the mass of learned and transmitted motor reactions, habits, techniques, ideas, and values – and the behavior they induce.... Culture is the special and exclusive product of men, and is their distinctive quality in the cosmos.... Culture ... is at one and the same time the totality of products of social men, and a tremendous force affecting all human beings, socially and individually."[18] Culture was at least implicitly, and sometimes explicitly, considered supra-societal; and arguments arose about this level of analysis which were not unlike those that arose about the term society.

According to Kroeber and Kluckhohn, the autonomy of culture as a level of analysis was first advanced by Frobenius as early as 1898; Spengler argued for it in 1918; and Kroeber advocated it in his 1917 paper. Kroeber and Kluckhohn recognized in the concept of culture the highest phenomenal level in human awareness. They pointed out the danger of going from the idea of culture as an emergent level of reality to a view of culture as an actual, substantive superorganism.

Kroeber summarized his position in the first paragraph of his 1952 essay on culture:

Primary, it seems to me, is the recognition of culture as a "level" or "order" or "emergent" of natural phenomena, a level marked by a certain distinctive organization of its characteristic phenomena. The emergence of phenomena of life from previous inorganic existence is the presumably earliest and most basic segregation of an order or level. Such emergence does not mean that physical and chemical processes are abrogated but that new organizations occur on the new level: organic manifestations, which need study in their own right or biologically, as well as physiochemically, because they possess a certain, though not an absolute, autonomy.[19]

Kroeber went on to warn against reification (regarding something abstract as a material thing), admitting that he had probably in the past failed to heed that warning carefully. Reification and mysticism are not necessary, he said, to recognize that cultural phenomena must be studied through a cultural approach. This resembles Durkheim's argument – in substance and in the strength of its espousal – that social facts must be used to explain social facts. Kroeber argued that cultural facts must be used to explain cultural facts.

Karl Marx

Marx (1818–1883) has held an equivocal position in the history of sociology. His relevance as a sociologist was recognized at least as early as the 1894 International Institute of Sociology Congress in Paris, where his works were discussed by scholars such as Tonnies and Lilienfeld. This recognition was manifested again when the Congress convened in 1900 around the Marxist theme, "historical materialism." But while Marx has been an ever-present figure in European sociology, he has not had the same degree of influence on the development of American sociology. Barnes' *History* does not include an essay on Marx, and there are only scattered references to him throughout the text. The treatment of Marx in introductory sociology texts rarely amounts to more than a brief acknowledgment of his "genius," a focus on his contribution to the conflict perspective on social stratification, and a comment on his "incorrect predictions."[20] Marx's sociology began to attract wider interest among American sociologists following the publication of J. Schumpeter's *Capitalism, Socialism and Democracy* in 1942. Schumpeter viewed the "economic interpretation of history" as one of the major achievements in sociology.[21]

Irving Zeitlin has drawn attention to the critical position of Marx in the history of sociology. He identifies a Marxian watershed between the romantic-conservative reaction to the French Revolution and modern sociology. Modern sociology, according to Zeitlin, is an outgrowth of a dialogue and debate with the legacy of Marx.[22]

The term sociology does not appear in any of Marx's published writings. One reason for this may be that Marx had a low opinion of Comte, his disciples, and positive philosophy.[23] Marx was not in the mainstream of the development of academic sociology. But he was in the vanguard of scholars whose work reflected the crystallization of sociological perspective in the nineteenth century. Marx was not as obsessed as Durkheim with establishing the validity and utility of sociology against the rival claims of other disciplines. But he strongly opposed attempts to treat individuals as isolated entities; at the same time, he criticized the idea of society as an empty abstraction.[24] There are many examples one could cite of the distinctly sociological emphasis of Marx's work: for example, (1) his view of the development of the division of labor as a function of different forms of ownership, (2) his idea that the quality of citizenship depended on the mode of property, and (3) his analysis of dependency relationships in feudal and bourgeois society, which parallels the Gemeinschaft-Gesellschaft analyses we have encountered in the works of Durkheim, Tonnies, and others.[25] More important than such specific examples of sociological perspective is the consistent stress throughout Marx's works on basic sociological assumptions and ideas. The life of the individual, indeed the very existence of the individual, according to Marx, expresses and confirms social life.[26] Marx did more than simply declare that human beings are social animals. He argued that human beings can only be individualized within society; the idea of becoming human outside of a social context is "preposterous," as much as the idea that an individual could learn to speak "without individuals who live together and talk to one another."[27]

Marx recognized that the means for actualizing human potential – "cultivating his gifts in all directions" – are rooted in community.[28] Here Marx distinguishes himself from the mainstream sociologists. Marx's sociology – and, more broadly, his political economy – rest on an "image of man." Marx was guided by the question, What does it mean to be a human being? Surely, Marx said, being human cannot mean being restricted to playing out the powerless role of the worker in capitalist society, nor even the powerful role of the capitalist who, though he or she is a master of production forces, fails to realize his or her full potential as a creative human being.

The study of human history reveals the principle that human consciousness is determined by the material conditions of human life:

> In the social production of their existence, men inevitably enter into definite relations, which are independent of their will, namely relations of production appropriate to a given stage in the development of their material forces of production. The totality of these relations of production constitutes the economic structure of society, the real foundation, on which arises a legal and political superstructure and to which correspond definite forms of social consciousness. The mode of production of material life conditions the general process of social, political and intellectual life.[29]

Social revolutions, according to Marx, occur when the forces of production and the relations of production come into conflict. Marx argued that historically this sort of conflict had been inevitable. Relations and forces that once fostered development would eventually inhibit it. The resulting economic changes in the inevitable social revolution sooner or later transform the entire superstructure and social consciousness. Marx identified four major epochs in the history of modes of production: Asiatic, ancient, feudal, and bourgeois. He believed that the modern bourgeois mode, capitalism, had created the material (including technological) conditions for solving the problem of class antagonisms once and for all. The present reveals the potential for transforming the conditions of human life so that human consciousness can begin to play a more important and eventually predominant role in structuring human activities. Advances in science and technology, Marx argued, have unveiled a vision of a realm of freedom where work is no longer necessitated by the need to subsist.[30] The realm of necessity is not transcended, but rather transformed from a struggle with nature and with other human beings into the cooperative venture of socialized (in the sense of socialism) humans. At this stage in human history, human beings achieve association as individuals, rather than as members of social classes. Beyond this lies the true realm of freedom in which the development of each individual becomes an end in itself. Marx is unequivocal about the domination of consciousness by the material conditions of life. In The German Ideology and the Preface to the Critique of Political Economy he writes, respectively, (1) "Life is not determined by consciousness, but consciousness by life;" and (2) "It is not the consciousness of men that determines their being, but, on the contrary, their social being determines their consciousness."[31]

But elsewhere Marx suggests that human beings are not entirely passive products of the material conditions of their lives. In *The Eighteenth Brumaire of Louis Bonaparte* he writes, "Men make their own history, but they do not make it just as they please; they do not make it under circumstances chosen by themselves, but under circumstances directly encountered, given, and transmitted from the past;" and, again, in *The German Ideology*, "circumstances make men just as much as men make circumstances."[32] Thus, for most of human history and for most of humanity, the material conditions of life – the necessities of producing for one's livelihood – have preoccupied and dominated human beings. But throughout, human beings have actively lived and worked under the given conditions of their lives, for the most part without overcoming or transcending them. In conjuring up a vision of the true realm of freedom, Marx suggests a new stage in human history where the mental powers of human beings emerge as a dominant force in organizing human activities. Indeed, Marx refers to human history as beginning in the post-capitalist epoch; all prior history, viewed from this perspective, is prehistory.[33]

One of the distinguishing features of Marx's sociology is its blend of past, present, and future. The unfolding of history is the context for appreciating the present; and the present is viewed in a way that reveals its potentialities for becoming the future. This potential is ever-present. History does not come to an end with communism. Marx does not look forward to an epoch when human potential becomes once and for all fully actualized. Rather, he views the socialist-communist transformation as the self-conscious entry of human beings into an open-ended future. In Marx's terms, historical necessities are not absolute necessities and should not be treated as universal laws; they should be viewed as "vanishing" necessities.[34]

History, for Marx, is a movement in which human beings are drawn into alienated, meaningless labor at the same time as they are creating the conditions (including the know-how) for emancipation. The vision of emancipation is one of human beings working to express their creative energies, living to work rather than working to live. Historically, the worker has increasingly come to exist for the productive process, and not the productive process for the worker.[35] Human beings become alienated from the product of their labor. They do not own the means of production, do not create whole products out of their own energies, and do not have power over the products they help to create. But alienation is not restricted to the means of production and the products of labor. Human beings become alienated from themselves, from other human beings, their labor, and the products of their labor, from nature, and from human life.[36] This idea of being a stranger in one's own life can only make sense if we are oriented to an image of what human beings and work ought to be. Marx's critique of history as class struggle, and of bourgeois society as the culmination of the alienating tendencies of history, rests on the belief that human beings are not what they should be, and that they should be what they could be.[37]

Work should be the creative involvement of human beings in exploring their world and developing themselves individually and collectively. But work as we generally experience it prevents the realization of this possibility, even while it creates the conditions for and consciousness of that realization. For Marx, communism is the beginning of a new stage in history in which human beings and not the production of things become the aim of life-work, and people cease being "crippled monstrosities" and become fully developed humans.[38]

Marx considered himself a scientist; but unlike many contemporary scientists, he did not divorce scientific activity from other activities, including moral decisions.

CONCLUSION

The origins of sociology as a discipline are firmly rooted in a conservative, sometimes reactionary, and quasireligious response to the changing conditions of Western society in the eighteenth, nineteenth, and early twentieth centuries. But sociological consciousness appears in the ideas of individuals of various political persuasions. In Marx, who never used the word "sociology," as well as in the academics who organized sociology as a discipline and profession, we see the crystallization of a realm of consciousness in which society and culture are recognized as valid levels of analysis, subject to changes, open to question, and proper subjects for human inquiry.

Since I am primarily concerned here with sociology as a perspective, I will not discuss the various and conflicting empirical, methodological, and theoretical developments in twentieth-century sociology. These are treated in most texts on method and theory, as well as in standard introductory texts. Instead, I want to conclude this chapter by articulating the sociological perspective in contemporary terms. In my view, the best contemporary statements on sociological perspective are rooted in the contributions of Marx, Weber, and Durkheim. They are the well-spring of conflict theory and constructivism, the two contemporary theoretical orientations that best articulate the sociological perspective whose biography I have just sketched.

Conflict theory stresses the historical importance of the coercive power of the state for upholding forms of property, such as slavery, feudal landholding, capital. Property divisions are reflected in class divisions, between slaves and slave-owners, serfs and lords, capitalists and workers. Classes oppose each other in the struggle for political power. Political power is the foundation on which people's access to the means of livelihood rests. The material resources available to social classes determine the extent to which they can effectively organize to establish, defend, and expand their interests.

The material conditions under which people live and work are the basic determinants of their styles of living and thinking. In general, people organize to identify, exploit, store, and utilize various resources they perceive to be relevant to their interests. We are led then to examine material conditions and how they affect social life. The basic principles of conflict analysis are:

1 people should be thought of as animals "maneuvering for advantage, susceptible to emotional appeals; they act in terms of self-interest, seeking satisfactions and avoiding dissatisfactions";
2 social interaction is affected by material or physical arrangements: physical places, modes of communication, weapons, tools, goods, "devices for staging one's public impressions." It is also affected by the resources available to people (material resources, the potential for physical coercion, sexual attractiveness, access to other people to negotiate with, and "devices for invoking emotional solidarity);"
3 inequalities in resources will, through conscious calculation or a basic attraction to situations which appear to provide the greatest immediate rewards, prompt dominant people or groups to try to gain advantage over subordinate people or groups;
4 the behavior that follows from how resources are distributed explains social structures; shifts in resource distributions following conflicts explain social change; and
5 interest groups that have the resources to make their viewpoints prevail are the social causes of ideals and beliefs.[39]

Constructivism is the thesis that our ways of living and thinking are socially constructed. On the surface, this thesis is simply a restatement of what the sociological perspective claims. But the term "social construction" has become a byword of the new sociology of science which has fostered the view that all knowledge, including scientific knowledge, is socially constructed. That is, knowledge emerges out of and incorporates social life. Knowledge is not revealed to us by a supreme being, nor is it the product of some sort of privileged relationship between certain people (e.g., scientists) and a directly accessible reality. In this context, the social construction thesis raises difficult epistemological problems which are outside the scope of this book. However, the idea that our views of reality are social constructs has a certain argumentative force. In the concluding chapters, I offer glimpses of the constructivist perspective on science and religion.

I have sketched the discovery of society in this chapter. In the next chapter, I explore the value dimensions of the study of society, and establish the humanistic orientation that characterizes the brand of sociology I defend in this book. The central messages of chapter 3 are that inquiry is not and cannot be value-free or value-neutral, and that a passionate, concerned sociology is a key to understanding and explaining society. As I pointed out in the Introduction, these messages are neither easy to grasp nor easy to practise.

NOTES

1 P. Rosenberg, "The Second Invention of Sociology," *The New York Times Book Review* (July 15, 1973), p. 21.

2 E. Durkheim, *The Rules of Sociological Method*, 8th edn (New York: The Free Press, 1964), p. 13.

3 M. Weber, *The Protestant Ethic and the Spirit of Capitalism* (New York: Charles Scribner's Sons, 1958), p. 182.

4 See R. Bendix, *Max Weber: An Intellectual Portrait* (New York: Doubleday Anchor, 1962), for a discussion of Weber and his works.

5 This section is based primarily on K. H. Wolff (ed. and trans.), *The Sociology of Georg Simmel* (New York: The Free Press, 1964).

6 Wolff, 1964: p. 53.

7 Wolff, 1964: p. 93.

8 Wolff, 1964: pp. 126–36.

9 H. Freyer, *Soziologie als Wirklichkeitwissenschaft* (Leipzig and Berlin, 1930), pp. 46–57.

10 Basic sources consulted in preparing this section were: P. Sorokin, *Contemporary Sociological Theories* (New York: Harper and Row, 1928); F. Tonnies, *Gemeinschaft und Gesellschaft*, 8th edn (Leipzig, 1935; originally published in 1887; an English translation, with supplementary material, was published in 1940 by C. P. Loomis); Rudolph Heberle, "The Sociological System of

Ferdinand Tonnies: 'Community' and 'Society'," in Barnes (ed.), 1966: pp. 144–65.

11 Sorokin, 1964: p. 492.

12 Sorokin, 1964: p. 491.

13 Jay Rumney, *Herbert Spencer's Sociology* (New York: Atherton Press, 1966), p. 32.

14 Rumney, 1966: pp. 45–48.

15 L. A. White, "Lewis Henry Morgan: Pioneer in the Theory of Social Evolution," in Barnes (ed.), 1966, p. 119.

16 White, 1966: p. 122.

17 A. L. Kroeber, "On Culture," in T. Parsons et al. (eds), *Theories of Society*, 2 vols (New York: The Free Press, 1961), p. 1032 (vol. 2). Reprinted from A. L. Kroeber, *The Nature of Culture* (Chicago: University of Chicago Press, 1952), pp. 4–10.

18 A. L. Kroeber and C. Kluckhohn, *Culture* (New York: Vintage Books, 1963), p. 84. The definition is taken from Kroeber's 1948 text, *Anthropology*.

19 Kroeber, 1961: p. 1032.

20 For a notable exception, see James B. McKee, *Introduction to Sociology* (New York: Holt, Rinehart, and Winston, 1969 and 1974).

21 T. B. Bottomore, "Introduction," in T. B. Bottomore and M. Rubel (eds), *Karl Marx: Selected Writings in Sociology and Social Philosophy*, translated by T. B. Bottomore (New York: McGraw-Hill Book Company, 1964), p. 46. Originally published in 1956.

22 Zeitlin, 1968: p. 322. Marx's visibility as a major figure in the history of sociology was heightened in the late 1960s and early 1970s by publication of the volume on Marx's writings in sociology and social philosophy edited by Bottomore and Rubel in 1956, Aron's inclusion of Marx along with Montesquieu, Comte, and de Tocqueville in the first volume of his *Main Currents in Sociological Theory* (1968), and publication of a volume on Marx in the University of Chicago Press series on "The Heritage of Sociology."

23 Bottomore, 1964: p. 13.

24 Karl Marx, *Grundrisse*, trans. by M Nicolaus (New York: Vintage Books, 1973), pp. 265, 496, and 483.

25 On (1), see Karl Marx and F. Engels, *The German Ideology* (New York: International Publishers, 1947), pp. 9–11; on (2) and (3), see Marx, 1973, pp. 487–8, and 164.

26 Karl Marx, *Economic and Philosophic Manuscripts of 1844* (Moscow: Foreign Languages Publishing House, n.d.), pp. 104–5.

27 Karl Marx, *Critique of Political Economy* (New York: International Publishers, 1970), p. 189.

28 Marx and Engels, 1947, pp. 74–5.

29 Marx, 1970, pp. 20–1.

30 Karl Marx, *Capital*, 3 vols (New York: International Publishers, 1967), vol. III, p. 820.

31 Marx and Engels, 1947, p. 15; Marx, 1970, p. 21.
32 Karl Marx, *The Eighteenth Brumaire of Louis Bonaparte* (New York: International Publishers, 1963), p. 15; Marx and Engels, 1947, p. 29.
33 Marx, 1970, pp. 21–2.
34 Marx, 1973, pp. 831ff.
35 Marx, 1967, vol. I, pp. 507ff.
36 Marx, n. d., p. 77.
37 E. Fromm, *Marx's Concept of Man* (New York: F. Ungar, 1966), pp. 42ff.
38 Marx, 1967, vol. I, pp. 360, 363. See the summary of Marx's sociology in C. W. Mills, *The Marxists* (New York: Dell Publishing Co., 1962), pp. 82–95.
39 R. Collins, *Conflict Sociology* (New York: Academic Press, 1975), pp. 60–1.

3

The Human Dimensions of Sociological Inquiry

Max Weber called the term "sociology" ambiguous. Simmel described the field as one surrounded by chaos, contradictions, confusion, and doubts. More recently, sociology has been described as a field in disarray: macrosociologists oppose microsociologists; activists contend with value-neutral observers; champions of social change argue with students of social order. Humanists, behaviorists, structuralists, symbolic interactionists and others compete for ascendancy.[1] But what some sociologists see as disarray others see as diversity.[2] In any case, the "adjectivization" of sociology has produced a sometimes confusing variety of "sociologies." The adjectives describe theoretical orientations (conflict and consensus theorists), viewpoints (e.g., materialism, ecologism, physiologism), and political commitments (e.g., bourgeois, Marxist, feminist, and Black sociologies).[3]

It would appear simple enough from a lexicographer's point of view to define sociology as "the science of the social." Here is a standard dictionary definition of sociology:

n(F *sociologie*, fr. *socio-* + *-logie -logy*)
1: the science of society, social institutions, and social relationships; *specif*: the systematic study of the development, structure, and function of human groups conceived as processes of interaction or organized patterns of collective behavior
2: the scientific analysis of a social institution as a functioning whole and as it relates to the rest of society.[4]

This is exactly the sort of definition one encounters in the opening pages of most introductory sociology textbooks. For example:

Sociology is one of the social sciences. Its long-run aim is to discover the basic structure of human society, to identify the main forces that hold groups together or weaken them, and to learn the conditions that transform social life. In this, sociology, like any pure or basic science, is a disciplined, intellectual quest for fundamental knowledge of the nature of things.[5]

Another text identifies the goal of contemporary sociology with the goal of classic philosophy: the search for understanding social organization and social processes, and the bases of social order and social change:

It differs from older forms of knowledge-seeking about society principally in that it uses the methods of science to arrive at increasingly valid and comprehensive explanations of social reality.[6]

The latter definition is elaborated by noting that sociology "clearly meets all the basic criteria for a science;" "its *aims* are to discover the nature of social phenomena, to describe social phenomena in terms of concepts and generalizations as accurately as the state of the discipline allows, and to construct systematic and logical theoretical explanations for discovered relationships;" methodologically, the descriptive and explanatory aspects of sociology are based on controlled observations which, by using the best available tools of inquiry, minimize the possibility of "accumulating spurious or erroneous data;" and epistemologically, sociology relies on "rigorous rules of evidence for testing the reliability of its hypotheses and generalizations."[7]
These definitions illustrate the idea, widely accepted among academic sociologists and especially authors of introductory texts, that sociology is a basic or pure science. An exclusive focus on the purity of sociology as a science, however, obscures the relationship between science and values. There is always the danger that such a focus will transform science into, or reflect an implicit or explicit commitment to, scientism.
Scientism can take on different forms. For example, one definition of scientism states that it is "a type of scholarly trespassing, of pseudo-exactitude, of embracing incongruous models of scientific method and

conceptualization." This definition is applied to sociologies that take a cynical view of the human being as "a rodent eager to learn the ins and outs of a maze." In this sense, scientism in sociology or in any other field is a symptom of insecurity and negativity about social life.[8] This conception of scientism may reflect a concern with the problem of trying to take on the trappings of science without meeting the substantive requirements of scientific inquiry. This in turn may imply some questionable assumptions, such as (1) that the physical sciences (especially physics) set the standards for what is to count as science, (2) that we know what those standards are in practice, and (3) that those standards are different (for example, that they are more rigorous) than the standards used in other fields of inquiry. In fact, sociologists of science have learned a great deal about how scientists in the traditional scientific fields (such as physics, chemistry, and biology) work and think, and what they have learned contradicts much traditional thinking (based on ideals and anecdotes) about the nature of science. Another problem with this conception of scientism is that it might be used to defend the idea that human behavior cannot be studied systematically.

Another definition of scientism is that it is "a boundary transgression or a misuse of otherwise legitimate procedures and attitudes of science."[9] The value *of* science – exact and dependable knowledge as a means to better understanding of our world, and as a basis for policy-making – is deformed by scientism into "Science" as an absolute authority commanding genuflection, and stamping anything it is associated with as excellent. But there are also values *in* science, and these vary depending on the subject matter; scientism in sociology means that what Werkmeister refers to as the "value-free concepts" of physics and chemistry are to be employed in sociology, "and that man himself is to be reduced – via a behavioristic psychology – to a purely physiochemical complexus of interrelated processes amenable to a complete explanation in terms of [these] concepts and categories."[10] Finally, there are values *for* science: standards of research; and "personal and societal biases and ideological prejudices." Scientism on this level refers to "the intrusion of ideological biases and personal prejudices – usually in a more or less subtle way – into the enterprise of science itself."[11]

A more or less scientistic perspective is implicit, if not explicit, in most treatments of sociology as a science. This is underscored when we consider those rare definitions of sociology which express a commitment to science, but add other dimensions. James B. McKee defines sociology as a science, but adds that it is also a humanistic and secular "effort to provide perspective on the collective enterprise that is society. It seeks to offer some knowledge by which people can be more rational and more humane in the decisions they make about the collective organization of their lives, its quality and magnitude and the direction of conscious change."[12] This definition introduces the adjective, "humanistic," and we next turn our attention to this perspective in sociology.

In his *Invitation to Sociology: A Humanistic Perspective*,[13] Peter Berger makes a firm commitment to science; but he argues that sociology is more than science. Sociology is a "game" for people who have an infinite, intense, and shameless interest in human behavior. Such people can focus on particular human activities as examples of the "infinite richness" of human life. But sociology is not a simple matter of playing a game; it is a process of "seeing through" social facades, "unmasking" and "debunking" social systems, and relativizing absolutest claims made by the "guardians of public order." The very process of studying society scientifically implies certain human values, according to Berger:

1 all human activity has potential significance for sociology;
2 the sociologist must master the art of listening without entering his or her own views; and
3 the sociologist is responsible, within the limits of his or her psychological capacities, for an unbiased, unprejudiced evaluation of his or her findings.
   Other aspects of sociology as a humanistic discipline are
4 a vital concern with the human condition;
5 a sensitivity to the human significance of social research;
6 open-mindedness and catholic vision; and
7 interpenetration with other human studies, especially philosophy and history.

The model sociologist, in Berger's view, is "a *condottierre* of social perception" who fights not for the oppressors of human beings but for their liberators. Berger's sociologist is a practitioner of a detached Machiavellianism, a virtue in the not uncommon situations in which people confront each others' "conflicting fanaticisms" in a morass of "ideological befuddlement" about what society is. Existentially, sociology can nourish motivation in terms of human needs, not "grandiose political programs;" it can encourage selective, economical commitments, rather than consecration to a "totalitarian faith;" and it can teach us how to be at once compassionate and skeptical:

Especially to those who have become disillusioned with the more fervent political eschatologies of our era, sociology can be of assistance in pointing to possibilities of political engagement that do not demand the sacrifice of one's soul and one's sense of humor.[14]

Elsewhere, Berger has outlined this political perspective and labeled it "conservative humanism." The basic tenets of this perspective are:

1 history is messy, and the idea of progress suspect;
2 innovation should be approached skeptically, and violent innovation with doubled skepticism;
3 human beings should be accepted as they are;
4 order, continuity, and triviality in social life should be valued;
5 we should be skeptical of "grand intellectual designs for the improvement of society;"
6 we should be skeptical of "movements;"
7 our tendency should be to leave people alone.

In addition, Berger offers the following maxims:

Learn how to refuse the existing orthodoxies. Learn also how to refuse the would-be orthodoxies of tomorrow. Participate in the lives of others, but think your own thoughts. Accept "alienation" – it is the price of freedom. *Learn how to stand apart.*[15]

Although the roots of his approach are conservative, Berger clearly challenges the conventional view of the necessary and logical separation of science, values, and politics.

C. Wright Mills inspired a "new sociology" in the late 1950s and early 1960s. His life and work are in part the foundation of some of the more recent "new" sociologies. Mills conceived a social science opposed to "bureaucratic techniques which exhibit social inquiry by 'methodological' pretensions, which congest such work by obscurant conceptions, or which trivialize it by concern with minor problems unconnected with publicly relevant issues."[16] In referring his conception of sociology to the promise of such classic social analysts as Durkheim, Marx, Weber, and Mannheim, Mills outlined the nature and foundations of "the sociological imagination."

Mills' sociology is characterized by:

1   a focus on the interrelation of the essential parts of whole societies, comparisons of whole societies, and analysis of the relationships between particular societal features and social continuities and changes;
2   placing given societies in the context of the total history of humanity, identifying how particular societal features are affected by, and affect historical periods, comparisons of the historical periods and their "characteristic ways of history-making," and analysis of the mechanics of societal change in history;
3   identification of the varieties of human beings which prevail, and "are coming to prevail," in given societies, the types of human beings found in given historical periods, an analysis of modes of selection, formation, liberation, repression, sensitization, and blunting of human beings, an uncovering of human nature as it is revealed in a given society or period, and the relationship between societal features and human nature.[17]

For Mills, the sociological imagination is the basis for grasping the nature of society – "what is going on in the world" – and for understanding ourselves "as minute points of the intersections of biography and history within society." The sociological imagination operates within two realms: "the personal troubles of milieu," and "the public issues of social structure." Troubles happen in the self and its relation to others in the self's "immediate milieu – the social setting that is directly open to his personal experience and to some extent his willful activity." Issues are public, related to the institutions of a total historical society, the overlapping and interpenetration of individual "immediate milieux," and the types of institutional crises Marxists refer to as "contradictions" or "antagonisms."[18] It will become clear as we proceed that Mills has had a strong influence on the development of the worldview of sociology developed in this book.

For radical sociologists like Frank Lindenfeld, sociology is pursued with the hope "that with greater understanding people will be able to confront and change the social reality that surrounds them, to make it a better environment for human beings."[19] From this perspective, the study of a particular set of problems requires that the sociologist be directed by questions and canons of theory and method, but simultaneously by questions of the human condition. In his reader on political sociology, for example, Lindenfeld orients himself to the question, "Why are some men and nations rich while others are poor? How long will 'the wretched of the earth' stand for their misery? And what can we do?"

The task of a radical sociology, according to David Horowitz, is "to study the structure of social oppression and to bring this knowledge, and the power it conveys, to the powerless and exploited social majority."[20] Radical sociology "begins with the specific, historically conditioned organization of the basic activities which sustain a social order;" this "leads directly to the question of how a social order may be reconstructed in order to better serve the needs of its members, rather than how its members and institutions may be adjusted and accommodated to the need to maintain social order and stability."[21]

Albert Szymanski's outline of the major tasks of radical sociology consists of two basic queries and three activities:

Queries

1   What are human nature, and human potential? How can we maximize actualization of human nature and potential?
2   What strategy can we develop to create a society oriented to actualizing human nature and potential?

Activities

1   Constant social criticism;
2   Relating personal, everyday troubles and concerns to social structures, thereby translating individual problems into political issues;
3   The formulation and propagation of a sociology relevant to practical human problems, and the creation of a "counter-definition of social reality."

Sociologists "must explain how badly the present society functions, how people's private frustrations stem from the social structure, how unnecessary and oppressive the present institutional arrangements are, and how much better an alternative social order would work."[22]

Marxist and socialist sociologies are often indistinguishable from each other or from radical sociologies. Their umbilical ties to Marx, Engels, and nineteenth-century socialism are, however, more evident. Marxist sociology is sometimes referred to as "historical materialism."[23] The outline of a Marxist approach to sociological theory and method is presented in box VI.

Marxist sociologists generally manifest the crudely conceived class struggle between the proletariat and the bourgeoisie in their intellectual struggle with bourgeois sociology. Zivkovic defines bourgeois sociology as "a positivistic, empirical social science without a philosophy."[25] Bourgeois sociologists are concerned with solving theoretical problems related to those practical problems which the

VI   OLEG MANDIC ON MARXIST SOCIOLOGY

Principles

1. The law of the relation between the social base and the superstructure – the way in which a society is organized for the production and distribution of material goods determines (directly or indirectly) its political, regulatory, ethical, cultural, and ideological achievements;

2. The law of the struggle of social groups – social evolution is the product of differences, contradictions, conflicts, and struggles within and between societies;

3. The law of revolutionary change in the evolution of concrete societies – there is a tendency for the evolution of relations of production to lag behind the evolution of forces of production. This gives rise to contradictions whose increasing intensity leads to revolutionary epochs and the emergence of new economic institutions and correspondingly new forms of social superstructure;

4. The law of the role of individuals in social events – an individual's activities in a given social situation are limited by the activities of other individuals acting in that situation: "... the common result originates in the dialectical negation of individual activities;"

5. The law of social progress – societies and their institutions evolve, proceeding from simple to complex forms. Progress in this context occurs to the extent that this evolution leads to social forms which are the most advantageous for the largest possible number of people, within given institutions, societies, or the world as a whole.

Methodology

1. All conclusions in social science must be rooted in "the concrete facts of social life;"

2. All aspects of social life are reciprocally linked, interrelated, and interdependent;

3. All social events change; they originate, evolve, and disappear;

4. Internal conflicts, influenced by external conflicts, are the causes of changes in social organization;

5. Every social phenomenon carries within itself "the core of future changes which will develop in one or another direction dependent on particular material conditions in the environment in which these phenomena are acting:"

6. The consequences of applying this method must be compared

with concrete facts to determine "if they exactly reflect social reality. Only such a comparison can determine whether the abstract conclusions are based on the firm ground of facts."[24]

---

dominant bourgeois class must solve. They are confined to solving problems within the class framework of bourgeois society; they thus consciously or unconsciously contribute to maintaining the given class order; they do not see in this class order "the trends that society carries beyond its borders into a new system, or the transition into the new system, or else [they do] not consider them to be inevitable nor even probable."[26] The virtue of the Marxist view, which sometimes disintegrates into a caricature of Marx (who lived long enough to protest, "Je ne suis pas Marxiste"), is that it draws our attention to the fact that sociologists *can* and *do* become intellectual "slaves" and "pawns" in the system of society that supports their activities, whatever the nature of the system.

Socialist sociology, in the work of Richard Flacks and others, is rooted in Marxist and radical traditions. Flacks uses the term socialism to convey "the vision of a society organized so that production is carried on for use rather than profit, class-based privilege and inequality is abolished, and men have equality of access to power and to the fruits of human labor."[27] Socialist sociology is a program for relating this vision to the social problems of capitalism. By leading to the development of concrete models or theoretical alternatives to the organization of human activities in the private, corporate society, socialist sociology:

1 stimulates debate and analysis in order to catalyze practical experimentation – all for the purpose of making alternatives to the status quo credible;
2 provides material to meet demands for institutional change which cannot be met "under capitalism;" Flacks refers to this as "structural reform." He notes that it is not the sociologist's job to formulate such a program ("although," he writes, "popular movements may find our skills useful"); "but the effort to concretize the meaning of socialism can help movement activists figure out the kinds of programs which will be both relevant to the felt needs of people and fundamentally challenging to the system;"
3 contributes to creating counter-institutions through utopian thinking:

In general, both the source and the test of the ideas of radical intellectuals lies with the movements for social change. As sociologists, what we can bring to such movements is this: some knowledge of the "literature" which might be relevant to political work; a certain degree of training to generalize from particular experience, to synthesize diverse experiences, to confront discomforting data, to examine underlying assumptions, to entertain alternative explanations for events; possibly some factual knowledge which might be of use.

Joyce Ladner, for example, presents Black sociology as a response to the biases of mainstream bourgeois, liberal, white sociology, and "a positive step toward setting forth basic definitions, concepts, and theory-building that utilize the experiences and histories of Afro-Americans." Black sociology is opposed to a white sociology that has generally supported the status quo and resisted the kinds of progressive social changes that would radically improve the living and working conditions of American Blacks. Ladner argues that sociologists are "the theorists and forerunners of social change," and therefore cannot ignore the goals of the masses. Black sociologists in particular must become advocates of the demands among Blacks and other oppressed peoples for freedom, justice, and self-determination.[28]

The imperatives Ladner sets forth for Black sociologists are an increased concern with Third World questions, and the relationship between race problems in America and in the Third World; and the development of new techniques and perspectives based on "a conciliation between culture (theory) and politics (practice):" "The myth of 'value-free' sociology becomes relevant to the Black sociologist, because he must become 'pro-value', by promoting the interests of the Black masses in his research, writings and teachings."

Reflexive sociology is a form of radical sociology. Its basic goals, formulated by Alvin Gouldner, are: (1) transforming the sociologist through a deepening of self-awareness, including awareness of how his or her work in sociology is affected by his or her social roles and activities, improving his or her ability to produce valid and reliable social knowledge, and facilitating openness to hostile information; (2) developing knowledge of one's influence on others rather than seeking to eliminate it, and of one's self as a knower and social change agent; (3) affirming individual creative scholarship that is opposed to organizational, professional, institutional, and cultural demands for conformity and routinization.[29]

Reflexive sociology is related to radical sociology, in Gouldner's view, by virtue of its critique of society-as-it-is, and its concerns with the "positive formulation of new societies, of utopias, in which men might live better." Reflexive-radical sociology integrates the personal-intimate with the collective-public, "everyday life with the occasionally 'political' act."[30]

The adjectival sociologies I have examined exhibit some of the multiple realities of sociological perspective. The humanistic viewpoint, and notably Gouldner's reflexive sociology, suggests that there is a profound and widely unrecognized relationship between open inquiry (science, in the best sense of that term) and humanistic or radical values. I examine this question further in the next section.

SCIENCE AND VALUES

The idea that scientific activity implies a certain set of values has been lucidly expressed by Jacob Bronowski. Bronowski noted that the values of science grow out of its practice:

> The values of science derive neither from the virtues of its members, nor from the finger-wagging codes of conduct by which every profession reminds itself to be good. They have grown out of the practice of science, because they are the inescapable conditions for its practice.[31]

Bronowski views science as "the creation of concepts and their exploration in the facts. It is no other test of the concept than its empirical truth to fact. Truth is the drive at the center of science." The "habit of truth" is a process, not a dogma. From this perspective, Bronowski invites us to consider an eminently sociological question: what kind of society have scientists "been compelled to form in this single pursuit?" He writes as if this society is a reality; it is better to consider it an ideal which is yet to be achieved, at least on a large scale. Briefly, Bronowski identifies several conditions for and characteristics of "good" science. They include independence in observation and thought, concern for originality, freedom, dissent, tolerance, respect for others and self-respect, organized orientation to correcting errors, prizing the scientist above science, and being flexible and single-minded at the same time as a scientist and as a scientific community.

The health and vitality of science cannot be taken for granted. Jerry Ravetz, for example, argues that there must be an "effective ethic," something more refined than a "professional ethic." The source of such an ethic, he suggests, lies in a sophisticated humanitarian commitment and not in religion, philosophy, or elitist codes of conduct.[32] The specification of the values which should comprise a humanitarian commitment is a relatively new task being carried forward by humanists. Maslow's work in this area stands out and is especially interesting on two counts: first, because it is congruent with a conception of nature as constantly evolving; second, because it encompasses many, if not all, the values associated by students of science from Merton to Bronowski with the scientific ethos. Maslow assumes the intrinsic value of truth, and views inquiry as a basic defining activity of human life. Among the Being-Values (values that promote a good life) Maslow associates with the good person and the good society are truth, goodness, beauty, wholeness, dichotomy-transcendence, "aliveness," uniqueness, perfection, necessity, completion, justice, order, simplicity, richness, effortlessness, playfulness, and self-sufficiency.[33]

The search for a humanistic ethos in science has often overlapped with some variety of radicalism. The association of science with radicalism may seem curious, but it really is not. The scientific ethos tends to conflict with the ethos of other social institutions.[34] This is, at least, part of an ideal view of science; on this view, only science is associated with a full, uncompromising, unfettered commitment to the pursuit of knowledge. Scientific inquiry must be constantly pressed forward, driven by skepticism and the idea that even fundamental assumptions are ultimately subject to criticism and change. Nothing is protected from the basic query, Why? No other social activity – and in reality not even scientific activity itself – operates fully according to this imperative to inquiry. But good inquiry must inevitably be perceived as a radical activity relative to the other social activities in a society. When Tom Hayden defined the "radical style" in the late 1960s, he came intriguingly close to a definition of ideal science or good inquiry:

Radicalism as a style involves penetration of a social problem to its roots, to its real causes. Radicalism presumes a willingness to continually press forward the query: Why? Radicalism finds no rest in conclusions; answers are seen as provisional, to be discarded in the face of new evidence or changed conditions.[35]

In addition to humanistic and radical commitments, a related value orientation that must be considered in constructing a scientific ethos is reflexion. Reflexive sociology, according to Gouldner,

> sees all men as profoundly shaped by their shared past, by their evolving culture and social systems. Yet it does not see men either as the helpless agents of some inexorable social force to which they must bow, or as the omnipresent overlords of an historical process that they can neatly engineer. A Reflexive Sociology believes that there is an inevitable "slippage" between man and society.[36]

Reflexion can be generalized as follows: a reflexive life is one in which the things of experience are all and always at least in part turned inward, and incorporated in our increasing awareness of who and what we are. Physics can be learned reflexively by analyzing our selves as physical systems. Astronomy and geology can be studied in terms of their meaning relative to our existence in and relationship to the universe – past, present, and future. The most abstract human endeavors have reflexive potential. Mathematics and logic, for example, can be explored as themselves explorations in the structure and processes of thinking. In this way, it becomes possible to realize that the self, as Alan Watts writes, resides "in the whole surge of energy which ranges from the galaxies to the nuclear fields in my body," but without the mystical sense Watts intends.[37] Reflexion is not a one-way process. Its relevance for a scientific ethos lies in the fact that increased awareness is a condition of new perceptions and ultimately new conceptualizations and comprehensions.

Humanistic, radical, and reflexive commitments are bases for the construction of a scientific ethos. In a sense, they are the specification and elaboration of values apparent in ideal science, and in good scientific research. This complex of values emphasizes open-endedness, process, and change.

THE SOCIAL ORGANIZATION OF SCIENCE

Proposals for resolving crises in science emphasize the necessity of achieving a closer realization of the ideal communal organization of science. These organizational proposals are usually linked, implicitly if not explicitly, to values which fit into the complex of humanistic, radical, and reflexive values discussed above. Examples of such proposals include Bernal's advocacy of "science as communism,"[38] Husserl's association of scientific culture with thoughtfulness and enlightenment, and Jaspers' conception of science as a basis for world-unity, friendship, and trust where the fundamental drive of science "binds men existentially – where their common work makes them friends."[39]

The "communistic" or "communal" theme is not radical in science; it has been identified as one of the norms of science. Merton used "communism" in "the nontechnical and extended sense of common ownership of goods," and referred to it as an "integral element of the scientific ethos."[40] Writing in 1952, Merton noted that concerns about the "frustration of science" reflected the conflict between the communistic ethos and "the definition of technology as 'private property' in a capitalistic economy." He noted a variety of responses to the conflict: defensively patenting scientific work to ensure its public availability (e.g., Einstein, Millikan, Compton, and Langmuir); urging the promotion of new businesses by scientists; and advocating socialism.

Wartofsky has outlined a rationale for socializing science. He claims that, although science is synonymous with reason, and the most advanced cognitive form humans have developed, it is now for the first time in danger of becoming maladaptive.[41] This danger is apparent from the viewpoint of global ecological and evolutionary history. Rationality, Wartofsky argues, now threatens our survival as a species. As science or reason have become the tools of conflicting powers and interests, the liberatory features of rationality have been transformed into repressive ones. Although Wartofsky's socialist argument is consistent with the communal ethos in ideal science, it diverges from it by strongly emphasizing social responsibility. The rational imperative in socialized reason or science is a responsibility for human welfare. Wartofsky emphasizes that this responsibility is not an ethical imperative but an imperative of (socialized) reason itself.

What are our social responsibilities as students of social reality, or more broadly, as scientists? Joshua Lederberg argues that scientists are responsible for "vigilant criticism," that is, for regularly informing themselves, each other, and the public of the nature, potential, successes, and failures of their work.[42] Robert Stebbins' prescription for biology teachers is applicable to all teachers: to instill a "fondness for nature" as well as to communicate a technical subject, is an ethical, moral, and political imperative for all teaching scientists; to teach accountability for human life in the present and in the future; and to promote self-criticism and self-evaluation regarding the values that direct one's scientific work, and one's life.[43]

Jim Shapiro, Larry Eron, and Jon Beckwith reminded us some years ago that scarcely 50 years separate Bequerel's discovery of radioactivity (1896) and Hiroshima.[44] Commoner, commenting on how narrow the gap between basic discovery and scientific application has become, notes that "Scientists can no longer evade the social, political, economic, and moral consequences of what they do in the laboratory."[45] Something approximating unadulterated inquiry may be possible under certain (utopian) conditions; in this world, at this time, pure science is more myth and ideology than it is disinterested research in the service of humanity or in the pursuit of "harmony." The painful questions raised by Tom Hayden 20 years ago remain largely unanswered in the scientific community:

> What has made me so strangely sensitive when my brothers seem so acquiescent; what has made me call insane what the experts call "the hard facts of power politics;" what has made me feel we are on the threshhold of death when others excitedly say we are on the New Frontier; and why have I turned with trembling and disgust from the Americans who do recognize peril and recoil into shelters full of the comforting gadgets the culture has produced?[46]

Fewer and fewer of us are privileged to avoid the consequences of ignorance, apathy, and withdrawal in the face of crises in science and society. There is a tragic promise in the routinized responses of rational humans. In an address delivered at the March 4, 1969 M.I.T. research "stoppage-strike," W. G. McMillan of RAND and UCLA promised his audience "a balanced perspective in your concern with the application of science and technology in our society."[47] He concluded by urging his listeners to "temper your impatience with the realization that things are as they are because it is exceedingly difficult for them to be otherwise."[48] Yet things as they are encourage an uninhibited impatience. Those among us who are temperamentally suited for it may wish to imitate Serge Lang's unwillingness to question "motivations;" he believes that "even though everyone is well-meaning and devoted, it doesn't prevent some form also being stupid and misinformed."[49] It is not, at any rate, unreasonable to conclude from an examination of what people and organizations do that the central values in our society and in most, if not all, of the rest of the world's societies, inhibit not only realization but comprehension of "the wish to humanize our existence."[50]

Making science a humanized and integral part of society is being experimented with on a small scale in a variety of alternative technology communities around the world.[51] In these communities, solar, wind, and water power are used as energy sources; and experiments are being carried out to develop new solar, wind, and water technologies. These technologies are integrated with a vision of a working ecological system that promotes human and communal development.

Contemporary China has provided examples of experimenting with a new worldview for science on a large scale. For centuries, until the scientific revolution in Western Europe, Chinese science and technology were the most advanced in the world. Nathan Sivin, an historian of Chinese science, has pointed out the unity of science and society in historical China and the importance of this for resolving current crises in science and society.[52] For a variety of reasons too complex to examine here, this unity worked against the emergence of a Chinese scientific revolution. Today, the unity of science and society in China is being carried out under new social conditions. In contemporary China, science "walks on two legs." This is a proverbial Chinese idea. Applied to science, it means that science is not the exclusive possession of a specially trained elite, and that it is not limited to promoting economic development. In practice, "walking on two legs" is manifested in the effort to provide the masses of Chinese people with access to science as a means for improving their everyday lives.

Science is defined more broadly in China than it is in the West; in this respect, it is to some degree compatible with the broadened definition of science I use. In China, science "is a process of thinking and developing rational knowledge through practice. As such it should not be something mysterious and special but a natural part of everyone's experience."[53]

It is difficult to say to what extent these ideas actually characterize everyday life in China today. And perhaps the Chinese are too tied to conventional ideas about scientific objectivity that can interfere with the pursuit of humanistic goals. Still, the idea that science (broadly conceived) walks on two legs should be part of any effort to humanize the conditions under which we live.

CONCLUSION

The message that emerges from the preceding discussion of humanistic and radical sociologies is that we need to free ourselves from the myths of value-free, value-neutral science. We are urged to show a concern for people rather than positions and roles. Our objective as sociologists should not be the cold, passionless, detached study of society. Rather, our objective should be to combat the fragmentation of persons that destroys the possibility of linking biographies, culture, and history in a network of empathy, compassion, and cooperation of human beings pursuing and creating liberating futures. Where wholeness exists, we should reinforce it. Combating fragmentation and reinforcing wholeness are not substitutes for but rather integral parts of the strategies for explanation and understanding I advocate.

A cautionary note is called for here. Science, as I pointed out earlier, should be viewed as a symbol for the best forms of inquiry we engage in. It should not be an object of adoration or worship, nor should it stand uncritically for *modern* science. Modern science has been an integral part of the cultural apparatus of political, economic, and military elites from its emergence in the seventeenth century to the present. And science in a variety of forms has, in general, always been a tool of ruling class interests. In this sense, adopting science uncritically means adopting a set of social and institutional trappings, such as hierarchical relationships, that serve established, elite, and ruling class interests. It is important, then, to carefully qualify what it is we mean when we claim to be scientific in a humanistic perspective. I have sought to sketch such a perspective on science in this chapter. A more detailed discussion is out of place here, but I have treated this in some detail elsewhere, and I encourage readers to consult the relevant sources.[54]

In chapters 1, 2, and 3, I have outlined the discovery of society and the value dimensions of sociology. In the following chapter, I focus on the theoretical issue of what society is. The reader has some background at this point on the general concerns of sociological inquiry. My objective in chapter 4 is to help the reader develop an image of society that adequately reflects the complexity and the dynamics of this core aspect of social reality.

NOTES

1 Bernard Rosenberg, *The Province of Sociology* (New York: Thomas Y. Crowell, 1972), pp. 1–2.

2 James B. McKee, *Introduction to Sociology*, 1st edn (New York: Holt, Rinehart and Winston, 1969).

3 W. L. Wallace (ed.), *Sociological Theory* (Chicago: Aldine Publishing Company, 1969).

4 *Webster's Seventh New Collegiate Dictionary* (Springfield, MA: G. & C. Merriam C., 1967), p. 828.

5 L. Broome and P. Selzmick, *Sociology*, 4th edn (New York: Harper and Row, 1968), p. 3.

6 M. DeFleur, W. D'Antonio, and L. DeFleur, *Sociology: Human Society* (Glenview, IL: Scott, Foresman and Company, 1973), p. 9.

7 DeFleur, et al., 1973: p. 27.

8 Helmert Schoeck, "Introduction," in Helmert Schoeck and James W. Wiggins (eds), *Scientism and Values* (New York: D. Van Nostrand Company, 1960), pp. IX–X.

9 W. H. Werkmeister, "Social Science and the Problem of Value," in Schoeck and Wiggins (eds), 1960: p. 1.

10 Werkmeister, 1960: p. 20.

11 Werkmeister, 1960: pp. 20–1.

12 James B. Mckee, *Introduction to Sociology*, 2nd edn (New York: Holt, Rinehart and Winston, 1974), p. 519.

13 Peter Berger, *Invitation to Sociology: A Humanistic Perspective* (New York: Anchor Books, 1963), pp. 166–9.

14 Berger, 1963: pp. 170–1.

15 Peter Berger, "Between System and Horde," in Peter Berger and R. J. Neuhaus, *Movement and Revolution* (New York: Anchor Books, 1970), pp. 29–30.

16 C. Wright Mills, *The Sociological Imagination* (New York: Grove Press, 1961), p. 20.

17 Mills, 1961: pp. 6–7.

18 Mills, 1961: pp. 8–9.

19 Frank Lindenfeld, "Preface," in Frank Lindenfeld (ed.), *Reader in Political Sociology* (New York: Funk and Wagnall's, 1968), p. ix.

20 David Horowitz, "General Introduction: Sociology and Society," in David Horowitz (ed.), *Radical Sociology* (San Francisco: Canfield Press, 1971), p. 5.

21 Horowitz, 1971: p. 7.

22 Albert Szymanski, "Toward a Radical Sociology" in J. D. Colfax and Jack L. Roach (eds), *Radical Sociology* (New York: Basic Books, 1971), pp. 105–6.

23 This is typical in the Soviet Union. See also the classic textbook by N. Bukharin, *Historical Materialism: A System of Sociology* (New York: International Publishers, 1925).

24 Oleg Mandic, "The Marxist School of Sociology: What is Sociology in a Marxist Sense," in Peter Berger (ed.), *Marxism and Sociology* (New York: Appleton-Century-Crofts, 1969), pp. 40–3.

25 Ljubomir Zivkovic, "The Structure of Marxist Sociology," in Berger, 1969: p. 98.

26 Zivkovic, 1969: pp. 122–3.

27 Richard Flacks, "Towards a Socialist Sociology," *The Insurgent Sociologist*, vol. II, no. 2 (Spring, 1972), pp. 26–7.

28 Joyce A. Ladner, "Introduction," in Joyce A. Ladner (ed.), *The Death of White Sociology* (New York: Random House, 1973), pp. xix–xxvii.

29 A. Gouldner, *The Coming Crisis of Western Sociology* (New York: Basic Books, 1970), pp. 494–8.

30 Gouldner, 1970: pp. 503–4.

31 Jacob Bronowski, *Science and Human Values*, revised and enlarged edn (New York: Harper Torchbooks, 1965), pp. 60–9.

32 J. R. Ravetz, *Scientific Knowledge and its Social Problems* (Oxford: The Clarendon Press, 1971), p. 313.

33 Abraham Maslow, *The Farther Reaches of Human Nature* (New York: The Viking Press, 1971), pp. 133–5.

34 R. Merton, *The Sociology of Science* (Chicago: University of Chicago Press, 1973), p. 266.

35 Tom Hayden, "A Letter to the New (Young) Left," in M. Cohen and D. Hale (eds), *The New Student Left*, Rev. and enlarged (Boston: Beacon Press, 1967), p. 6.

36 Gouldner, 1970: p. 507.

37 A. Watts, *The Book* (New York: Collier Books, 1967), p. 10.

38 Bernal, 1939.

39 E. Husserl, *The Crisis of European Sciences and Transcendental Phenomenology* (Evanston, IL: Northwestern University Press, 1970). Originally published in 1950; K. Jaspers, *The Future of Mankind* (Chicago: University of Chicago Press, 1963), p. 200.

40 Merton, 1973: pp. 273, 275.

41 M. Wartofsky, "Is Science Rational?," in W. H. Truitt and T. W. G. Solomons (eds), *Science, Technology, and Freedom* (Boston: Houghton Mifflin, 1974), pp. 203, 208–9.

42 Joshua Lederberg, "Food Additives," in M. Brown (ed.), *The Social Responsibility of the Scientist* (New York: The Free Press), 1971, pp. 129–30.

43 Robert Stebbins, "The Loss of Biological Diversity," in Brown (ed.), 1971: p. 171; See for example, George Wald, "A Generation in Search of a Future," in J. Allen (ed.), *Scientists, Students and Society* (Cambridge, MA: MIT Press, 1970), pp. 106–15.

44 J. Shapiro, L. Eron, and J. Beckwith, "Correspondence," in M. Brown (ed.), 1971: p. vii. From a letter to *Nature*, December 27, 1969.

45 Barry Commoner, "The Ecological Crisis," in Brown (ed.), 1917: p. 174.

46 Hayden, 1967: p. 4.

47   W. G. McMillan, "The Scientist in Military Affairs," in Allen (ed.), 1970: p. 15.
48   McMillan, 1970: p. 24.
49   Serge Lang,. "The DOD, Government, and Universities," in Brown (ed.), 1971: p. 52.
50   Brown, "Epilogue," in Brown (ed.), 1971: p. 272.
51   D. Dickson, *Alternative Technology* (Glasgow, Scotland: Fontana, 1974).
52   Nathan Sivin, "Preface," in N. Sivin and S. NaKayama (eds), *Chinese Science* (Cambridge, MA: M.I.T. Press, 1973), p. xxx.
53   SESPA, *China: Science Walks on Two Legs* (New York: Avon Books, 1974), pp. 211–12; and see M. Livingston and Lowinger, *The Minds of the Chinese People* (Englewood Cliffs, NJ: Prentice-Hall, 1983).
54   S. Restivo and M. Zenzen, "A Humanistic Perspective on Science and Society," pp. 82–116 in W. K. Fishman and C. G. Benello (eds), *Readings in Humanist Sociology* (Bayside, NY: General Hall, 1986); and S. Restivo, "Modern Science as a Social Problem," *Social Problems* 35, 3 (June 1988), pp. 206–25.

Part II

Society, the Self, and Social Relationships

4

Imagining Society

In Part I, I sketched the development of sociology as a science of society. In this chapter I construct a picture of the most general core concept in sociology, "society." The resources I draw on are dialectical sociology, open systems theory, and ecological-evolutionary sociology. My objective is to draw on approaches that convey the complexity and dynamism of society, and complement each other in ways that can lead to a general theory of society. This should not be interpreted as a call for consensus and order in sociological theory, but rather an evaluation of the possibility of constructing an explanatory theory of society.[1]

The dangers of general theory – Grand Theory, Unified Theory, disciplinary imperialism – are real and should not be minimized. But there are also problems with being theoretically timid, empirically parochial, tied to facts in themselves, or a slave to quantitative data. General theory should not represent a search for a single, ultimate, all-encompassing explanatory system. Rather, it should be viewed as an effort to construct a temporary, comprehensive unification with the expectation that such a theory will eventually become diversified, or one in a set of theories that yield a new unification. Inquiry is an unending process of theoretical unifications and diversifications, and an evolution of worldviews.

The following outline of dialectical sociology is designed to evoke an image of society as a complex system in motion. The terms "dialectic" and "laws" should be understood loosely as references to, respectively, the causal roots and basic principles of social change. The dialectical model provides a picture of society that comes closer than other models to getting across the levels and the motions of society. It should not be viewed as a dogma, or a fully tested, empirically grounded set of principles. The various principles of dialectical sociology are, in general, approximations to the most general principles governing the most general aspects of social life.

DIALECTICAL SOCIOLOGY

In Marxist theory, "dialectics" refers to the general process of motion, development, and change in nature, society, and thought. The three main laws of dialectics are: the transformation of quantity into quality, and of quality into quantity; the interpenetration of opposites; and the "negation of the negation." Engels described the law of the negation of the negation as an extremely general, comprehensive, and important law of development that holds in biology, zoology, geology, mathematics, history, and philosophy. This law, or metaphor, is the cornerstone of the dialectical imagination. Engels emphasized that a negation must be carried out in a certain way if it is to result in development. Negation does not mean simply saying no, declaring that something does not exist, or destroying something in an arbitrary way.[2]

Engels offers many examples of dialectical processes in his lengthy notes on dialectics. Some of the examples fit the negation of the negation rhetoric better than others. And nowhere in the writings of Engels or Marx is there a systematic statement of dialectics as a *sociological* theory. But Engels' work does evoke a dynamic image of society. The dialectical conception of society guides the work of scholars from Hegel to Merleau-Ponty and Herbert Marcuse. The translation of this conception of society into a form relevant to sociological theory has proceeded haltingly. Nikolai Bukharin and Georges Gurvitch have made important contributions to giving theoretical substance to dialectical imagery.

Bukharin conceives dialectical methods to be based on two considerations: that all phenomena are interrelated; and that they exist in states of motion.[3] Society, according to Bukharin, is always in motion; it is always undergoing alterations. We do not always observe society "growing." But motion and alterations are constant features of social life. They take society through different states and forms which can reflect evolution or devolution. The equilibrium we observe in society (and in nature) is an equilibrium in flux; it is constantly being established and destroyed, re-established on new bases and disturbed again. This process is a reflection of the internal conflicts and contradictions that are the motive forces of social change; this process is sometimes described in terms of *thesis* (original equilibrium), *antithesis* (disturbance), and *synthesis* (resolution of contradiction and emergence of a new unification and equilibrium, that is, a new thesis).

Society, like all other things, is a whole made up of interrelated parts, or elements, that is, a system. The system of society is surrounded by natural systems that constitute its environment. Contradictions between society and environment are referred to as external contradictions; those between society and its elements (or between and among the elements) are referred to as internal contradictions.

There are three types of relationships between society and its environment. In stable equilibrium, the situation remains unaltered; or if prevailing conditions are disturbed, they are re-established. This is an ideal state, which does not exist in reality. In unstable equilibrium with positive indication (an expanding system), contradictions and conflicts are resolved in ways which bring about increase and development in the society (that is, evolution). Finally, with unstable equilibrium with negative indication (a declining system), the resolution of conflicts and contradictions leads to the devolution of the society.

Internal or structural equilibrium is a function of external equilibrium. And just as in nature, gradual changes prepare the ground for sudden changes – evolution leads to revolution. (This idea has received some support from the contemporary evolutionary theory of punctuated equilibrium).

Bukharin's conception of dialectical sociology is an early effort to articulate a view of society based on dialectical principles. More recently, Georges Gurvitch has made some progress in transforming dialectical imagery into sociological theory.[4]

Gurvitch's goal was the construction of a general theory encompassing all the specialties in sociology. His descriptions of social reality vividly capture the dialectical image of society. He views society as a set of interpenetrating levels, strata, planes, and layers which are in constant conflict. Social reality is characterized by tension, fluctuations, movement, renewing, and the threat of revolutions. It is complex, dynamic, paradoxical, irrational, progressive. The basic unpredictability of this complex social reality is, according to Gurvitch, tempered by essential patterns that make tentative generalizations possible.

Dialectics is not a logic or a method in Gurvitch's sociology; social reality *is*, he argues, dialectical; the uncontainability of experience, he asserts, necessarily means that the researcher is part of this dialectic.

There are five "operational procedures of the dialectic" in Gurvitch's theory: (1) complementarity, (2) mutual implication, (3) ambiguity, (4) polarization, and (5) reciprocity of perspectives. Complementarity covers those cases where contradictory alternatives turn out to be complementary, two polarities are connected by a continuum, and polar points pull together in a compensatory action. Mutual implication refers to situations in which things that are heterogeneous or opposites exhibit mutuality and interdependency. They turn out to be at least partially immanent in one another. Ambiguities exist in social relationships, between and among individuals, individuals and groups, and within individuals. They can develop into ambivalences and polarizations; feelings of love, for example, can turn into feelings of hate, or love and hate can co-exist more or less uneasily.

The mutual tensions between the various elements of social reality vary in intensity, and sometimes these tensions polarize a set of elements. Paradoxes tend to resist polarizations. Reciprocity of perspectives refers to situations in which the total identification or total separation of elements is denied. The emphasis is on mutual immanence, parallelism, and symmetry.

Gurvitch did not argue for the universal applicability of the dialectic. The dialectic, in his program, applies to the natural sciences only to the extent that they are affected by human factors. (Herbert Marcuse has a similar view of the dialectic.)[5] But the physicist David Bohm has proposed a dialectical view of physical reality that provides support for those who, like Engels, see dialectics as a general theory applicable to all aspects of reality.[6] In any case, the image of society in dialectical sociology captures the complexity and dynamics of society in a way that few other perspectives, theories, or models have, or could.

A similar image of society is conveyed in a more coherent and abstract fashion by general systems theory. It is easy to see why general systems theory and dialectical sociology are not usually thought of as compatible. The term "systems theory" (in both general systems terms and in terms of its more familiar association for sociologists with the work of Talcott Parsons) is often considered a synonym for "conceptual closure," and this violates the open-endedness of dialectics. But Alfred Kuhn's conception of systems as "products of the interaction of polar opposites" evokes the dialectic. And in fact the idea of relating dialectic and general systems theory is not new in sociology. It has been suggested, for example, that general systems theory can demystify dialectical sociology; and on the other hand, it has been proposed that the dialectic orientation can help to sharpen notions such as feedback for sociologists. A rationale for considering the relationship between general systems theory and dialectical sociology is already implicit in Bukharin's references to systems, equilibrium, and positive and negative indications (or feedback). In the next section I outline the general systems orientation, and draw attention to its compatibility with dialectical sociology.[7]

GENERAL SYSTEMS SOCIOLOGY

General systems theory is widely viewed as applicable, actually or potentially, to physical, biological, and social systems. One version of general systems theory, for example, involves definitions and postulated relationships that are applicable to mechanical, electrical, biological, psychological, and social levels of analysis.[8] Two things about general systems theory might make it attractive for sociologists. It deals with the recognized needs to tie various disciplines together, and to develop a holistic, empirically testable orientation to sociological problems, and the open system approach in general systems theory avoids the pitfalls of the closed system approach to social organization; it deals with the internal and external environments of organizations, and feedback mechanisms.[9]

The promise of general systems theory for sociology can be summarized as follows:

1 a common vocabulary that unifies the various behavioral disciplines;
2 a technique for treating large, complex organizations;
3 a synthetic approach which takes into account the intricate interrelationships of parts within wholes;
4 a perspective that deals with the heart of sociology because it draws attention to the sociocultural system as sets of information and communications nets;
5 a focus on relations, process and transition probabilities; and a method for dealing with flexible structures which have many degrees of freedom; and
6 "An operationally definable, objective, non-anthropomorphic study of purposiveness, goal-seeking system behavior, symbolic cognitive processes, consciousness and self-awareness, and sociocultural emergence and dynamics in general."[10]

General systems theory has the capacity for dealing with some of the fundamental qualities that dialectical sociologists are concerned with: openness, emergence, and dynamics in sociocultural systems. These qualities have been widely considered to be incompatible with systems theories. In fact, the process model (which includes the dialectical process model) transcends the weaknesses of mechanical and organismic societal models, and even anticipates cybernetic principles.

The compatibilities between general systems theory and dialectical sociology become apparent once it is recognized that the concept of system does not logically entail closure, staticism, rigid stability, or an unchanging equilibrium. To illustrate this, consider the following definition of a system as "a set of components interacting with each other and a boundary which possesses the property of filtering both the kind and rate of flow of inputs and outputs to and from the system."[11] This is a structural definition. Functionally, a system processes inputs and produces output which is different in some detectable way from the inputs. Since function without structure is impossible, the structural definition has primacy. This idea of system is comparable to the idea of dialectics as an interpretation of

> the self-motion of the structure in terms of the nature and development of the contradictions inherent to it. It is predicated on an analysis of the functional correlation of the elements of the structure. The analysis of these functional relationships proceeds from the assumption that each element as part of a substructure is related to the other elements as substructures and to the environment as a whole.[12]

Such statements are not unusual in dialectical sociology; they are not by themselves, however, convincing examples of compatibility. But general systems theory includes open systems theory, which evokes a dialectical imagery.[13]

Systems theorists distinguish between open and closed systems. A closed system is an ideal (in the abstract sense) system. It is conceived to be completely isolated. It may undergo internal changes, but it does not exchange energy or information with its environment.[14] Real systems are never completely isolated; they are open to varying degrees. To say that a system is open means that it exchanges energy and information with its environment, and that this exchange process is essential for the system's viability, continuity, and capacity for change.[15] Bertrand identifies the following characteristics of open (social) systems: input, throughput, output cycles of events, negative entropy (negentropy), feedback and coding, boundary maintenance, steady state, storage and memory, variability and adaptation, elaboration, equifinality (capacity for reaching different states along different causal paths), tension, common goals and functional utility, and totality.[16] Totality, the idea that the system is more than the sum of its parts, is consistent with dialectical sociology. Elaboration, which refers to processes that generate new and modify old structural relations, is consistent with the emphasis on growth and development in dialectics. Of all the characteristics Bertrand lists, "tension" is perhaps the essential link between open systems and dialectical sociology. Tension is a generic term that encompasses the dialectical sociologist's ideas on immanence, negation, and conflict.

Here is Buckley's description of tension:

the source of action and interaction of the parts of mechanical systems is expressed in the physical concept of energy, whereas in complex, adaptive systems raw energy plays a less and less important role as it gives way to a more complex form of organized and directed motive force that we refer to as the inherent "irritability of protoplasm," tension or stress in animals, and psychic energy or motive power in men. "Tension," in the broad sense, of which "stress" and "strain" are manifestations under conditions of felt blockage, is ever present in one form or another throughout the sociocultural system – sometimes as diffuse, socially unstructured strivings, frustrations, enthusiasms, aggressions, neurotic or normative deviation; sometimes as clustered and minimally structured crowd or quasi-group processes, normatively constructive as well as destructive; and sometimes as socioculturally structured creativity and production, conflict and competition, or upheaval and destruction.[17]

Open systems theorists place as much emphasis on internal contradictions as dialectical sociologists do. Berrein, for example, refers to "unavoidable built-in conflict" in social systems caused by movements on behalf of preserving subsystem identities in opposition to the growing control of the suprasystem. More significantly, he considers it possible that "the form of growth in social systems is in part determined by certain nascent conditions embedded within the 'charter' members of a new group."[18]

Berrein's imagery is hardly less dialectical than Gurvitch's. He refers to the "continuing interaction" between a social system and its sub-and supra-systems,[19] to the development of social systems from the simple to the complex, with the concomitant development of emergent characteristics, and to the association of increasing uncertainty with increasing complexity.[20] Evidence about reality in general compels us, Berrein argues, "to view the subject matter of all science as consisting of interdependent circular transactions among linked systems in which cause cannot be distinguished from effect except by doing violence to the phenomena themselves."[21] Berrein specifically eschews the mechanistic viewpoint in favor of what amounts to a dialectical-systems theory. This is the consequence of working out the properties of "open systems."

The compatibility of open systems theory and the form of dialectical sociology outlined in the works of Bukharin and Gurvitch is expressed in the fact that both have a macrolevel, systemic orientation, emphasize complexity and its association with uncertainty, eschew mechanism, challenge traditional notions of cause and effect, and emphasize immanence, inherent conflict, and the importance of emergent characteristics. The theoretical advantage of general (open) systems theory over dialectical sociology is that it provides a logically consistent, technically well-defined conceptual system.

There is a third candidate for paradigm status in sociology that has important characteristics in common with general systems and dialectical sociology. In the next section, I examine compatibilities between ecological/evolutionary sociology, and general systems and dialectical sociology.

ECOLOGICAL/EVOLUTIONARY SOCIOLOGY

Sociologists Gerhard Lenski and Jean Lenski, and economist Edgar Dunn, Jr, have independently proposed the modern synthetic theory of organic evolution as a basis for a general theory in social science. The Lenskis view the ecological/evolutionary approach as a promising basis for integrating the basic findings of sociology, and of the social and biological sciences in general.[22] Dunn views the synthetic theory as the source of general principles relevant to all the social sciences and in particular to studying processes of social change.[23] He suggests that there is an "emerging paradigm" in social science based on the synthetic theory. This paradigm is characterized as a "process of social learning" metaphor. Dunn points out certain parallels between this metaphor and general systems theory, without going into the details of consistency, convergence, or compatibility. He also points out some parallels between the social learning metaphor and Marxian theory.

But his evaluation of Marxian theory is based on a narrow review of Marx's ideas; he does not consider the contributions by Engels, Bukharin, Gurvitch and others to dialectical sociology. His viewpoint is therefore more limited than the one I outline in this chapter.

The Lenskis' paradigm has four aspects: humankind's relations to the biotic world; universals of life; a basic analogue (symbol systems are functionally analogous to genetic systems;) and the theory of sociocultural evolution. In relation to the biotic world, humankind shares some attributes with all, and other attributes with some, living things; in addition, humankind possesses some attributes that no other living things share. The Lenskis list eight universals of life, ranging from the basic requirement for food, water, and air to reproductive and evolutionary capacities. The basic analogue states that symbol systems and genetic systems both facilitate the adaptation of populations to environments "through the acquisition, storage, transmission, and use of relevant information."[24] This leads to the second-order analogue relating sociocultural and organic evolution.

The theory of sociocultural evolution outlined by the Lenskis refers to four basic processes: continuity (the persistence of phenomena); innovation (the emergence of phenomena); extinction (the disappearance of phenomena); and evolution. Evolution is the result of the combined operation of continuity, innovation, and extinction. It is a cumulative process involving the addition of new elements to a persistent base of elements.[25] The major points of convergence between Lenski's eco/evolutionary sociology and dialectical and general systems sociology are: a macrosociological focus; an emphasis on process; a developmental (evolutionary, progressive) hypothesis; a systemic view of society and culture; and a consideration of emergent phenomena. The general systems theorist Berrein refers to emergence in his discussion of the evolution of organizational systems: the formation of suprasystems of subsystems results in the appearance of new properties, "emergent qualities," not found in the inputs to the system. He notes that emergence appears to be characteristic of "biological, conceptual, and probably social evolution."[26]

A notable feature of the Lenskis' theory is a definition of progress: "a raising of the upper level of the capacity of populations to mobilize energy and information in the adaptive process." Progress is one of two basic trends in sociocultural evolution that parallel the basic trends of organic evolution. The other is diversification. The Lenskis also define learning as "that process which manifests itself by changes in behavior (usually adaptive in nature) based on prior experience."[27]

VII   THE PRINCIPLES OF SOCIAL LEARNING

1. Social learning takes place at individual and group levels;

2. Social behavior and social learning are not identical; there are sets of behavior directed to maintaining essentially homeostatic social processes. There are two categories of social behavior: evaluative and organizing;

3. Evaluation and organizing operate in social learning, but they are transformed into aspects of behavior-changing behavior;

4. In social learning, problem-solving involves hypothesis-testing; but in contrast to classical experimentation, social learning involves an experimenter who is endogenous to a system that is not fully deterministic;

5. Social learning is a normative process which leads to the evolution of social values; and

6. Social learning has normal and extraordinary modes. The normal mode applies to reorganizing subsystem boundaries in terms of system goals. The extraordinary mode involves reformulating system goals.[29]

Edgar Dunn has developed a similar notion of learning into a social learning metaphor. Dunn's central thesis is that a process of behavioral development or social learning is implicit in behavior.[28] This process of social learning is a form of evolutionary experimentation, and Dunn explains it using a synthetic evolution metaphor. The metaphor allows him to deal with the stochastic and the purposive aspects of behavior-changing behavior. The major principles of social learning are outlined in box VII.

The normative basis of the social learning metaphor or model is the primacy of growth motives in individuals, or what I refer to as the primacy of the person. In applying the social learning metaphor, the design of adaptable networks always has precedence over "optimum transfer networks;" history is conceived as a source of tests and a stimulus for reinterpreting social learning; social action and analysis are merged; goals and controls are regularly evaluated, and reformulated whenever necessary; and cooperative connections are designed linking the sciences in order to provide information for social learning.

Dunn adds some detail to the more general evolutionary theory the Lenskis develop; the compatibility of the two perspectives is obvious. But the Lenskis link evolutionary theory to ecology, something Dunn does not do.[30] Their treatment of ecology is, however, sketchy, and in the next section I fill in the salient features of the ecological program.

THE ECOLOGICAL PROGRAM

The central focus of human ecology is human organisms interacting with environments.[31] In particular, human ecologists examine how people adjust to their environments, and how environments affect intergroup relationships. The central question in human ecology is: how do populations cope with specific environmental conditions in the course of satisfying subsistence needs and insuring their perpetuation?

In addition, the following assumptions, according to Micklin, are widely accepted in human ecology:

1　Populations use social organization to coordinate social skills and activities necessary for prolonged survival. Patterns of social organization are persistent over time, but can be more of less readily modified.
2　Spatial and temporal patterns of relationships are characterized by regularities and variations;
3　Ecological relationships are represented by sets of activities; these might be viewed as social roles on the individual level, and as social processes on the collective level;
4　Shifts occur in ecological organization based on the capacity in social organization for changing and adapting to external conditions.

There are three more assumptions which I wish to add here following Micklin; these are probably not as widely accepted as the prior assumptions:

5　Human activity is affected by both material conditions and ideas;
6　Conflict is intrinsic to social life. Ecological analysis focuses on conflicts that arise out of the different criteria groups use to define optimal adaptation to environments, and the different means groups use to achieve ecological goals.
7　Ecological analysis focuses on two analytically distinct outcomes of ecological systems: (1) quantitative survival criteria, for example, size of population supported, and life expectancy; (2) qualitative survival criteria.[32]

VIII THEORY OF SOCIOCULTURAL EVOLUTION

1. Definitions: specific evolution refers to the "phylogenetic, adaptive, diversifying, specializing, ramifying aspects" of the total evolutionary process: general evolution refers to "the emergence of higher forms of life, regardless of particular lines of descent or historical sequences of adaptive modification."

2. Principles:
   (a) The principle of stabilization – adaptation is a self-limiting factor in specific evolution;
   (b) The phylogenetic discontinuity of progress – new stages in evolution begin in new lines rather than in predominantly advanced lines;
   (c) The local discontinuity of progress – successive new stages of evolution are likely to begin in different localities;
   (d) The law of evolutionary potential – "The more specialized and adapted a form in a given evolutionary state, the smaller is its potential for passing to the next stage."[35]

The ecological evolutionary program can be rounded out with McHarg's outline of the basic characteristics of healthy and unhealthy ecological systems,[33] and the law of evolutionary potential formulated by Sahlins and Service.[34] McHarg associates ecological health with evolution. A retrogressive, unhealthy ecological system is characterized by simplicity, uniformity, independence, instability, a low number of species, and high entropy. An evolving, ecologically healthy system is characterized by complexity, diversity, interdependence, stability, a high number of species, and low entropy.

Sahlins and Service have tried to capture the broad sweep of evolution in a set of definitions and principles. These definitions and principles are generally consistent with the ideas of the Lenskis and Dunn, and provide a useful summary statement which can orient analyses and critical discussions on sociocultural evolution. The Sahlins and Service theory of sociocultural evolution is summarized in the definitions and principles outlined in box VIII.

There is at least an implicit theory of knowledge underlying dialectical, general systems, and ecological-evolutionary sociology. A rough idea of what that theory might look like can be gathered from Sutherland's epistemological program for general systems theory.[36] I find the rhetoric here a little too positivistic and rigid, but the program is worth sketching for illustrative purposes; see box IX.

IX AN EPISTEMOLOGICAL PROGRAM

1. Phenomenal isomorphism is a scientifically useful idea;
2. "Scientific truth" is based on an empirico-theoretical approach;
3. Analogic models are critical in studying complex phenomena;
4. In the social and behavioral sciences, "organic" referents are preferred over "mechanical" referents;
5. Analytical holism (based on the hypothetico-deductive approach) is preferred over reductionism-inductivism;
6. Macrodeterminacy is an isomorphic property of many, or most, complex systems, and a starting point for analysis;
7. Ideal-typical and taxonomic constructs are the basic modes of phenomenal analysis in the social and behavioral sciences.

In particular, his notions of "organic referents," "analytical holism," and "macrodeterminacy" seem well suited for dialectical and evolutionary-ecological sociology.

The theoretical perspectives I have reviewed can be the basis for constructing a general theory of society. But for the present, they at least provide three interrelated ways of imagining society. The materials I have reviewed can, in their present form, provide a coherent – if slightly eclectic – basis for general theorizing in macrosociology. They may, moreover, prove useful for presenting sociology in a manner that reflects the improving power of sociological explanations. The progress of sociological inquiry would be facilitated by recognizing that sound contributions have been made in identifying and articulating the basic assumptions, concepts, principles, and epistemology of macrosociology. Working toward a general theory from the set of contributions I have outlined is a preferable alternative to multiplying special and ad hoc theories, idiosyncratic vocabularies, and theoretically weak empirical studies.

In the next section, I identify some of the more important commonalities and complementarities that link the perspectives I have outlined and provide the foundations for a general theory of society.

COMMONALITIES AND COMPLEMENTARITIES

The particular versions of dialectical, general systems, and ecological/evolutionary sociology I have outlined have the following general features in common:

1 a macro-level focus;
2 a vision of a unified sociology (e.g., Gurvitch), social science (e.g., Dunn), or science (e.g., Berrein);
3 a holistic, systemic, and dynamic view of social reality;
4 an emphasis on immanence, inherent conflict, process, change, and emergence;
5 a capacity for dealing with evolving and increasingly complex systems, as well as with devolution; and
6 an epistemological foundation that transcends simplistic conceptions of cause and effect, mechanism, and physicalism. These general features are, as I have indicated, manifested in compatible imagery, conceptual parallels, and analogous assumptions and principles. Perhaps the most important commonality, however, is the value imperative which the three approaches share.

Dialectical, general systems, and ecological/evolutionary sociologists vary in the degree to which they contend that certain values (e.g., for survival, liberation, or evolution) follow from their theoretical orientations. But the approaches I have outlined imply that human survival with "quality of life" requires doing all we can, individually and collectively, to continually broaden and deepen our experiences and our consciousnesses.

Buckley argues that modern systems analysis suggests that "A central feature of the complex adaptive system is its capacity to persist or develop by changing its own structure, sometimes in fundamental ways."[37] This idea is stated by the Lenskis as "the evolution of evolution" hypothesis: human beings may have to gain "rational control" over "the entire process of societal evolution" in order to survive.[38] Dunn is more specific; he identifies three major thresholds in sociocultural evolution: a phylogenetic raising of the generalizing capacity of animal nervous systems and the emergence of symbolization and speech; the emergence of social organization as a factor in social maintenance; and the development of the classical scientific method. Dunn then suggests that we may be on the verge of a fourth threshold. Beyond this threshold we would have the power to transcend "environmentally patterned behavior" and to shape "behaviorally patterned environments" in the interest of actualizing human potential.[39]

Taking account of growth and decline in sociocultural systems, dialectical, general systems, and ecological/ evolutionary sociology can provide us with information on how we must live if we are going to survive, adapt, and evolve.[40] Survival, adaptation, and evolution require an orientation to and preparation for process and change. Open-ended living means living in accordance with the principles of ecology and evolution, and the more general principles of open systems, all of which stress the importance of complexity, flexibility, and diversity as conditions for healthy development in human systems. And it implies an orientation to a dialectical reality with a stress on the idea that survival and evolution depend on liberating ourselves from the oppressions that burden us, and perceiving ourselves as self-actualizing entities immersed in process and change.[41]

POWER, ECOLOGY, AND EVOLUTION

Power is related to the capacity for survival, actualization of potential, and evolution at the individual and sociocultural levels. *I* have power to the extent that I can do what I need to do in order to (a) survive, and (b) self-actualize. A *sociocultural system* has power to the extent that it is capable of being perpetuated and changed.

Weber defined power as "the chance of a man or number of men to realize their own will in a communal action even against the resistance of others who are participating in the action."[42] Most contemporary sociological definitions of power are consistent with Weber's definition. They emphasize power as latent, or as a potential; and they incorporate the idea of resistance.[43] One of the important developments in the conceptualization of power has been to tie it to the idea of resources. Etzioni, for example, suggests that we can predict the power of a social unit "by studying its assets, its total structure, and its past performance."[44] In this sense, power has a cost: assets become depleted, and if they are not replenished, power declines. Etzioni identifies three types of assets: utilitarian (economic resources, technical and administrative capabilities, human resources), coercive (means of violence), and persuasive (symbols).

The most general way of conceiving the bases of power is in terms of resources. Power can then be defined as the potential in an entity (e.g., individual, social group, collectivity) for identifying, acquiring, mobilizing, and, generally, controlling resources necessary and/or sufficient for satisfying entity needs and achieving entity goals. We can then identify three levels of power. Primary power refers to the potential for satisfying needs and achieving goals at the level of basic survival (subsistence). Secondary power refers to post-subsistence needs and goals. And meta-power refers to needs and goals related to actualizing human and sociocultural potential.

Power can be viewed as the potential for progress, or general evolution. Elaborating the Lenskis' definition (introduced earlier), I define progress as a *raising of the upper limit within living systems (individual and collective) of the capacity to conceptualize, standardize, exploit, mobilize, process, retrieve, and utilize resources in the adaptive process, and to bring these resources to bear on increasing adaptability.* Progress, in short, is the process of increasing the power of living systems.

Power is a function of the quantity, quality, distribution, variety, demand for, and recycling and renewing rates of resources. It also depends on the capacities of organisms (individually and collectively) for receiving, storing, retrieving, and processing information; the strength of the survival motive; and the strength of the meta-survival (that is, self-actualization) motive. Another factor is the degree of cooperation and the capacity for optimizing options in sociocultural systems. Power must also be considered a function of the time available for exercising or actualizing it. In general, power depends on diversity, complexity, and flexibility in living systems; the degree to which the various elements are cooperatively engaged; the capacity for absorbing costs; and the capacity for overcoming resistance (to barriers limiting perception, for example, as well as to more widely recognized forms of resistance).

The conception of power I have sketched underscores the dependence of self-actualization and sociocultural evolution on our individual and collective capacities for cooperatively controlling resources. These capacities are in turn dependent on the degree to which individuals are optimally healthy and, therefore, maximally aware of themselves and their environs. The ideas of self-actualization and cooperation are discussed in detail in chapters 5 and 6.

CONCLUSION

In general, the interrelationships between and among the three theoretical approaches I have reviewed can be conceived in terms of Gurvitch's operational procedures. The dialectical interaction of the three approaches in teaching and research can be an important stimulus to the development of a general theory. In the short run, each approach retains its relative autonomy and is independently subject to criticism, development, and application. In the long run, the three approaches become integrated into one general theory.

Each approach has special contributions to make in the process of constructing a general theory. I conceive dialectical sociology (as formulated by Bukharin and Gurvitch) as the primary source of the imagery common to the three approaches. Open systems sociology might be the source of a conceptually clear, well-defined, self-consistent, and systematic vocabulary for expressing the dialectical imagery. The development of an open systems nomenclature may solve some of the terminological difficulties that are bound to arise in constructing conceptual and theoretical systems across conventional disciplinary boundaries. In addition, open systems sociology is a natural basis for formalizing and mathematizing the general language of macrosociology when and where such processes are appropriate. The Lenskis' work is the most promising source of a general language, that is, a specialized sociological vocabulary linked to empirical social realities.

The teaching imperative is to utilize the ideas, principles, and images of the three approaches as outlined above for analyzing and comprehending the variety of sociocultural, institutional, and organizational phenomena. In the introductory text or course, for example, a general theoretical orientation can be established and applied to particular cases instead of treating each institution or social problem in terms of unrelated or unintegrated empirical studies and special, or ad hoc, theories.

With respect to the research imperative, the goal of a general theory can only be achieved if there is a commitment among some (not necessarily all) sociologists to constructing general theory within each of the three theoretical areas discussed in this chapter. In addition, some of these sociologists in turn will have to perceive that there are compatibilities between their particular theoretical approach and one or both of the other two approaches. Such a commitment will have to attract a core of sociologists who will work on theory (including conceptual clarification, standardization of nomenclature, and formalization), and who will use this theoretical work as a reference source and guide for empirical studies.[45]

NOTES

1 For endorsements of general theory as a goal in sociological inquiry, see R. Collins, *Conflict Sociology* (New York: Academic Press, 1975), p. ix; G. Lenski and J. Lenski, *Human Societies*, 2nd edn (New York: McGraw-Hill, 1974), pp. ix–x; R. Merton, 'Structural Analysis in Sociology', in P. Blau

(ed.), *Approaches to the Study of Social Structures* (New York: The Free Press, 1975), p. 52, and see M. Harris, *Cultural Materialism* (New York: Vintage, 1980).

2 F. Engels, *Anti-Duhring* (New York: International Publishers, 1939), pp. 153–155. Trans. by E. Burns; ed. by C. Dutt. Originally published in 1885; and F. Engels, *Dialectics of Nature* (New York: International Publishers, 1940), 26. Trans. and ed. by C. Dutt. Originally written between 1872 and 1882.

3 N. Bukharin, *Historical Materialism: A System of Sociology* (New York: International Publishers, 1925), p. 67. The following summary is based on Bukharin's discussion of dialetical sociology on pp. 68–82.

4 The following discussion is based on Georges Gurvitch, *La Vocation Actuelle de la Sociologie*, 2nd edn, 2 vols (Paris: Presses Universitaires de France, 1957 and 1963), vol. I, p. 63; P. Bosserman, *Dialectical Sociology: An Analysis of the Sociology of Georges Gurvitch* (Boston: Porter Sargent Publishers, 1968), pp. 223–7, 260; G. Gurvitch, *Dialectique et Sociologie* (Paris: Flammarion, 1962), pp. 180, 190–213.

5 "Every fact can be subjected to dialectical analysis only in so far as every fact is influenced by the antagonisms of the social process." H. Marcuse, *Reason and Revolution*. (Boston: Beacon Press, 1960), p. 315.

6 David Bohm, *Causality and Change in Modern Physics* (Philadelphia: University of Pennsylvania Press, 1971); and "Quantum Theory as an Indication of a New Order in Physics, Part B: Implicate and Explicate Order in Physical Law," *Foundations of Physics*, vol. 3, no. 2 (1973), pp. 139–68. Bohm argues that physical phenomena have to be conceptualized in terms of a new view of reality. His conception of physical reality is consistent with the conceptions of social reality found in the three approaches discussed here. Bohmian reality is complex, dynamic, and holistic. Bohm's descriptions of physical reality evoke distinctly dialectical images. In the "new order of physics," according to Bohm, facts, methods, and theories are seen as different aspects of an "individual wholeness;" the universe is an infinity of things in becoming in which "everything implicates everything."

7 A. Kuhn, *Unified Social Science* (Homewood, IL: The Dorsey Press, 1975); R. W. Friedrichs, *A Sociology of Sociology* (New York: The Free Press, 1970), p. 53; W. Buckley, *Sociology and Modern Systems Theory* (Englewood Cliffs, NJ: Prentice- Hall, 1967), p. 37; L. Schnieder, "Dialectic in Sociology." *American Sociological Review*. vol. 36, no. 4 (August, 1971), p. 677. F. K. Berrein, *General and Social Systems* (New Brunswick, NJ: Rutgers University Press, 1968), p. 8. See also K. Boulding, "General Systems Theory – The Skeleton of Science." *Management Science*, vol. 2, no. 3 (April, 1956), pp. 198–200.

8 F. K. Berrein, *General and Social Systems* (New Brunswick, NJ: Rutgers University Press, 1968), p. 8. See also K. Boulding, "General Systems Theory – the Skeleton of Science," *Management Science*, vol. 2, no. 3 (April, 1956), pp. 198–200.

9 A. L. Bertrand, *Social Organization* (Philadelphia: F. A. David and Co., 1972), p. 96.

10 Buckley, 1967, p. 39.

11 Berrein, 1968, pp. 14–15.

12 Milos Kalab, "The Specificity of the Marxist Conception of Sociology," in P. L. Berger (ed.), *Marxism and Sociology* (New York: Appleton-Century-Crofts, 1969), pp. 72–3.

13 Cf., A. S. Iberall, *Toward a General Science of Viable Systems* (New York: McGraw-Hill, 1972), pp. 4–5.

14 V. L. Parsegian, *The Cybernetic World* (New York: Doubleday Anchor, 1973), p. 28.

15 Buckley, 1967, p. 50.

16 Bertrand, 1972, pp. 97–103.

17 Buckley, 1967, p. 51.

18 Berrein, 1968, p. 135.

19 Berrein, 1968, p. 158.

20 Berrein, 1968, p. 199.

21 Berrein, 1968, p. 201.

22 Lenski and Lenski, 1974, p. x. References to Lenski in the following notes are to the *first* edition of the book, published in 1970.

23 E. Dunn, Jr., *Economic and Social Development* (Baltimore: The Johns Hopkins Press, 1971), p. 3.

24 Lenski and Lenski, 1974, p. 19.

25 Lenski and Lenski, 1974, p. 51.

26 Berrein, 1968, p. 62.

27 Lenski, 1970, p. 59; Lenski and Lenski, 1974, p. 14.

28 Dunn, 1971, pp. 11; 238–54.

29 Dunn, 1971, p. 242.

30 Lenski, 1970, p. 25.

31 M. Micklin, "A Framework for the Study of Human Society," in M. Micklin (ed.), *Population, Environment, and Social Organization* (Hinsdale, IL: The Dryden Press, 1973), p. 3.

32 Micklin, 1973, pp. 3–4.

33 Ian McHarg, "An Ecological Method for Landscape Architecture," in P. Shepard and D. McKinley (eds), *The Subversive Science* (Boston: Houghton Mifflin Company, 1969), p. 332.

34 M. Sahlins and E. Service (eds), *Evolution and Culture* (Ann Arbor: The University of Michigan Press, 1960), p. 16.

35 Sahlins and Service, 1960, pp. 95–9.

36 J. W. Sutherland, *A General Systems Philosophy for the Social and Behavioral Sciences* (New York: George Braziller, 1973), pp. 19–20; 34.

37 Buckley, 1967, p. 206.

38 Lenski, 1970, p. 491.

39 Dunn, 1971, pp. 262–4.

40 Cf., Bosserman, 1968, pp. 263–4.

41 I discuss values for survival and evolution in more detail, and with specific

reference to the scientific ethos, in chapter 7 of *The Social Relations of Physics, Mysticism, and Mathematics* (Dordrecht: D. Reidel, 1983). The value complex I associate with "openended living" is humanistic, radical, and reflexive.

42 Max Weber, *The Theory of Social and Economic Organization* (New York: The Free Press, 1964), p. 152.

43 Marvin Olsen (ed.), *Power in Societies* (New York: Macmillan, 1970). See especially Part I, which includes essays by Hawley, Etzioni, Dubin, Weber, and others on the concept of power.

44 Amitai Etzioni, *The Active Society* (New York: The Free Press, 1968), pp. 314–23, 357–61; reprinted as "Power as a Societal Force" in Olsen (ed.), 1970, pp. 18–27.

45 This "strategy" is an alternative to the disciplined pluralism championed by Robert Merton, "theories of the middle range." Merton has recently described this approach in terms of making "modest theoretical consolidations toward the ultimate and still very remote ideal of a unified comprehensive theory." This view is problematic on two accounts. First, it endorses general theory as an ideal, but fails to indicate or suggest a path out of middle-rangism that will take us to that goal. Second, the vision of an ultimate unity contradicts Merton's lucid discussion of the functions of theoretical diversity; Merton, 1975, pp. 29 and 52. Our goal should not be a "final" unified theory; see note 1.

5

The Social Structure
of the Self

My objectives in this chapter are to sketch a view of the self as a social structure, show that the self is problematic, that is, that its development and continuity cannot be taken for granted, identify conditions for stability and change in the self, and discuss the self as a creator, agent, and product of society, culture, and sociocultural change.

THE SELF AS A SOCIAL STRUCTURE

Some notion of "self" is necessary to account for the individual's experience of unity and continuity in him or herself and others. Conceptions of the self prior to the emergence of the social sciences ranged from metaphysical and theological ideas about the soul to views of the individual as a collection of somative sensations. This individualistic orientation was influential during the early history of psychology. A great deal of attention was devoted to the problem of consciousness. Titchener's conception of the self as a complex of kinesthetic and organic sensations, for example, was based on an introspective analysis of consciousness.[1] In the late nineteenth century, some students of consciousness began to explore the self from a social perspective.

William James recognized the significance of social factors for understanding the self, but he did not examine the relationship between self and society in depth. James Baldwin was more explicit about the self as a social product. He argued that sociocultural factors such as language, play, and art are necessary means for the growth of the self. His concept of the self growing out of the constant interaction between individual and environment suggested that the self could be viewed as a social process.[2]

Charles H. Cooley argued for individualistic and social analyses of the self. He resolved the self into an "I" (the individualistic component) and a "We" (the social component). The consciousness of "I," according to Cooley, belongs to an advanced stage of development in the individual, and is not a part of all stages of consciousness.[3]

George Mead provided a general synthesis of the ideas of self formulated by James, Baldwin, Cooley, and others.[4] His symbolic interactionist approach stressed social factors in the development of the self. He did not, however, discard the individualistic perspective. According to Mead, the self has three components. Individuals get a variety of messages from people they come in contact with. They generalize these messages to construct that part of the self Mead referred to as "the generalized other." The "me" component is made up of internalized, accepted behavioral prescriptions and proscriptions. Spontaneity, creativity, impulsiveness, anti-social behavior, and deviance manifest the third component of the Meadian self, the "I."

Mead concluded that the self is a social structure. This idea has been interpreted psychologically by many sociologists. They have generally defined the self as an individual's "consciousness-of-being," or equated the self with the individual's "self-concept." The idea of the self as a social structure, however, can be interpreted in a more strongly sociological way as a set of social relationships that changes over time. This view of the self brings the individual into sociological focus without "psychologizing" the concept of social structure.

A sociologist who wants to construct an image of a self (his or her own, or someone else's) sets out to construct a set of social relationships. The self is a more or less organized set of social relationships, a social structure. It can be revealed through a combination of observations, self-reports, queries in questionnaires and depth interviews, and projective and introspective techniques and probes such as those used in psychology, psychoanalysis, and psychotherapy. Goffman's imagery vividly illustrates the social structural view of the self.

Erving Goffman sees the self as a collaborative product which is hung on the peg we think of as the person. The self is constructed and maintained with resources available in social establishments:

There will be a back region with its tools for shaping the body, and a front region with its fixed props. There will be a team of persons whose activity on stage in conjunction with available props will constitute the scene from which the performed character's self will emerge, and another team, the audience, whose interpretive activity will be necessary for this emergence. The self is a product of all these arrangements, and in all of its parts bears the marks of this genesis.[5]

Goffman's dramaturgical imagery suggests that the self can be viewed as a set of relationships between the person and his or her world. The core of the person as an organism is the Goffman peg. People, symbols, and objects are attached to and detached from this peg, and constitute the changing self.

The idea of a changing self has not been stressed in sociology. Mead, for example, felt that once the self had "arisen" the developmental phase of selfhood ended. But he also provided a rationale for a more dynamic view of the self. He noted that the unity and structure of the complete self mirrors the unity and structure of "the social process as a whole."[6] A necessary condition for the development of a self is a stable society characterized by stable social processes. Mead emphasized stability in his analysis of communication. Symbols used in communication, he noted, should arouse in us what they arouse in others. Such reciprocal arousal must be our goal and our expectation in communication.[7]

The self grows out of the person's ability to anticipate reactions and responses from objects and people he or she encounters. This ability to anticipate is a consequence of constancies in images, concepts, objects, and persons.[8] The unity and structure of the self reflect the unity and structure of the social world in which the person lives. This social world (and, more broadly, the environment) is however, never, perfectly unified or structurally static. It changes during the person's lifetime, just as the environment within which a social group or society operates changes over time. Social worlds vary with time and across geographical and sociocultural boundaries. There are thus as many types of selves as there are social worlds. A person born into eighteenth – century Indian society would develop a different self than he or she would develop in contemporary France, or Brazil. Such differences, changes, and variations have not, until recent times, shaken the belief in a basic, unchanging, core self akin to a soul. The modern experience with large-scale, rapid social change, alienation, and dehumanization has undermined that belief and provided a basis for viewing the self as problematic.[9]

Marx's observations on the alienation of the worker, and Weber's more general concern with the alienating effects of rationality and bureaucracy, were among the first signs of an awareness among social scientists that the self could not be taken for granted. The constancy principle had to be reinterpreted in order to account for the possibility of rapid change in the self associated with changes in society, culture, and the environment. A certain degree of constancy is necessary for the self to arise. Society and culture, however, exhibit conflicts, tensions, and contradictions. The degree of sociocultural change varies, but can be considered ubiquitous. We should therefore expect varying degrees of conflict, tension, and contradiction in selves. The constancy principle sets limits on the amount of change a self can experience without undergoing major changes itself, including deterioration, or death. But change has healthy as well as pathological consequences in the self as in society.

The rapid changes in social organization and technology associated with industrialization have exposed increasing numbers of human beings to conflicting and internally inconsistent value systems. One of the positive consequences of these changes is that we have become more acutely aware of the dynamic nature of reality. The self is in motion as an agent of, in resistance to, and as a passive reactor to sociocultural and environmental changes. This idea is dealt with in a separate section further on. First, I want to consider an important issue raised at least implicitly in the preceding discussion. Does the idea that the self is a product of society imply that the self is programmed?

THE SELF AS A PROGRAM

If the self is not present at birth and if it is dependent for its existence, continuity, and change on outside factors, can we say that the self, like the computer, is programmed? The analogy between humans and computers occurs to us for at least three reasons: some people seem to act mechanically; computers seem to do fundamentally human things like prove mathematical theorems, write poetry, and compose music; and human beings obviously do not become human – in fact, do not survive – unless they are exposed to sociocultural inputs; and these inputs, reflected in personality traits, modes of thought, linguistic usage, and general behavior, seem to be analogous to computer programs.

The literature on the computer-human being analogy is extensive. On the pro-analogy side it ranges from Arthur Burk's argument that a finite deterministic automaton can perform all natural human functions to Helier Robinson's thesis that it may be possible to program a computer for consciousness and morality. The opposition ranges from theologians who believe that humans, unlike all other living and material things, are endowed with souls to computer scientists who argue that humans differ from machines by virtue of such qualities as courage.[10]

J. Weizenbaum draws the distinction between people and machines in a manner that is not completely free of difficulties, but is consistent with the view of the self sketched in this chapter.[11] He likens the unconscious to "a turbulent sea," and the border between the conscious and the unconcious mind to "a stormy coastline." It takes courage, he argues, to probe, reveal, and explore what the unconscious contains. This is so because the unconscious contains not only "the material of creativity," but also "the darkest truths about one's self." To become a whole person means to confront one's inner and outer worlds. In order to become whole, we must be free to explore these realities. This is an image of a life filled with risks; but we can courageously accept these sorts of risks because, like explorers, we can learn to trust our capacities for endurance and overcoming. Weizenbaum concludes this description of the whole person with the question: "What could it mean to speak of risk, courage, trust, endurance, and overcoming when one speaks of machines?"

Perhaps, to answer Weizenbaum's question, we are just the sort of machine that can do the sorts of things he identifies as human. Are we, then, organic machines; and if so, does that settle the question of whether machines can think? One of the things we may need to do in order to fairly test the expectations of the artificial intelligence experts is to give intelligent non-organic machines some mobility: first, the capacity to move physically about an environment, second, to do something they already do, only better, move electronically through information and knowledge environments. Mobile machines interacting with mobile machines may be just what is needed to generate artificial intelligence.

The heuristic value of the programming analogy is that it helps us to see that people's experiences can be more or less expansive or narrow, open or closed. The narrower and more closed a person's experiences are, the more predictable, controlled, and controllable his or her activities are. By contrast, actualizing the human potential for growth and development by expanding the field of a person's experiences and alternatives narrows the potential for rigorous control and predictability.

One fundamental distinction between computers and humans may turn on the distinction between open and closed systems. Put simply, closed systems are ideal systems which do not exchange energies across their boundaries. Open systems, by contrast, do exchange energies across their boundaries. In reality, all systems are open. However, some approach closure to a greater degree than others.

The way in which a human being is socialized or programmed determines the extent to which he or she will behave in ways that appear robot-like or in ways that reflect independence and uniqueness. Human beings can be programmed to be more or less open. The experience of freedom (free will) is dependent on the extent to which the person is socialized open-endly. Open-ended socialization requires a social situation which offers alternatives and encourages individual choices bounded by constraints of cooperation, decency, and dignity.

THE SELF IN MOTION

Getting to know your self or someone else's self involves constructing a social structural image. Such an image is built up from answers to such questions as (1) who do you know; (2) how often do you interact with others; (3) what activities do you engage in (alone as well as with others); (4) are the people, things, and ideas you relate to central or peripheral in your life; (5) which of these components are stable, and which are changing? A sixth and therapeutic question is: Which experiences are out-of-mind, hidden away, and faded, as repressed or suppressed memories? Your ability to answer these questions about yourself or others depends on how well-developed your self is. If your self is underdeveloped, this will be reflected in the fuzziness of your self-image or consciousness. The degree of your self-development sets limits on the degree to which clear images of your self can be constructed by others.

The self has a development. Internally, it exists when and to the extent that an individual is conscious of his or her separateness, distinctiveness, and uniqueness. Externally, it exists when and to the extent that an individual can convey, verbally and non-verbally, information about his or her self to others. It is obvious from question six above that someone else might be able to form a clearer image of your self, in some respects at least, than you are able to form.

The degree to which a self exists can also be evaluated in terms of autonomy. Each of us integrates the people, things, and ideas we experience in different ways and to different degrees. If we are acutely aware of certain components of our selves, and of their specific influences, integration is low and the self is underdeveloped in terms of autonomy. This is the case if, when you make a decision, you can see, for example, your mother, or father, or teacher, or some symbol like a flag or God, inside your head urging, or warning you about the "proper" thing to do. If you can make decisions without such distinct images "popping up" inside you, your self is wholly integrated and autonomous. Your behavior is then better described as a matter of conscience rather than a matter of guilt or shame.[12]

The development of the self is affected by external stimuli. Unless you receive adequate levels of sensory stimulation, you will deteriorate, and die prematurely, or function below your potential. These consequences will follow from either too much or too little stimulation. It is impossible to determine optimum levels of stimulation with any precision. We do know, however, that mental and physical well-being is dependent on regular sensory stimulation. Stimuli must be, to a certain degree, consistent and patterned; and they must be, to a certain degree, dynamic. An unchanging stimulus gradually loses its power to generate significant responses.

Another factor is social change. Social changes can threaten the self. For example, moving from a steady job, a family, and a community of friends into a concentration camp can destroy one's self and create a new one. The continuity of your self depends on your staying in touch with the present, remembered, and anticipated realities of the social world which you take for granted. When that continuity is threatened you can utilize two interrelated strategies for protection: you can try to symbolically and actually continue to act as you have in the past (play the same roles), and you can draw on your imagination (strategy of will) to generate stimuli you are being deprived of, and to transform or override the threatening stimuli you are encountering. Thus, if I found myself in a concentration camp I might try to continue to be a sociologist by observing, recording, and thinking about patterns of social interaction in the camp. This would not be an easy strategy to carry out. The severity of the camp conditions and my levels of physical and mental tolerance for deprivation, punishment, and terror would determine the degree to which I could successfully carry out my strategy. The strategy would be useless unless combined with a strategy for physical survival. And, finally, the degree to which I would be interfering with the human rights and dignities of others would have to be considered. For example, in the interest of the survival of my self, would it be appropriate to interview someone who was starving, or who had been tortured, rather than to offer comfort? Obviously I would want to develop a strategy for playing sociologist consistent with my involvement with and commitment to those confined with me. I shall leave it for you to consider further the moral dilemmas such a situation would generate. The choices you make, and the choices forced on you, the severity and length of confinement, and the degree of support you can give to and receive from others will all determine whether you will survive the experience physically, and how your self will be affected.

THE SELF, SOCIAL ISOLATION, AND DRASTIC CHANGE

The dependence of the self on social relationships is dramatically illustrated in cases of human isolation. Lucien Maison examined three "feral children" cases he considers "as dependable as any historical record."[13] In 1828, Kaspar Hauser, 17 years old at the time, was found living in a hole or cage unable to speak, and extremely backward in his ability to use his hands. He was taught basic skills, including language, and learned Latin and arithmetic before he was murdered in 1833. One-year-old Amala and eight-year-old Kamala were discovered in a cave near the Indian village of Codsmur in 1920 with a she-wolf and two wolf cubs. They moved about on their knees and elbows, ran four-legged on their hands and feet, panted, bared their teeth, lapped up liquids, snarled, and exhibited other "wolf-like" characteristics. Amala died in 1927. Kamala learned how to speak, walk, run simple errands, and drink from a glass. She had a 50-word vocabulary when she died in 1929. Victor of Aveyron was found naked and alone in the woods outside a small French town in 1800. He was about 11 years old when he was put under the care of doctors at the National Institute for the Deaf and Dumb in Paris. Originally considered a congenital idiot, Victor eventually learned to communicate by pointing; he never learned to speak. He behaved selfishly, helping only when his immediate needs were served. Victor died in 1840. Maison's conclusion, based on a review of these and other cases, is that there is no such thing as human nature. Each human being has a history. There are no predetermined human characteristics; and human possibilities are unlimited.

Anna and Isabelle, both illegitimate children, were discovered when they were about six years old, under similar conditions of isolation, in the late 1930s. Anna got just enough care from her grandfather to keep her alive. She was kept in isolation in an upstairs room. Anna was unable to walk or talk, and did not exhibit any basic intelligence. She died four and a half years after being found, by which time she had learned to behave to a certain extent like a normal two- or three-year-old. Isabelle had more opportunity for interaction during the years she lived in a dark room with her deaf and mute mother. Initially, she was able to make croaking sounds only, and showed signs of feeble-mindedness, Isabelle reached a normal educational level before she was nine.[14]

A stronger illustration of the dependence of the self on social and broader environmental conditions is provided by the cases of the Ik and the Kaiadilt. The Ik were forced to change from a life of hunting in an environment of abundance to a life of scarcity farming by decree of the government of Uganda. When the anthropologist Colin Turnbull went to live among them in 1964, the forced changes in their life had put them on the edge of extinction. Starving, aging rapidly, Ik adaptive strategies led to bizarre behavior: adults laughing as a child crawls toward a fire and grabs a hot coal; laughing boys and girls drumming their weakened grandfather on the head with sticks and pelting him with stones. Life had not always been like this. A generation earlier, people had laughed for joy. Now, laughter had become part of an attempt to adapt to harsh, even impossible, new conditions of living. A people's character – the character of being an Ik – had been transformed by manipulating environmental conditions, and changing traditional social organization by forcing the Ik into crowded encampments. The Kaiadilt, an Australian aborigine group, have undergone a radical transformation due to a combination of inhumane treatment and environmental disaster. The experiences of the Ik and the Kaiadilt suggest that human values are not inherent in humanity. In Turnbull's words:

The Ik teach us that our much vaunted human values are . . . associated only with a particular form of survival called society, and that all, even society itself, are luxuries that can be dispensed with. That does not make them any the less wonderful or desirable, and if man has any greatness it is surely in his ability to maintain these values, clinging to them to an often very bitter end, even shortening an already pitifully short life rather than sacrifice his humanity. But that too involves choice, and the Ik teach us that man can lose the will to make it.[15]

The self is fragile. It is a veneer painted on the organism by society and culture. And it is not indelible. Imagine how quickly the veneer that is your self would vanish if you were sealed into a room with only enough air for a few hours, and no food or water. Imagine yourself in such a room with other people; and consider how your relationships would change as the conditions of deprivation worsened. Thinking about extreme situations like this, and like the concentration camp, should help you understand why the self is problematic. On the other hand, we tend to take for granted aspects of our everyday lives that help to sustain our selves, our consciousness of who and what we are. Every time we pass someone we know and are recognized, every time someone refers to us by our name, our selves are reinforced.

The strategies for protecting the self under negative conditions are likely to be implemented in confronting any major change in living conditions. In the next section, I want to discuss the problem of how positive change and continuity are combined in a humanistic image of the self.

SELF-ACTUALIZATION

All of us are aware of different needs and desires, of varied ways in which we can satisfy them, and of the many ways we can be deprived and frustrated. We also know that we can get too much of even those things that are absolute necessities for survival, such as food and water. The consequences of frustration, deprivation, or over-stimulation vary radically depending on the particular needs or desires, circumstances, and time. Deferred gratification may in some cases be necessary for reasoned living; and certain levels of deprivation or frustration may foster creativity. We must always be aware, however, of the irreversible damage our selves can undergo as a result of prolonged deprivation and frustration. Protein deficiencies early in life, for example, may result in irreversible damage to brain cells and affect intellectual potential. Sensory deprivation may lead to hallucinations in the short run, and to irreversible physical and mental deterioration in the long run. Pain, discomfort, and inefficiency are consequences of deprivation and frustration; deterioration and death in a matter of seconds, minutes, months, or years are also possible.

In addition to some sense of the realistic necessities of life, people have ideas or ideals about what constitutes optimal or maximal well-being. In athletics or physical culture, people strive for excellence in physical power and endurance. Knowledge is available about how to work toward optimizing our physical abilities, through diet, exercise, rest, relaxation, and sleep. What about our selves; are there ideals and means for approximating them in self-development? Your first response might be that self-development is not the same as physical development. It is more complex, more variable, and less subject to consensus regarding means and ends. Yet self-actualization theory represents an attempt to confront the difficult problem of what it means to be human, and how to achieve "human-ness." Abraham Maslow was a pioneer in this type of research.

Maslow conceived the humanistic orientation to be toward the Big Problem of creating the Good Person in the Good Society. He conceived the Good Person as one who feels responsible for his or her evolution (i.e., individual growth and development), is "fully illuminated or awakened or perspicacious," and is "fully human." The Good Person is self-evolving, or self-actualizing.[16] Maslow identifies eight characteristics of self-actualization:

1 "full, vivid, selfless experiencing, with full concentration and absorption;"
2 making choices that, on the average, promote growth; choices based on defense, safety and fear are generally regressive choices and therefore opposed to self-actualization;
3 "listening to the impulse voices" instead of the introjected voices of parents;
4 taking responsibility, looking within oneself for answers, being honest rather than dishonest "when in doubt;"
5 "daring to be different, unpopular, nonconformist;"
6 "working to do well the thing one wants to do;"
7 ridding oneself of illusions and false notions; and
8 "identifying and then giving up defenses."[17]

Maslow distinguished five types of human needs and ordered them in a hierarchy as follows: physiological, safety, love, esteem (or respect), and self-actualization. Alderfer tried to clarify this typology by expanding it to seven categories: physiological, safety-material, safety-interpersonal, respect for others, respect from others, self-esteem (or self-respect), and self-actualization.[18] The simplest interpretation of this model is that, as lower-level needs are satisfied, higher-level needs emerge. Higher-level behavior depends on being able to regularly satisfy lower-level needs without inordinate expenditure of time and energy.

Another viewpoint is that all seven needs are ever present, and that the degree to which they are part of our motivational system is situational. Self-actualization, for example, is not and cannot be a primary motive or value in subsistence societies. This viewpoint suggests that we are not fully human or optimally healthy if we are prevented (for whatever reasons) from experiencing and satisfying our needs on all seven levels, and if we are prevented from devoting most of our energy to self-actualization. This in no way slights the humanness of people who live in subsistence societies, or the victims of oppression in contemporary society who are relegated to lives of misery in the midst of an abundance of resources thoughtlessly exploited and wasted for reasons of profit and power. Neither does it automatically uphold conventionally successful individuals or history's traditional heroes as models of self-actualization. It simply draws attention to the potentials we have, and to the value of working to identify and actualize them. We cannot be satisfied with subsistence, nor retire to the material comforts of modern life, and hope for any kind of growth, development, or evolution. Self-actualization is an endless striving for change in the interest of life and consciousness. Ultimately, it is this quality, and not an individual's socio-economic or material situation, that defines self-actualization.

Ideally, self-actualization requires:

1　regular satisfaction of all lower-level needs;
2　awareness of and motivation to satisfy self-actualization needs;
3　dealing with lower-level needs in terms of self-actualization: for example, physiological needs are originally satisfied on a trial and error basis, later in terms of standard cultural prescriptions, still later in terms of the systematic application of medical and nutritional knowledge, and eventually in terms of criteria for optimal or maximal well-being; we do not simply eat for its own sake, merely in order to get on to safety, love, and self-actualization needs but rather in accordance with our need to self-actualize; and
4　relying on a generally humanistic value orientation for guidance; this will rule out, for example, classifying acts of dehumanization as self-actualization.

Maslow's ideas, along with those of other students of good, positive, or mature human behavior, have been incorporated into a model of psycho-social development by Charles Hampden-Turner.[19] He argues that the identification and actualization of human potentials in one human being are interdependent with the identification and actualization of such potentials in other human beings. This is ideally a continuous process which Hampden-Turner summarizes in a cycle model.

There are eight basic aspects of self-actualization in Hampden-Turner's model. The first is a capacity for recognizing injustices and absurdities, and an orientation to overcoming them rather than accepting them as unalterable conditions. This means, for example, internalizing the "full enormity" of nuclear annihilation, and then living "in ceaseless agitation for a saner world." The second is an orientation to continually expanding one's areas of competence, anticipation, and expectations. A high level of motivation constantly generates new goals, and prevents stagnation. An authentic and intense investment in and commitment to others is the third aspect. This means going out from your individuality "to participate in other beings." Authenticity and intensity underscore the humanistic imperative that we act in terms of conscious moral choice and true feelings, and not in the immoral or amoral, overcomforming, compulsive and mechanical manner of an Eichmann "filling cattle trucks with Jews marked for extermination."

The fourth aspect of self-actualization is a deliberate and temporary suspension of basic assumptions and meanings with the attendant risks of exposing an undefended self to others. This is necessary for two reasons: to continually open up the self to new perceptions, conceptions, and possibilities for higher syntheses of experiences; and to confront and overcome or defy death (as a threatening, extinguishing and eternal ending) by investing and risking oneself in things valuable to others and to humanity as long as one is alive.

The fifth aspect is reaching out to people defined or labeled as deviants, minorities, or enemies "to make contact, to bring compassion, and to discover novel life." Continual striving for self-actualization is the sixth aspect. The seventh, struggling to understand and be understood, arises out of confrontations with self and others; this leads to high synergy cooperation. Synergy measures the degree of mutual enhancement in interpersonal relations. The eighth aspect is the integration of the first seven aspects into ever greater complexities. This model clearly defines self-actualization as an interpersonal process, an idea which I explore in the next chapter. But first, I want to expand the context within which I believe the self has to be viewed.

ECOLOGY, EVOLUTION, AND THE SELF

The self is usually experienced in a more or less well-defined space with birth at one end and death at the other. The boundaries and qualities of this space are generally constructed out of the everyday world of families, friends, jobs, career aspirations, and personal hopes and tragedies. Strategies for survival are developed within the constraints of this space; we make choices which seem to make sense in terms of the beliefs, goals, and alternatives we encounter in that space. The life-to-death spaces within which we move, however, are embedded in a much broader space whose boundaries and qualities are defined by ecological and evolutionary factors. Our everyday consciousness and strategies for survival take on a different appearance when considered in the broader ecological-evolutionary space. Let's see what the self looks like as part of an evolutionary play in an ecological theatre.[20]

The earth is an ecological theater

The earth is a complex array of diverse and interdependent living things and environments described by ecologists as a landscape of relationships and a dance of energy and information. Ecological consciousness affirms our integrity as individual human beings, but roots that integrity in a comprehending and caring orientation toward ourselves and our living and non-living surroundings. It is a radical counterpoint to the overindividualized images of being human that have been created around and reinforced in self-centeredness, isolation, alienation, and loneliness.

History is an evolutionary-devolutionary play

In addition to living in a network of various and overlapping ecological communities, human beings are also historical entities. Each of us is an end-product of an evolutionary process. That process has overridden devolutionary processes which have carried most forms of life to extinction.

We are all carriers of evolutionary and devolutionary potentials. Our lives are more than eating and sleeping, waking and striving, loving and hating, enjoying and suffering; they are biographies in evolutionary-devolutionary history. Whatever else our lives are, and however we see them in everyday terms, they are also tests of the survival and evolutionary value of ways of thinking and behaving.

CONCLUSION

Human beings, like other animals, have potentials for awareness and action relevant to survival. We are unique in our potentials for self-consciousness, consciousness of and communication with others, comprehension of reality, and seeking and constructing meaning. This uniqueness is the basis for defining the fully human person as one engaged in identifying and actualizing his or her potentials, and conscious of the ecological-evolutionary dimensions of living. From a humanistic perspective, this process entails an unequivocal commitment to the priority of human beings over abstract, dogmatic, and arbitrary ideals, systems, boundaries, and symbols such as Profits, Property, Capitalism, Democracy, Apple Pie, Socialism, Free Enterprise, Patriotism, Nationalism, God, or Mother.

The image of the self I have sketched is not intended to be perfectionist or idealist; rather, it is designed to keep us as open as possible to the surprises and shocks that surely lie ahead of us, individually and collectively. Ultimately, the relevance of this image to survival, growth, and evolution will have to be demonstrated in the outcomes of struggles among individuals, classes, and cultures guided by different, sometimes radically opposed, values.

I cannot overemphasize the importance of being able to remain an effective group member without giving up your identity, your individuality, to it. This is not only a condition, even a definition, of what it means to be human from a humanistic perspective; it is a fundamental prerequisite for open, honest inquiry. The problem here is not whether we can build machines that think and act like people, but whether we can build people who are self-governing. People who are not self-governing are ready candidates for programming and control by others. It is important to keep in mind the notion of an open system. All of us are programmed. That is not at issue. But on the level of everyday life, we know and feel the difference between being ordered around, abused, oppressed, and exploited and being politically and economically free, that is, *experiencing* freedom. In our own and other societies, the child who exhibits a high level of self-esteem, a strong ego, is often a source of trouble from the perspective of parents, teachers, and other authorities. If they can make such a child submissive and accepting, such authority figures will consider themselves successful. The result, however, is a child who will grow up to be a pawn of social forces which he or she will not recognize to be the collective acts of assertive, aggressive minorities taking full advantage of the relatively passive masses. By passing on conservative values at every turn, parents, teachers, and others are passing along defective values.

The political implications of self-actualization follow from the premium placed on self-determination and self-government. This means abolishing situations in which people are used – and allow themselves to be used – as instruments in violation of their interests. This in turn requires social relationships quite different from those we readily encounter today. In the next chapter, I explore the idea of opening relationships and how people and social interests can be mutually related and reinforcing. The conceptual vehicle for this exploration is the idea of love. The sociological relevance of love lies not in its connotations and denotations regarding romance or maturity, or its role in the ideology of marriage and the family, but rather its role as a form of cooperation. This sense of love makes it a critical topic for sociology, and especially for sociology with a human face.

NOTES

1 See the discussion of Titchener in J. P. Chaplin and T. S. Krawiec, *Systems and Theories of Psychology* (New York: Holt, Rinchart and 177 Winston, 1960), pp. 40ff.
2 William James, *Principles of Psychology* (New York: Henry Holt and Company, 1890). See the discussion on James and Baldwin in S. Stansfeld Sargent, *Social Psychology* (New York: The Ronald Press, 1950), pp. 202ff); also James M. Baldwin, *Mental Development in the Child and in the Race* (New York: The Macmillan Company), 1895); and James M. Baldwin, *Social and Ethical Interpretations in Mental Development* (New York: The Macmillan Company, 1897).
3 C. Cooley's major works are: *Human Nature and the Social Order* (New York: Charles Scribners and Sons, 1902); and *Social Organization* (New York: Charles Scribners and Sons, 1909).
4 My remarks on G. Mead are based on his major work, *Mind, Self and Society*, ed. C. W. Morris (Chicago: University of Chicago Press, 1934), pp. 135–226. The material from these pages is reprinted in edited form in A. Strauss (ed.), *George Herbert Mead on Social Psychology*, Revised edn (Chicago: University of Chicago Press, 1964), see esp. pp. 199 and 204.
5 Erving Goffman, *The Presentation of Self in Everyday Life*, revised and expanded (New York: Doubleday Anchor Books, 1969), p. 253.

6 Strauss (ed.), 1964, p. 208.
7 Strauss (ed.), 1964, pp. 211, 213.
8 T. R. Sarbin, "Role Theory," in G. Lindzey (ed.), *Handbook of Social Psychology*, 2 vols (Reading, Mass.: Addison-Wesley Publishing Co., Inc., 1954), pp. 238–44 (vol. I); Milton Rokeach, *The Three Christs of Ypsilanti* (New York: A. A. Knopf, 1964), esp. pp. 19–36; P. A. Bertocci, "The Self in Recent Psychology of Personality," Eastern Division, 59th annual meeting, December 27–29, 1962: abstracted in *The Journal of Philosophy*, vol. 59 (1962), p. 685.
9 Helen Merrill Lynd, *On Shame and the Search for Identity* (New York: Harcourt, Brace, 1958), pp. 45–7. The work on alienation and the search for identity is summarized (along with a bibliography) in Eric and Mary Josephson (eds), *Man Alone: Alienation in Modern Society* (New York: Dell Publishing Co., 1962).
10 A. Burks, "Logic, Computers, and Men," *Proceedings and Addresses of the American Philosophical Association* (Clinton, NY: Hamilton College, 1972–1973), pp. 39–57. See Burks' references to the literature on computers and human reasoning; H. Robinson, *Renascent Rationalism* (Toronto: Maclean-Hunter Press, 1975).
11 J. Weizenbaum, *Computer Power and Human Reason* (San Francisco: W. H. Freeman, 1978), p. 280.
12 I am indebted to David Cooper's *The Death of the Family* (New York: Vintage Books, 1971) for this imagery. Cooper speaks of the need to "depopulate the room" that is, to rid one's consciousness of all the specific images that generate guilt and shame. The alternative, in my view, is an integrated self characterized by self-motivation and conscience.
13 L. Maison, *Wolf Children and the Problem of Human Nature* (New York: Monthly Review Press, 1972).
14 K. Davis, "Extreme Social Isolation of a Child," *American Journal of Sociology*, vol. 45 (January, 1940), pp. 554–64; K. Davis, "Final Note on a Case of Extreme Isolation," *American Journal of Sociology*, vol. 50 (March, 1947), pp. 432–7.
15 Colin Turnbull, *The Mountain People* (New York: Simon and Schuster, 1972), p. 294. On the Kaiadilt, see J. Cawte, *Cruel, Poor and Brutal Nations* (Honolulu: The University Press of Hawaii, 1972).
16 A. Maslow, *Toward a Psychology of Being* (New York: D. Van Nostrand Company, 1968), p. 25.
17 A. Maslow, *The Farther Reaches of Human Nature* (New York: The Viking Press, 1971), pp. 45–50.
18 C. P. Alderfer, *Existence, Relatedness, and Growth* (New York: The Free Press, 1972).
19 C. Hampden-Turner, *Radical Man* (Cambridge, Mass.: Schenkman, 1970), pp. 31–65. The following discussion is taken from these pages.
20 The phrases "evolutionary play" and "ecological theatre" appear in the editor's introduction to chapter 1 in P. K. Anderson (ed.), *Omega: Murder of the Ecosystem and Suicide of Man* (Dubuque, Iowa: W. C. Brown, 1971), p. 1.

6

The Sociology of Love

The philosopher Voltaire complained that the name of "love" is given to "a thousand chimeras." But if we sort through the thousand chimeras, it turns out that they are generally examples of three basic forms of love: political love, romantic love, and mature love. Political and romantic love are part of the ideology of love, marriage, family, and sex that has expressed, justified, and reinforced patriarchy from ancient times to the present. Political love in its most advanced form is practised by political elites, usually men, and links sex, ruling power, and truth. Romantic love involves idealizing love, loved ones, and physical passion, and is a resource for oppressing and exploiting men, women, and children, but especially women. Mature love is based on equality and caring; it is independent of the sanctions of church and state, and transcends conventions about the sex, age, and number of lovers. My first objective in this chapter is to identify some of the major sources and expressions of political and romantic love; they are part of our patriarchal tradition, and continue to play a crucial role in modern lives. My second objective is to explore mature love in a way that links self-actualization, loving relationships, and the Good Society.

The classic source for ideas about political love in the West is Plato's *Symposium*.[1] In this dialogue, a rich variety of ideas about love are discussed. Phaedrus affirms Love as a mighty god, the eldest of the gods. There are no memorials to Love's parents. In Hesiod's words, "First Chaos came, and then broad-bosomed Earth, The everlasting seat of all that is, And Love." Parmenides sings of Generation fashioning Love first in the "train of gods." Phaedrus takes note of this, and goes on to praise Love as the guiding principle for men who want to live noble lives. Pausanias amends this praise by distinguishing two kinds of love based on the existence of two love goddesses. There is the heavenly love of the elder Aphrodite, motherless daughter of Uranus; and the common love of the younger Aphrodite who is the daughter of Zeus and Diane. Common love is mean, and can have as its object women as well as youths, that is, young men and boys. Its object is the body rather than the soul. Because common love pursues its objects without thoughts of noble means, it can lead indiscriminately to good and evil. Heavenly love is love of youths. The love of young men and boys was not a matter of homosexuality in any simple sense; it was one important ingredient in the social production and reproduction of political and domestic domination by males. Even the term "bisexuality" is misleading in this context. The elite men had sexual relations with adult women as well as with youths; but sex in this context was primarily a matter of male power and solidarity and not a matter of right and wrong objects of desire.

Eryximachus comments on the universality of "double love," which he finds not only in our affection toward things but in the bodies of animals, in the earth's production, and "in all that is." Aristophanes next discourses on the power of Love to heal us, and make us "happy and blessed" by leading us back to our true nature and original state. This idea reflects his theory that there were originally three sexes: male, female, and their union. The primeval creature was round with four hands and four feet, one head with two faces exactly alike and looking in opposite directions, four ears, two sexual organs, and so on. In a struggle with the gods, the human-creatures were each split in half. Love, from this perspective, manifests in part the fact that each of us is incomplete, and always looking for his or her other half: half-men searching for men, half-women searching for women, and half men-women, Aristophanes' third sex, searching for women if they are the male half and for men if they are the female half.

Agathon, in his turn, challenges Phaedrus by claiming that Love is not the oldest but the youngest of the gods and eternally youthful. Love is the source of every good in heaven and on earth, overruling since his birth the once prevailing Necessity that set the gods upon "dreadful deeds." He quotes a poet who describes Love as the god responsible for peace on earth, the god who "calms the stormy deep," "stills the winds," and bids the sufferer sleep." Socrates' questioning leads Agathon to conclude, contrary to his original position, that Love is neither beautiful nor good. Socrates then recites a dialogue between himself and his "instructress in the art of love," Diotima of Mantinea. The conclusion of this dialogue is that Love is not divine; rather, he resides in the world of spirits, intermediate between the worlds of the divine and the mortal. The power of Love resides in his ability to interpret between gods and men. Diotima tells Socrates that the art of love allows us to progress from the perception of the beautiful on earth, from the perception of one beautiful thing to two beautiful things and to "all fair forms," and thence in sequence to fair practices, fair notions, and, finally, to absolute beauty. True love transcends gold, garments, and fair boys, and is the way to a noble life, true virtue, friendship with God, and perhaps even immortality.

The rich variety of ideas on love in the *Symposium* is further reflected in the Greek vocabulary which contains three words for love: *philos*, referring to friendship, love between equals, and brotherly love; *eros*, referring to physical love; and *agape*, referring to unconditional pure love. The word *eros* was used in the Homeric epics to refer to sexual passion; *agapetos* means "beloved son," and *agapenor*, "manly," or "loving manliness." The act of falling in love has connotations of madness in Greek: *eromaneo* (n. *eromania*) means "to be mad for love" or "in love."

There is an important change in Greek erotics that Socrates and Plato introduce. For Aristophanes and others, the problem of true love was a matter of knowing whom to love, and the conditions under which love can be honorable for both the lover and the beloved. These sorts of questions do not disappear in the erotics of Socrates and Plato, but they become subordinated to a primary concern with the essence of love. The Greeks' reflections on love were aimed at developing – for an elite, of free adult males – an "aesthetic of existence." As Foucault has pointed out:

> Their sexual ethic, from which our own derives in part, rested on a very harsh system of inequalities and constraints (particularly in connection with women and slaves); but it was problematized in thought as the relationship, for a free man, between the exercise of his freedom, the form of his power, and his access to truth.[2]

This connection between love and power will become clearer as we proceed.

There is another tradition of political love in Western culture that is derived from Ovid. Ovid's *Art of Love* was written in Augustan Rome about 500 years after the period during which Socrates, Plato, and Aristotle flourished. In contrast to the Platonic tradition, the Ovidian tradition deals with love in a simple, earthy, even base, manner. Attending to what Plato referred to as "common heterosexual love,"

Ovid characterized love as sensual, anti-romantic, anti-intellectual, and oriented to the satisfaction of physical needs rather than to the development of durable, spiritually inspired commitments. The Ovidian lover is a soldier; for "The age which suiteth war is also favorable to Venus."

> Soldier and lover have, each, their vigil to keep; both couch upon hard ground; both have their watch to keep, the one at the door of his mistress, the other at the door of his general ... The one is sent forward as a scout towards the enemy; the other keepeth watch upon his rival as upon a foe. The one lays siege to warlike cities, the other to the dwelling of his inexorable mistress. One beats down the gates, the other doors.[3]

Plato and Ovid represent the culture of the upper and ruling classes. The love affairs they relate are generally non-marital, and rooted in the social production and reproduction of male prerogatives and power. The ideas on political love in Plato and Ovid influenced the twelfth century classic, *The Art of Courtly Love*, apparently written by a chaplain, Andreas Capellanus.[4] He outlined the rules of love that prevailed in the French courts where noblewomen and their friends regularly debated and issued decrees on the nature of love. Capellanus follows Plato in conceiving love as "the root and principal cause of everything good;" he is closer to Ovid in his definition of love as "a certain inborn suffering derived from the sight of and excessive meditation upon the beauty of the opposite sex, which causes each one to wish above all things the embraces of the other and by common desire to carry out all of love's precepts in the other's embraces."

The courtly code emphasizes the limited nature of love and the function of jealousy as a proof for the existence of love. Courtly love was an idealized, extra-marital relationship which was not supposed to be physically consummated. The code is based, as I noted earlier, on the ideas of noblewomen. These women had the power to discourse on love, and even to exercise political power to some extent. For example, Eleanor of Aquitaine (1122–1204), her daughter Mary Comtesse of Champagne, another daughter who became queen of Spain, and a granddaughter who became queen of France, practised an intense "marriage politics." But while marriage politics was part of the arena within which courtly love and the chivalry that accompanied it arose, it did not change the patriarchal social order. Courtly love was not only restricted to a small section of the aristocracy, primarily in France; it did not signal equal rights in love for even the men and women in that minority. Capellanus comments that "immodest things" are available to men but disgraceful to women; women who indulge their passions promiscuously are considered "unclean" and "unfit to associate with other ladies."[5]

The spirit of male domination that runs through the courtly code reflects the role of a new aristocracy of knights that began to develop in the twelfth century:

> The requirements of courtly love and the courtesies of chivalry that went along with it were ways that these newly established aristocrats tried to distance themselves culturally from the crude soldiers they had so recently been. Bowing and deferring politely to ladies was one of the marks of their new refinement.[6]

For the bulk of the population, of course, sex, love, and marriage continued to be grounded in practical economic necessities. And women, aristocrats and peasants alike, continued to be dominated by men.

There are a number of related factors that we need to consider to explain the development of romantic love between the tenth and twelfth centuries in Europe: the rediscovery of the early Greek and Roman texts; the need to counter widespread brutality; anti-Church sentiments; and the preponderance of bachelor knights and the scarcity of noblewomen in the castle-culture.[7] But in general it should be stressed that these factors only make sense as part of the history of patriarchal political economy.

Cappelanus summarized the principles of courtly or romantic love in a set of 31 statements. The list includes: marriage is not an excuse for not loving; love is impossible without jealousy; a double love is impossible; a true lover does not desire to love anyone but "his" beloved; people vexed by love eat and sleep very little; lovers turn pale and their hearts palpitate on seeing their beloved ones; and "Nothing forbids a woman being loved by two men or one man by two women, though not actively by both at the same time."

The twelfth century courtly code straddles two eras. In the tenth and early eleventh centuries, abduction, arrangement, and incest were basic features of marriage among warriors and kings. Concubinage was common and open; and husbands readily disposed of old wives for new ones. These social relationships reflected concerns about dynasties, family alliances, and lineage.

By the thirteenth century, significant changes had occurred in the social structure of marriage. The basic features of the Christian marriage system were in place. Marriage had become a sacrament based on a theology of sex and consent. Among young men, the games of courtly love and jousting replaced abduction. Married men accepted monogamy; and they allowed the Church a role in the dissolution of marriage (by sanctioning divorce, for example, if the unwanted wife could be shown to be a cousin). At the bottom of these changes was a principle of hierarchy that gave the husband authority over his wife, and the Church authority over community marital and spiritual matters.[8]

The construction of the modern system of sexual economy begins in concert with the construction of a political and ecclesiastical economy of feudal property. In fact, the beginnings of modern monogamy as a method for controlling the continuity of aristocratic lineages is already evident in the ninth century. We will see later that social scientists have generally ignored the political economy of love and marriage.

The East has its own tradition of political love. In ancient China, for example, a debate arose between Confucianists and Mohists (followers of Mo Tzu, Confucius' "first opponent"). Mo Tzu was born among the *hsieh*, a professional class of knights-errant whose basic ethic was that they should "enjoy equally and suffer equally." Mo Tzu's concept of "all-embracing love" is an attempt to generalize the precept that everyone should love everyone else equally. This principle alone could lead to a world of peace and harmonious living, he argued. The "calamities of the world" – small states attacked by large ones, small houses disturbed by large ones, the weak oppressed by the strong; the few misused by the many; the simple deceived by the cunning, and the humble disdained by the honored – all are consequences of living according to the "principle of discrimination:" that it is absurd to care for friends as one cares for oneself, and to care for their parents as for one's own.[9]

The Confucianists, by contrast, believed that there should be degrees of love. Mencius studied under a disciple of Confucius' grandson. He developed an idealistic version of Confucianism; and he outlined the Confucianist view of love as follows:

The superior man, in his relation to things, loves them but has no feeling of human-heartedness. In his relation to people, he has human-heartedness, but no deep feeling of family affection. One should have feelings of family affection for the members of one's family, but human-heartedness for people; human-heartedness for people, but love for things.[10]

Love should be extended, according to this view, until it includes people distant from the immediate family, a practice advocated by Confucius in the principle of *ching* (conscientiousness) and *shu* (altruism). The conservative social and political functions of Confucian love for male-dominated Chinese culture were of a piece with the general conservativism of the Confucian system.

This debate, and the Confucian emphasis on filial piety, do not exhaust the subject of love in the East. The idea of romantic love appears as early as 3,000 years ago in the Chinese Book of Odes, and romantic love stories are found throughout the great Hindu epics, *Ramayana* and the *Mahabharata*.

Some scholars have suggested that romantic love flourished in ancient China and India. But the Confucian emphasis on filial piety and rules of propriety, and the denunciation of *gandharva* marriage (based on mutual love) in the Hindu Laws of Manu, essentially outlawed romantic love. There was great skepticism regarding what Plato calls "heavenly love." But there was always an opportunity for men at least to have an extra-marital life; the courtesan is a frequent heroine in Chinese love stories. In Japan, the tradition persists that a man has a dutiful unexciting marriage at home and a romantic relationship at the geisha house. In America, northwestern Europe, and Polynesia, love has generally (and more recently) been viewed as a condition for marriage. Other cultures have stressed love as a product of marriage. In East and West, however, the patterns of political and/or romantic love have prevailed in one form or another from ancient times to the present. The concept of mature love, like the concepts of social and political equality, is also ancient, but it has not been a common feature of any complex society, ancient, modern, or contemporary.

Christianizing marriage, as we have seen, was part of the pattern that gave rise to the ideals of romantic love. The voices of the early Christian tradition (St Paul, St Jerome, Tertullian, and others) referred to marriage as the Devil's work, something to be tolerated because it provides us with virgins, and a shameful necessity. A more positive orientation toward marriage, coupled with sanctions against intermarriage, arose as church leaders recognized the need to propagate new generations of souls, and to stay competitive in the race for souls by various religious and non-religious groups. But nothing in the Church's changing strategies in the interest of institutional survival challenged the Biblical foundations for the oppression and exploitation of women.[11] Sermons about love have thus tended to reinforce the patriarchal functions of political and romantic love.

If political and romantic love are stock features of patriarchy, we should not be surprised to find sociologists and other social scientists in patriarchal societies legitimizing them in their research and theory. This is generally true. The issue is not very complicated in the case of conservative social scientists; they simply embrace patriarchal ideas about love, marriage, family, and sex. But liberal and radical social scientists who defend one or another form of mature love often do so in a conservative heterosexual couples framework.

SOCIOLOGICAL PERSPECTIVES ON LOVE

Sociologists tend to psychologize love by defining it in terms of feelings. Many definitions of love in the sociological literature stress the strong emotional bond between two people which satisfies their need to give and to receive. Even when they focus on love as a relationship, sociologists tend to define it as a psychological state. The prevailing paradigm in the sociology of love is further characterized by an emphasis on the romantic aspects of love, often to the point of equating love with romantic love.[12] Some sociologists have noted the need to broaden the study of love, and to treat it in more strongly sociological terms.[13] The efforts to develop a strong sociology of love, however, have been constrained by a focus on (1) heterosexual relationships, courtship, and marriage, and (2) the male-and-female couple as the basic unit of sexual intimacy, marriage, and the family.

Cavan points out that the verb "to love" is loosely applied to pleasurable feelings. In order to achieve a better understanding of love, she focuses on "the interpersonal bond that unites people."[14] She defines love as "a pleasurable or joyous feeling aroused by some stimulus." Sexual love is defined as "intimate love between a man and woman who find sex a means of expression for their love." According to Cavan, the capacity for love is innate. It is important to distinguish love from infatuations. And "mature love" (Cavan's term for "conjugal love") must be distinguished from extreme romantic love. Mature love works well in marriage; "it is less demanding, less exclusive, and more tolerant" than romantic love.

Bell focuses his attention on conjugal love: "a strong emotion directed at a person of the opposite sex and involving feelings of sexual attraction, tenderness, and some commitment to the other's ego-needs."[15] He summarizes the literature on love by noting that most definitions of love present it as "a strong emotion between two individuals which involves and satisfies the need of giving and receiving."[16] Some of the common ingredients in these definitions are idealization, respect, sexual attraction, companionship, selflessness, and maturity. It is important to notice that love is equated in the definitions Bell reviews with heterosexual love.

Some writers refer to love as something that can grow. Bell, however, prefers to look at love in terms of change rather than growth. Whereas growth suggests adding to what already exists, change implies that aspects or elements of a love relationship can be important at one stage, but discarded and replaced at a later stage.[17] A love relationship begins with a self-definition of being in love. This is followed by some action; Bell suggests, for example, that if a person defines him or herself as in love, that person will commonly become oriented to getting married since love is a precondition for marriage. Falling out of love also goes through naming or labeling stages.

Sociologists have viewed love from a variety of theoretical perspectives. Love has been treated as a type of primary relationship (Reiss), a case of intrinsic attraction in an exchange relationship (Blau), a game based on cost-benefit accounting (Scanzoni and others), and a form of property (Collins).[18] Most of these accounts focus on the microsocial level, and usually on two-person relationships. There are no indications that these diverse efforts are leading to the development of a general, widely accepted microsociological theory of love. At the same time sociologists have given little thought to the possibility of a macrosociological theory of love. This possibility is more clearly realized in the humanist and anarchist literature on love.

Sociologists specializing in marriage and the family generally define love in psychological terms, and focus on love as a heterosexual, romantic, and marital phenomenon. Some sociologists adopt a broader humanistic orientation to love as a factor in self-actualization, caring, cooperation, adaptability, and evolution. The humanistic approach, however, also stresses psychological definitions, and individual needs in heterosexual couples. My aim in this section is to sketch a sociological rationale for the conception of love as a factor in human survival, self-actualization, and social and cultural evolution. The idea that love is a social fact is the basis for conceiving love as a manifestation of a cooperative principle that has become increasingly important in social and cultural evolution.

BEYOND THE IDEOLOGY OF ROMANTIC LOVE

"I love you" has been a part of the ideology of the institutions of marriage and the family as we know them today for several hundred years. Love in that setting is a fragile veil of romanticism that hides the terrible costs to human beings and human feelings in even so-called "happy marriages."[19] "I love you" in this context is not a sign of trust, caring, or friendship but a resource you use to help you get such things as sex, forgiveness, security, financial support, and so on. The ideology of love conditions our behavior toward each other in adult relationships, and toward our children. Children, like husbands and wives, are considered property. And it is to property relations that we must look to explain the apparent paradox between loving someone and abusing them. In the case of children, for example, it is clear that many parents are not doing a good job of loving. If they are not abusing their children physically (including sexually), they are abusing them verbally. Control and discipline are by words of childrearing in many homes. Overprotecting children could also be considered a form of abuse.

A humanistic approach to intimacy requires that people give careful thought to whether to have children or not, to why they want or need children. Children should not be taken for granted. When they are taken for granted, when you have children because "everybody else does," or "it's natural," or "it fulfills you," then the children will inevitably suffer.

Love relationships fall short of their potential for improving our lives when we love someone because we are afraid of being alone. Getting married will lead to problems if you are getting married out of fear of living alone, fear of what people will say if you live with someone, fear of spiritual consequences such as eternal damnation, or fear of being deserted if the love bond is not legally sanctioned. For love to be a positive force in human lives, it must be rooted in ability rather than need. A person with a weak ego is always in danger of falling in love, just as he or she is susceptible to intoxication, and in extreme cases, to psychosis. In traditional marital or intimate relationships, love can be an addiction. Marriage vows, far from proving mutual love, are more likely to be disguised expressions of distrust, emotional blackmail, and a response to social pressures.

If love is based on need, and in particular the need for security, then the fear of losing the beloved will generate feelings of jealousy. Jealousy arises out of feelings of inadequacy and feelings of ownership. It is a consequence of treating "loved" ones like pieces of property.

When we turn our anthropological telescope to the cultural landscape, we find diversity across time and space in the form of what we are in the habit of calling "the family." We find explicable connections between these family forms and ideas about intimacy on the one hand, and the conditions under which people live on the other. We also find that those forms and ideas change systematically over time. We can thus conclude that forms of and ideas about marriage, sex, love, and intimacy in general are best understood as strategies for dealing with human needs and problems. It seems reasonable to conclude that when these particular needs and problems no longer exist, or when they can be more effectively satisfied or solved outside traditional boundaries, or when the values guiding tradition need to be modified because they interfere with the fullest possible development of individual and society, then the traditional forms and ideas become unnecessary and undesirable.

We are now at a point in our development as a world society in which there is increasing awareness of and concern for individual rights, ecological balance, and problems of authority at all levels of social life. It is therefore important to encourage and not merely tolerate consideration of the variety of forms of and ideas about intimacy that are part of the world picture. For adult intimate relationships (homosexual or heterosexual) the options available today include conventional monogamy, modified monogamy (e.g., non-exclusive sexually, child – free, contractual), non-monogamous matrimony (polygamy, group marriage, communal living), non-marital arrangements (free from legal, religious, or conventional social constraints, non-binding, and readily terminable), and celibacy. These are the types of alternatives identified by people critical of the limitations of traditional monogamy. They make too many concessions to the prevailing social order and to monogamy too. Freeing ourselves entirely from this context would lead us to think in terms of forms of friendship.

In the following section, I explore the nature of love and intimacy in terms of the Good Person in the Good Society. It should be clear from the preceding discussion why love can be so brutal in normal society, and at the very least an emotional roller-coaster. On the level of individual relationships, the problem is that love is the product of successfully negotiating one's way through sexual and emotional marketplaces. But in a modern industrialized society where the marketplaces for sexual and emotional goods and services are open and accessible 24 hours a day, sustaining a conventional love-as-property relationship is not easy; and it is probably a contradiction in terms. It is time now to see if there is anything about love that we can salvage in the interest of improving our relationships, our society, and our environments.

THE HUMANISTIC CONCEPTION OF LOVE

Humanists offer an alternative to the conventional sociological treatment of love. Maslow, for example, treats love as part of his program for the Good Person and Good Society.[20] This orientation contrasts sharply with the prevailing orientation in the sociology of love which tends to ignore or draw attention away from the relationship between love and humanistic concerns about self-actualization and the Good Society. The feminist movement and related efforts to foster sexual equality, erase traditional gender stereotypes, and humanize male-female and human relationships have certainly had an impact on the marriage and the family literature. But the constraints mentioned earlier continue to operate and to limit the depth and scope of criticisms of traditional forms of sex and loving. The focus rarely shifts from the heterosexual couple. And even where there is an explicit concern with issues of self-actualization and liberation, the treatment tends to be limited and hesitant. Alternatives are generally framed in traditional, couple-centered, male-female terms.[21]

The most notable exception to these tendencies among persons concerned with mutual love is found in the anarchist literature. The anarchists recognized that traditional patriarchy was a social construction, and they attacked the institutions of state, church, sex, family, love, and marriage. They also formulated an alternative political economy of intimacy. Michael Bakunin (1814–1876), for example, proposed: "Only when private property and the State will have been abolished will the authoritarian juridical family disappear ... No longer will anyone be deterred from living together without civil or religious marriage. All the old impediments to the full sexual freedom of women will no longer exist."[22]

Later, another anarchist, Emma Goldman (1869–1940), argued that while the demand for equal rights in every vocation is "just and fair," the right to love and be loved is the most "vital" right: "Indeed, if partial emancipation is to become a complete and true emancipation of woman, it will have to do away with the ridiculous notion that to be loved, to be sweetheart and mother, is synonymous with being slave or subordinate."[23]

From a humanistic perspective, love is a condition of self-actualization. Love of self and love of others are viewed as the necessary foundation for a life oriented to identifying and actualizing human potentials. Fromm made an important contribution to the development of this perspective in *The Art of Loving*.[24] He conceived love as a solution to the problems of existence that affirms the person's "aliveness," and promotes self-actualization. In Fromm's analysis, mature love (distinguished from symbiotic love) is based on the Delphic motto, "Know thyself." The components of mature love are caring, respect, responsibility, and knowledge.

The existential emphasis in Fromm's analysis should not obscure the fact that love is a social activity and process. The relationship between love and self-actualization is not confined to the self's existential space. It is a social relationship that has a development over time. Maslow, for example, notes that the love relationship in self-actualization is a fusion of the ability to love and respect for oneself and others. His emphasis on love as a dynamic relationship designed to foster mutual growth is more fully sociological than ideas on love as an emotional or psychological state. Furthermore, Maslow relates love to society.[25]

Maslow associates B-Love (Being-Love, or what Fromm calls "mature love") with the anthropologist Ruth Benedict's concept of high synergy. Benedict suggested that non-aggression is conspicuous in societies where an individual's acts simultaneously serve his or her interests and group interests. Individuals in such societies are not selfish; rather, social arrangements make individual and group interests identical. In such "high synergy" societies, "institutions insure mutual advantage from their undertakings;" in "low synergy" societies, "the advantage of one individual becomes a victory over another, and the majority who are not victorious must shift as they can." In physiology, the term "synergy" is used to refer to the "co-ordinate action of separate elements." The American sociologist Lester Ward seems to have been the first scholar to suggest that the term synergy be used in sociology "to denote the unintended cooperative action [and the organization and other cultural products resulting from such cooperative action] in which people often engage as they pursue their own individual interests." Benedict's usage seems to have this denotation. Maslow's usage more clearly reflects the conception of synergy as enhancement, in the sense that the whole is greater than the sum of its parts. This implies that "true" cooperation, that is, conscious, planned cooperation, can have synergistic effects.[26]

Maslow considers high synergy a good definition of Being-Love. He refers to Being-Love as "the high love relationship," and defines it as "the expansion of the self, the person, the identity."[27] Love of the self and love of the other are viewed as interdependent; Being-Love stresses the dependence of self-actualization on facilitative love relationships. By linking individuals (self-actualizers) and evolving societies (high synergy societies), Maslow associates love with adaptability at the individual, group, and sociocultural levels. This provides an initial rationale for considering the evolutionary significance of love. The variety of phenomena generally referred to as "love" may reflect the presence of a potential in human beings for high levels of communication and cooperation. New levels in the actualization of this potential, reflected in new levels of interpersonal intimacy, may be a necessary condition for the further evolution of life and consciousness on earth.

The B-Love relationship is full, deep, and intense. On the adult level, the question arises whether more than one such relationship is necessary or possible, at any one time, or over a lifetime. Given limited time and energy, the need (given the ways in which people are socialized in modern societies) to break down barriers (defenses) within, between, and among people that obstruct honest, valid, meaningful comunication and perception, and the idea that some type of deep, full intense relationship is a necessary condition of self-actualization, lifelong, monogamous relationships would seem to have significant advantages over other forms of intimate relationships. Such core relationships do not have to be exclusive in any of the traditional ways associated with monogamy (e.g., sexually). They are, however, conceived to be exclusive in the depth, fullness, and intensity of the love commitment shared by the core partners. This does not preclude B-Love outside the core; but no relationship outside the core will manifest the same degree and extent of commitment and communication. A core commitment is also possible among three or more highly self-actualized persons. Obviously, given present social and cultural conditions, such a core would be, in general, more difficult to establish than a two-person core, and more difficult to sustain. I discuss these issues further later in this chapter.[28]

The importance of monogamy and a lifelong core is, it is important to emphasize, a function of prevailing sociocultural conditions, and historical contexts. It is not clear, for example, that core relationships that dissolve after a certain number of years should be viewed as failures. The structure of the core can be radically transformed over time, or even dissolved, without destroying friendships or family ties. Children can be raised in a variety of equally healthy cores, and in cores that have been transformed into more diffuse and peripheral relationships through separation, if the separation is based on the sorts of incompatibilities in relationships that do not threaten friendships. The point is that not only is this an age in which many alternatives are possible (due to positive and negative social changes with the potential for positive and negative consequences); it is also a time in which we are learning about the necessity of such alternatives and of flexibility in our views about relationships. The idea that friendship is at the root of intimacy and of individual and social well-being, and not legal institutions such as marriage, is not only liberating for individuals but a condition for liberating ourselves from the oppression of all forms of authority. Since we are no longer bound to think of relationships solely in reproductive terms, what I have said applies to homosexual as well as heterosexual relationships.

The focus on friendship also means a focus on forms of sensuality in general rather than an exclusive focus on genital sex. The positive personal, social, and cultural value of alternative relationships should not therefore depend on the prevalence and virulence of sexually transmitted diseases. Alternative forms of loving friendships go hand in hand with alternative forms of sensuality.

LOVE AND SOCIOCULTURAL EVOLUTION

Pitirim Sorokin, and more recently, Roderic Gorney, have explicitly linked love to sociocultural evolution. Sorokin used the term love loosely.[29] He did not define love formally, but referred to it as "the concentrated form of life." Sorokin noted a tendency in modern society to be skeptical of, and to disbelieve in, the power of "creative love." Love was widely considered "epiphenomenal and illusory," and referred to (with other virtues such as friendship, cooperation, truth, goodness, and beauty) as a rationalization, self-deception, derivation, ideology, or "idealistic bosh."[30] Sorokin referred to "a vast body of evidence" supporting his notion of the power of creative love, friendship, non-violence, and non-aggression in society. He cited typical cases illustrating the power of creative love to stop aggression and enmity, promote vitality and longevity, restore health and well-being, support social movements, foster individual growth, and generate more love; love begets love, and hate begets hate. Sorokin's view of love as the mainspring of life and evolution is supported by many advocates of love as a survival value.[31] Most of them share Sorokin's propensity for generalizing on the basis of variable and sometimes questionable empirical examples, and without the benefit of a well-formulated theoretical position. Until recently, it is true, this area of inquiry has had to be sustained by provocative hypotheses in the face of under-developed and controversial theories of biological and sociocultural evolution. Recent advances in evolutionary theory have not entirely resolved the problems and controversies of the past. They have, however, made it possible to consider the relationship between love and sociocultural evolution somewhat more systematically. Roderic Gorney's work illustrates some of the progress that has been made.

Gorney argues that love as a factor in evolution has its roots in the emergence of cell-proximity in primitive organisms as a survival mechanism.[32] More complex forms of "colonial cooperation" followed: cell collaboration and the emergence of multi-cellular animals; and internal fertilization among amphibia and reptiles. More advanced cooperation made its appearance among the mammals. The placenta, mammary glands, and long gestation and dependency periods added a new dimension to the struggle for survival; the survival of the young became dependent on extended caring behavior by one or more adults. Gorney refers to this new dimension as "individual love."

Grouping behavior and sociation in the lower animals were transcended by the societal behavior of the higher mammals, which in turn was transcended by human societal organization and culture. Gorney concludes that the next stage in human evolution will free love from its traditional reproductive and nurturing functions, and incorporate it into "that part of the self-validating function which advances the fullest flowering of human potential by bringing individual people into intimate personal caring relationships with one another." He rejects traditional and romantic conceptions of love, as well as attempts by social scientists to define love in behavioral, attitudinal, or operational terms. Gorney follows Montague in defining love as "the conferring of survival benefits upon another in a creatively enlarging manner."[33] This suggests that love, in all its manifestations (in a variety of aborted, distorted and embryonic ways), reflects a cooperative principle that is becoming increasingly critical as a condition of sociocultural evolution. A sociological rationale for this idea is developed in the following section.

AN EVOLUTIONARY SOCIOLOGY OF LOVE

Sociologists have not generally defined society in evolutionary terms. But as Lenski argues, society is an adaptive mechanism which has increased the survival and reproductive chances of certain organisms.[34] Lenski thus adds society to the list of more familiar adaptive mechanisms in animals such as speed, strength, agility, intelligence, and coloration. Society is characterized by relatively sustained ties of interaction, a high degree of interdependence among its members, and a high degree of autonomy. This form of organization, among all primates, including humans, has survival value because it enhances learning opportunities.

Lenski defines learning as "that process which manifests itself by changes in behavior (usually adaptive in nature) based on prior experience."[35] Learning depends on some degree of cooperation between and among individuals. There has been some debate, however, concerning the relative importance of cooperation and competition in evolution. At least since Piotr Kropotkin's work on *Mutual Aid* (1902), there has been interest in study of, and speculation about, the proposition that cooperation in the animal world has been equal to or exceeded competition as an important principle of survival and adaptation.[36] Proponents of this position can draw on innumerable cases of parasitism, symbiosis, and even the eugenic improvement of a species on account of a predator's success in killing inferior individuals. All animals, including humans, have developed substitutes for life-and-death struggle ranging from population control to the use of threat and retreat instead of war.

Etkin, in a study of social organization among vertebrates, points out a paradox. Natural selection, he writes, "must be expected to favor self-seeking, 'antisocial' actions by the individual." This would tend to be socially disruptive. But group formation is quite common in vertebrates. Etkin concludes that there must be controls that keep aggressive, competitive behavior from interfering with sociality. He cites dominance hierarchy and territoriality as two such controls.[37] His attempt to dismiss "earnest and well-meant efforts to show that cooperative behavior has survival value" is not convincing. The evidence he cites suggests that controls against aggression and competition emerge with social organization. It is plausible to argue that these controls can, at the sociocultural level, be elaborated to the point where a transition occurs; cooperation becomes more important in survival than competition. Furthermore, a change in the nature of natural selection can be expected, such that groups or collectivities are selected by virtue of the relevance of their values and modes of social organization to survival. The process becomes quite complex when we add consciousness, and human efforts to select in terms of what they understand to be values and organizations that have high adaptive potential. Of course, the selection process might work in favor of individuals or collectivities whose short-term adaptive capacities are good (at least to the point of insuring their success in the struggle for survival), but whose evolutionary potential is low.

Assuming that the selection process works in favor of increasing evolutionary potential, the ascendency of cooperation principle does not imply an end to competition. Under the conditions outlined in this chapter, competition shifts to the collective level and involves struggles for power (command over resources) between more or less distinctive groups characterized by high and low levels of cooperation. Salk's view of this process as a struggle between two value systems, one with high and one with low survival potential (in the long-term evolutionary sense) is somewhat oversimplified but instructive.[38] The most compelling arguments for "the ascendency of cooperation" assumption derive from ecological consciousness. A variety of crises in the animal, plant, and human communities has in recent times stimulated widespread awareness of the importance of cooperation in survival and evolution.[39]

Lenski defines sociocultural evolution as raising "the upper level of the capacity of human societies to mobilize energy and information."[40] Cooperation is an evolutionary mechanism to the extent that it improves the capacity for mobilizing energy and information. The challenge to human survival which we see emerging and emergent in the world today is a challenge to our individual and collective capacities to mobilize energy and information through new forms and levels of cooperation. This implies new forms and levels of personal, interpersonal, and sociocultural organization. Maslow's ideas on high synergy can be interpreted as specifying the conditions which must be fostered in individuals, groups, and societies if new levels of energy and information mobilization are going to be reached. Love enters this argument as a significant bond between and among human beings. Sex may have been the basic bond that, early in the evolutionary process, made new levels of cooperation possible. (But, as I point out in my conclusion, sex is already a social construction; therefore, something more "primitive" must be looked to, perhaps the need for touching).[41]

In the evolutionary process, mutation is the most important way in which simpler organisms cope with changing environments. For more complex living systems, the exchange of "genetic information" – *recombination* – among different organisms is the most important coping mechanism. More popularly, recombination is referred to as sex.[42] It is plausible to hypothesize a third coping mechanism associated with the emergence of culture as a vehicle of evolution; the exchange of information in symbolic communication between and among human beings. This can be viewed as an elaboration of recombination, or sex. One of the consequences of sexuality is that it makes extended intimacy possible. Through extended intimacy, human beings can expand their knowledge of themselves, others, and reality in general. This is, admittedly, a large intuitive leap. However, the notion of intersubjective testing in science may reflect the advantage of – and perhaps the necessity of – having plural relatively autonomous systems intercommunicate in order to maximize the capacity of individual minds to grasp the nature of reality. I am suggesting that the intersubjective bond, which is most effective when communication is open, honest, and, in a sense, intimate, can be viewed as a development from more primitive bonds, including sex. In any case, this notion is not crucial to my argument; the existence of conditions for extended intimacy, whatever they are, is what is important here. Among humans, intimacy has been fostered by the generalization of sexual cycles, sexual codes, and the sexual imperative (reproduction). Human sexual relations are independent of an estrous cycle; they can be expressed in a wide variety of cultural ways besides monogamy and heterosexuality; and the imperative for sex can be pleasure.

Phenomena defined as "love" represent a first order cultural elaboration of sex. The identification of love with self-actualization, B-Love, and high synergy societies can be viewed as a second order cultural elaboration of love. This elaboration involves defining love as a social relationship and social process in which the objective is to facilitate the viable functioning and development of individuals and groups, and equating loving and knowing; "I love you" comes to mean "I want to know you, and I want you to know me," in the fullest sense of knowing. This implies gaining a perspective on the sociocultural, environmental, global, and ultimately cosmic settings of self and others. The elaboration and generalization of sex and love result in an expansion of the possibilities and expectations associated with loving relationships. Maslow's conception of B-Love defines a relationship that is more complex, diversified, and flexible than D (Deficient, or immature)-Love, or the love associated with traditional, relatively closed, and exclusive monogamous marriages. Complexity, diversity, and flexibility are widely recognized by students of ecological and evolutionary theory to be associated with adaptive and evolutionary potential in animal, plant, and human communities.[43] In brief, the opportunities for learning are enhanced in B-Love. Enhanced learning promotes adaptability. The consequence of associating B-Love with the synergic society, as Maslow does, is to create a link between love and the process of raising the information carrying capacity of human societies.

B-Love entails ecological and evolutionary consciousness. If we are committed, facilitative, and caring with respect to ourselves and others, we must necessarily be so with respect to human beings as ecological entities living in a global network of ecological communities. And if we are involved in the process of identifying and actualizing human potentials, we must be aware of conditions that facilitate this process; and this necessarily involves seeing ourselves as active in and agents of an evolutionary process. This is a good time to remind ourselves that the earth is an arena for the interplay of devolutionary *and* evolutionary forces, and that there is no guarantee that the future will be better than the past, or even that there will be a future. The evolutionary framework is an orientation; it does not entail unilear progress, or any sociobiological imperatives. We should not forget that the past offers us models and possibilities for the present and the future. In practical terms, for loving relationships of all kinds and at all levels this perspective encourages us to adopt the following patterns of behavior: flexible roles, constructive discussion, creative and imaginative management of all aspects of the relationship, checking assumptions about partners, and not doing things just because everyone else expects you to. The best way to ensure that loving someone else is going to have humane consequences is to love yourself, care about and take care of yourself; remember that you are an organic and a social machine. Build your relationship on the strengths of independence. And above all, aim to be friends.

LOVE AND HUMAN LIBERATION

Love has historically been a form of property; and it continues to play that role in many, if not most, modern lives. In the view adopted here, the abolition of traditional property relations which is associated with the Good (liberated) Society transforms love from a property relation to a committed, facilitative caring relationship between or among persons who also love themselves. It is a social process in which people get to know one another more and more intimately. This process, predicated on the self-actualization of the participants, is optimally lifelong. This generalization of love makes it independent of particular sexual, marital, or cohabitive styles and preferences, and of age differences. The precise nature of any love relationship can be considered a function of the psycho-social development of the participants. Love relationships will not always involve people at similar levels of psycho-social development, or with equitable access to and control over personal and material resources. A polar case of inequitable love is the love relationship between an adult and an infant or child. Differences in power do not mean inevitable exploitation but rather different forms of love guided by different levels of responsibility.

In summary, love can be considered a special case of cooperation. Cooperation is a social process in which individuals or groups work together toward a common goal or goals. Love is a cooperative process involving two or more persons committed to facilitating each other's self-actualization, and achieving higher and more extensive degrees of intimacy. Intimacy refers to the degree to which barriers to (defenses against) intra- and interpersonal knowing have been broken down. I use the term "persons" purposefully (instead of, for example, "individuals") to emphasize that we are dealing with the fullest representation of human beings. In a core commitment, the love relationship is long-term (perhaps life long). In general, two persons make the "best" core, but only in the context of the present state of societies. The difficulties involved in breaking down intra-and interpersonal barriers make it unlikely that a group of three or more persons could individually attain the degree and extent of intimacy possible in a two-person core. But nothing precludes three-or-more person cores; they are simply more difficult and complex experiments in intimacy.

THE FUTURE OF INTIMATE RELATIONSHIPS

Ideas about the future of marriage and the family tend to reflect (1) American or Western values, (2) dissatisfaction with the present institution of marriage, (3) projections of current trends, (4) the desire to increase opportunities for individuals to choose marital, family, and sexual lifestyles, and (5) a concern for increasing the warmth and intensity of human relationships. The sociocultural contexts of marriages and families are rarely analyzed in depth. The implications of ecology and evolutionary theory for thinking about the future of marriage and the family have been virtually ignored.[44] The perspective outlined in this chapter suggests that we need to broaden our conception of marriage and family; for this reason, I prefer to think in terms of intimate relationships. Ecology and evolutionary theory draw our attention to the fact that intimate relationships are ways in which human beings interact within the global ecosystem. Human survival and the enhancement of human living are threatened by increasing stresses in the global ecosystem. To relieve these stresses and create a viable world, we need to identify and experiment with alternative ways of relating to each other. We need to support experimentation with a wide variety of life styles. This experimentation is the process through which appropriate forms of social organization have been and will continue to be developed in response to new ecological and evolutionary challenges. In supporting a variety of values and life styles, we can and should be guided by criteria for evaluating their viability as adaptive and evolutionary systems. We should be ever-mindful of two questions: (1) to what extent do given ways of living promote full, intense, and humanizing intimacy between and among human beings; and (2) to what extent do they conform to the general principles for viable adaptive and evolutionary systems? The criteria for viability are being developed in ecological and evolutionary theory, and general systems and information theory. These theoretical developments support the need for open-ended living oriented to process and change.

Summary

Traditionally, sociologists have generally thought of love in terms of a psychological-marital-heterosexual-romantic paradigm. The more general humanistic conception of love as a committed, facilitative, caring relationship lends itself more readily to an evolutionary interpretation. Working from such a conception of love, Sorokin and Gorney suggest that love is an evolutionary mechanism. I have sketched a sociological rationale for an evolutionary view of love. This rationale is based on the idea that society and culture are evolutionary mechanisms; and that this reflects the increasing importance of a cooperative principle in an evolutionary process now dominated by sociocultural factors. I suggested that (1) love is a first order cultural elaboration of sex, (2) the generalized humanistic conception of love is a second order cultural elaboration, (3) loving enhances learning and knowing, and (4) love is a manifestation of the cooperative principle in sociocultural evolution. The central idea that love is an evolutionary mechanism remains rooted in the speculative sociology inherited from Sorokin. There is, however, increasing evidence for this idea and an imperative for further discussion and research on love and sociocultural evolution. Theoretical bases for thinking about the future of intimacy and lifestyles can be expected to emerge out of such discussions and research.

CONCLUSION

We live in a gendered society. Culture puts a gloss on the biological given, sex (but see below), and creates the qualities we think of as masculine and feminine. As gender terms, masculine and feminine can apply to either males or females. In general, however, the terms are derived from and will tend to characterize the actual behavior of males and females respectively. Cultural differences across time and space are reflected in differences in what counts as masculine and feminine in any given society at any given time.

Since men tend to dominate and even literally own women, the qualities of both masculine and feminine tend to be defined by men in their own terms. That is, men directly and indirectly define what is to count as feminine. To the extent that women accept their subordinate position in a male dominated society, they will also accept as their own men's definitions of what counts as feminine. When women do not accept men's definitions, they can be made socially invisible, punished, or killed by men or their women allies. Women can also organize around their own definitions (alone, or with supportive men), given the appropriate social and material resources. They can organize to protect and foster their own interests as women with a women's agenda, as women who want the same prizes the men have access to, or as women representing the interests of human beings in general with a new cultural agenda.[45]

The demarcation between sex (male/female) and gender (masculine/feminine) is complicated by the fact that sex itself is not simply given but socially constructed. The categories "male" and "female" are social constructs. In order to see why the idea that "men are men" and "women are women" may be less obvious than you imagine, try examining the photographs in a textbook on hermaphroditism. This should shake your confidence in your ability to easily tell men and women – males and females – apart. The fact that hormones and so-called secondary sex characteristics have a *distribution* in the male and female populations, and that the two distributions overlap, is another indication that maleness and femaleness are matters of degree.[46]

Sexual intercourse offers a more direct example of something that may at first seem to be a biological given, an instinct perhaps. But we know that sexual behavior is learned behavior. On another level, although sexual intercourse might at first sight appear to be a completely private and intimate part of our lives, it turns out on reflection to be a very public matter. The relationship between sex and society – and especially between sex and power – is no secret to sociologists of sex, marriage, family, and friendship. But few, if any, of them have depicted that relationship as powerfully and dramatically as the feminist writer and activist, Andrea Dworkin. Her focus is on "the act" of intercourse. It is "Society," she argues, that "says with the authority of its police power how intercourse will and will not occur." One nonobvious implication of this social reality is that the essentially legal meaning of "sexual privacy" is that a man has the right "to use his wife the way he wants." In sexual matters as elsewhere, the law creates legal *and* illegal activities. The law "creates gender, female inferiority, and an ecology of male power;" and in legal and illegal spheres, "intercourse is political dominance; power as power or power as pleasure." (No wonder one of my former colleagues, a lawyer and sociologist, was fond of defining law as the institutionalization of the social injustices of a society).

That intercourse is a social fact is illustrated by such things as sodomy statutes, and the interest communities have in the proper consummation of marriages. What do privacy and intimacy mean when, as in some traditional communities, the newly married woman and the couple's bedding are examined by a group of older women on behalf of the male-dominated community the morning after the wedding? The regulation of sex offers a particularly dramatic example of the often invisible relationship between private and public orders: "The principle that 'the personal is political' belongs to patriarchal law itself, originating there in a virtual synthesis of intimacy and state policy, the private and the public, the penis and the rule of men."[47]

Inequalities in wealth and power follow gender lines. Clearly, such inequalities stand in the way of realizing the types of selves and relationships I argue for in this chapter and throughout this book. Erasing sex and gender inequalities must therefore be a major part of the emancipatory political agenda implied by the humanistic agenda I adopt. The single most important change we should work for on this score is the abolition of marriage, family, sex, and intimacy as relationships of property, possession, and power.

One final point. I have referred throughout this chapter to male domination and patriarchy. It should be stressed – and this is part of the general message of the Copernican revolution in sociology – that these are facts of social life, social constructions. That is, we have to turn to social organization and culture to explain why they prevail. We cannot explain them by looking to the biology of males and females. The rest of the message is that social organization and culture can be changed; not anyway and anytime we wish, but under the right conditions, and with the appropriate resources.

The view of love I have sketched here is grounded in a basic opposition to all forms of authority. There is both a theoretical and a practical basis for linking resistance to authority and open, healthy, adaptive living, loving, and inquiry. Historically, religion has played a central role in most societies as a real and symbolic expression of authority. Because it has been anchored in a transcendental or supernatural realm it has given the appearance of being more resistant to critical inquiry than it really is. The idea that religion, belief, and faith are somehow outside the jurisdiction of critical (scientific) inquiry is a pervasive and pernicious myth. In chapter 6, I review some of the basic findings of the sociology of religion. The primary finding or discovery is that religions, gods, beliefs, and faith are products of earthly interests, problems, and opportunities. The very idea of a supernatural or transcendental realm is a social construct, not a cosmic reality. Perhaps no area of social life brings us face to face with the revolutionary implications of the sociological worldview as dramatically as religion.

NOTES

1   Plato, "The Symposium," pp. 42–56 in I. Schneider (ed.), *The World of Love*, vol. I (New York: G. Braziller, 1964).
2   M. Foucault, *The Use of Pleasure: The History of Sexuality*, vol. 2 (New York: Vintage, 1985), pp. 252–3.
3   Ovid, *The Art of Love* (Bloomington: Indiana University Press, 1957), pp. 21–2.
4   A. Capellanus, *The Art of Courtly Love* (New York: Frederick Ungar, 1959), pp. 184–6.
5   Capellanus, 1959, pp. 161–2.
6   R. Collins, *Sociology of Marriage and the Family* (Chicago: Nelson-Hall, 1985), pp. 418–22.

7   I. Reiss, *The Family System in America* (New York: Holt, Rinehart and Winston, 1971), p. 76.

8   G. Duby, *The Knight, the Lady, and the Priest: The Making of Modern Marriage in Medieval France* (New York: Random House, 1983); S. Wemple, *Women in Frankish Society: Marriage and the Cloisters, 500 to 900* (Philadelphia: University of Pennsylvania Press, 1981); and to broaden the perspective on this period, see John Boswell, *Christianity, Social Tolerance and Homosexuality: Gay People in Western Europe from the Beginning of the Christian Era to the Fourteenth Century* (Chicago: University of Chicago Press, 1980).

9   Fung Yu-Lan, *A Short History of Chinese Philosophy* (New York: Macmillan, 1960), pp. 49, 53–4.

10   Yu-Lan, 1960, pp. 71–2.

11   K. Harris, *Sex, Ideology and Religion: The Representation of Women in the Bible* (Totowa, NJ: Barnes and Noble, 1984).

12   See, for example, Reiss, 1971, pp. 95–6. For a notable exception, see G. P. Fullerton, *Survival in Marriage* (New York: Holt, Rinehart and Winston, 1972), pp. 342–57.

13   W. J. Goode, "The Theoretical Importance of Love," in M. E. and T. E. Lasswell (eds), *Love, Marriage, Family* (Glenview, IL: Scott, Foresman and Company, 1973), p. 169; and I. Reiss, "Toward a Sociology of the Heterosexual Love Relationship," in Lasswell and Lasswell (eds), 1973, pp. 170–7.

14   R. S. Cavan, *The American Family*, 4th edn. (New York: T. Crowell, 1969), pp. 375ff. See also J. Ramey, *Intimate Friendships* (New Jersey: Prentice-Hall, 1976), p. 214.

15   R. R. Bell, *Marriage and Family Interaction*, 3rd edn, (Homewood, IL: Dorsey Press, 1971), p. 104.

16   Bell, 1971, p. 114.

17   Bell, 1971, p. 115.

18   Reiss, 1971; P. Blau, *Exchange and Power in Social Life* (New York: John Wiley, 1964), p. 76; J. Scanzoni, *Sexual Bargaining* (Englewood Cliffs, NJ: Prentice-Hall, 1972), p. 72, as well as J. Bernard, "The Adjustment of Married Mates," pp. 675–739 in H. Christensen (ed.), *Handbook of Marriage and the Family* (Chicago: Rand McNally, 1964), and F. L. Nye and F. M. Berardo, *The Family* (New York: Macmillan, 1973), p. 124; R. Collins, *Sociological Insight* (New York: Oxford University Press, 1982), pp. 119–58. A psychology of love as a phenomenon of reward and punishment has been proposed by H. Miller and P. Seigel, *Loving* (New York: John Wiley, 1971). They define love as a learned form of approach behavior. Love has also been analyzed from a phenomenological viewpoint, as an exercise in communication, and from a developmental interpersonal perspective in, respectively: C. Wilson, "Love as an Adventure in Human Freedom," pp. 49–65 in H. Otto (ed.), *Love Today* (New York: Dell Publishing Company, 1972); H. Otto, "Communication in Love," pp. 66–72 in Otto (ed.), 1972, and D. E. Orlinsky "Love Relationships in the Life Cycle: A Develop-

mental Interpersonal Perspective," pp. 135–50 in Otto (ed.), 1972. For more formal and quantitative approaches, see P. D. Bardis, "Erotometer: A Technique for the Measurement of Heterosexual Love," *International Review of Sociology* (March 1, 1971), pp. 71–8; and W. R. Burr, *Theory Construction and the Sociology of the Family* (New York: John Wiley, 1973).

19　For more background and details on the ideas discussed in this section, see S. Peele, *Love and Addiction* (New York: New American Library, 1975); and D. Cooper, *The Death of the Family* (New York: Random House, 1970).

20　See the discussion of Maslow below. An early example of a marriage and the family textbook that does treat love in relation to self-actualization is J. T. Landis and M. G. Landis, *Building a Successful Marriage* (Englewood Cliffs, NJ: Prentice-Hall, 1958), pp. 132–4. The authors identify four characteristics of love: (1) cooperation; (2) friendship, of the same kind that can unite two people of the same sex; (3) growth, through increased awareness of surrounding meanings, needs, and opportunities; (4) mutual support, in good and bad times. Landis and Landis conceive love as a "mutual concern": "You love a person if his well-being, his growth toward his greatest potential in all facets of his personality, matters to you as much as your own, probably not more, but as much."

21　For some exceptions see the articles in the journal *Alternative Lifestyles* (Beverly Hills, CA: Sage Publications).

22　M. Bakunin, "Manifesto of the Russian Revolutionary Association to the Oppressed Women of Russia on Women's Liberation," pp. 395–8 in S. Dolgoff (ed.), *Bakunin on Anarchism* (Montreal: Black Rose Books, 1980), p. 397.

23　Emma Goldman, "Love Among the Free," pp. 266–83 in I. L. Horowitz (ed.), *The Anarchists* (New York: Dell, 1964), p. 274; and see the classic fictionalized account of the emancipation movement in Russia in the 1860s that focuses on open love relationships, N. Chernyshevsky, *What is to be Done?* (New York: Vintage, 1961). Originally published in 1863, this novel was an inspiration for many of the Russian revolutionaries of the late nineteenth and early twentieth centuries, including Lenin.

24　E. Fromm, *The Art of Loving* (New York: Harper and Row, 1956).

25　A. Maslow, *Motivation and Personality* (New York: D. Van Nostrand Company, 1954).

26　A. Maslow, *The Farther Reaches of Human Nature* (New York: The Viking Press, 1971), p. 202; T. Hoult, *Dictionary of Modern Sociology* (Totowa, NJ: Littlefield, Adams and Company, 1969), p. 327.

27　Maslow, 1971, p. 209.

28　On the theory of monogamous commitment, see G. and N. O'Neill, *Open Marriage* (New York: M. Evans, 1972), and R. Mazur, *The New Intimacy* (Boston: Beacon Press, 1973). For a theory of self-disclosure that asserts that well-being depends on being able to disclose oneself fully and honestly to at least one other person, see S. Jourard, *Self-Disclosure* (New York: Wiley-Interscience, 1971). For a humanistic view of multilateral ("group") marriages, see L. and J. Constantine, *Group Marriage* (New York: Macmillan, 1973).

29   P. Sorokin, "The Power of Creative Love," pp. 238–44 in C. C. Bowman (ed.), *Humanistic Sociology* (New York: Appleton-Century-Crofts, 1973).

30   Such pessimism and cynicism about love and evolution continue to be expressed in discussions of altruism and evolution. R. D. Alexander, for example, in "The Search for a General Theory of Behavior," *Behavioral Science*, vol. 20 (1975), pp. 77–100, hypothesizes that biological evolution has selected humans for the quality of being able to repress consciousness of selfishness, thereby producing a form of "sincere hypocrisy" which stands for altruism. See D. T. Campbell, "On the Conflicts Between Biological and Social Evolution and Between Psychology and Moral Tradition," *The American Psychologist*, vol. 30, no. 12 (December 1975), p. 1112; and M. T. Ghiselin, *The Economy of Nature and the Evolution of Sex* (Berkeley, CA: University of California Press, 1974), p. 247.

31   See, for example, A. Montague, *The Direction of Human Development*, rev. ed. (New York: Hawthorne Books, 1970), pp. 2–3; Otto, 1972, p. 10.

32   R. Gorney, *The Human Agenda* (New York: Bantam Books, 1973), p. 47.

33   Gorney, 1973, pp. 452–3; Montague, 1970, pp. 288–317.

34   G. Lenski, *Human Societies* (New York: McGraw-Hill, 1970); G. Lenski and J. Lenski, *Human Societies*, 2nd edn (New York: McGraw-Hill, 1974). This is not the same as a theory of societal evolution, which has been a part of the sociological scene from Marx and Spencer to Parsons. Lenski is clearer than his predecessors about defining society as an adaptive and evolutionary mechanism rather than merely a passive unit of some sort of unilinear evolutionary principle.

35   Lenski, 1970, p. 17.

36   P. Kropotkin, *Mutal Aid* (London: W. Heinemann, 1902); C. D. Darlington, *The Evolution of Man and Society* (New York: Simon and Schuster, 1971), p. 458; K. F. Mather, "The Emergence of Values in Geologic Life Development," in E. Laszlo and J. Wilbur (eds), *Human Values and Natural Science* (New York: Gordon and Breach, 1970), pp. 7, 13.

37   W. Etkin, "Cooperation and Competition in Social Behavior," in W. Etkin (ed.), *Social Behavior and Organization Among Vertebrates* (Chicago: University of Chicago Press, 1964), pp. 6, 7, 33.

38   On this point, see L. Wispe and J. N. Thompson, "The War Between the Words," *The American Psychologist*, vol. 31, (May 1976), p. 344; J. Salk, *The Survival of the Wisest* (New York: Harper and Row, 1973); E. O. Wilson, *Sociobiology* (Cambridge, MA: Belknap Press, 1975); Campbell, 1975; E. Dunn, *Economic and Social Development* (Baltimore, MD: The Johns Hopkins Press, 1971); Lenski, 1970, Lenski and Lenski, 1974. The recent literature on group selection and the genetics of altruism, especially in Wilson and responses to Wilson and to the general concept of sociobiology, is relevant

to my argument, but cannot be treated here. Without the space for commenting on the altruism literature, I will simply note that the view of love I am presenting here can be interpreted as an emergent of (1) biological altruism, in which the individual sacrifices for the benefit of genetically related others in the group, and the later development of (2) human altruism, in which the interests of the other take precedence over self-interest. Fully developed, love as an evolutionary mechanism becomes manifested in a high synergy relationship wherein the distinction between selfish and selfless behavior is transcended or made irrelevant by social structural arrangements. This argument takes account of biology, but does not reduce sociological realities to sociobiological ones. On the ideological functions of sociobiology, and a sociologically grounded alternative view of human nature, see R. C. Lewontin, S. Rose, and L. J. Kamin, *Not in Our Genes* (New York: Pantheon, 1984).

39 For a view of the current human crises as a problem in the ecology of consciousness, see F. Barron, "Towards an Ecology of Consciousness," *Inquiry*, vol. 15, nos 1 and 2 (Summer 1972), pp. 95–113.

40 Lenski, 1970, p. 63.

41 For another perspective on this see Susan Cavin, *Lesbian Origins* (San Francisco: Ism Press, 1985). Cavin posits that "female homosocial relations form the original base and constant cement of society" (p. 6). In this "grand theory" approach to sociology, Cavin discusses the roles of societal sex ratios, female sexuality, and sex segregation in the origin of society and in the origin of women's oppression. Even patriarchies, she contends, are grounded in female society (p. 4).

42 Cavin, 1985, p. 52; E. Mayr, "The Evolution of Living Systems," in H. K. Bleibtreu (ed.), *Evolutionary Anthropology* (Boston: Allyn and Bacon, 1970), pp. 25–6.

43 P. K. Anderson (ed.), *Omega* (Dubuque, IA: W. C. Brown, 1971), pp. 18, 33; I. McHarg, "Values, Freedom and Form," in R. Disch (ed.), *The Ecological Conscience* (Englewood Cliffs, NJ: Prentice-Hall, 1969), p. 332; M. Sahlins and E. Service (eds), *Evolution and Culture* (Ann Arbor, MI: University of Michigan Press, 1960); Salk, 1973.

44 For illustrative traditional approaches to the future of marriage and the family, see R. Hamil, "Alternative Models for Modern Marriage," *The Futurist*, vol. V, no. 4 (August 1971), pp. 166–8; L. Davids, "North American Marriage: 1990," *The Futurist*, vol. V, no. 5 (October 1971), pp. 190–4; J. Bernard, *The Future of Marriage* (New York: Bantam Books, 1972). Collins, 1982, pp. 473–4, in what is perhaps the best marriage and the family textbook on the market today, is rather optimistic about the future of the family; for a more pessimistic – and perhaps more realistic view – see M. Harris, *Why Nothing Works: The Anthropology of Daily Life* (New York: Simon and Schuster, 1987), chapter 5. This is an updated version of *America Now*, published in 1981.

45   Cf., M. Frye, *The Politics of Reality: Essays in Feminist Theory* (Trumansburg, NY: The Crossing Press, 1983).

46   See J. Money and A. A. Ehrhardt, *Man and Woman, Boy and Girl* (Baltimore: Johns Hopkins, 1972).

47   A. D. Dworkin, *Intercourse* (New York: The Free Press, 1987), p. 158, and pp. 147–67.

Part III
Knowledge and Belief

7

The Social Construction of Religion

Religious beliefs and institutions were an important concern of the nineteenth-century social thinkers who fashioned the sociological perspective. However, because of the central functions of religion as a tool of state power and a source of individual and community solidarity, the most profound results and implications of their work on the social construction of gods, religious beliefs and institutions, and faith have been basically ignored. This chapter is an introduction to the sociological way of looking at and talking about religion.

TYPES OF SOCIETIES AND TYPES OF RELIGIONS

One of the most important tools we have for gaining an explanatory perspective on our ways of living and thinking is the comparative method. Examining a significant number of societies across time and space is the basis for the observation that different types of societies generate different types of gods and religions. The nature and extent of the division of labor, the degree of social differentiation, the type of stratification system, and social changes (within and across societies) are some of the factors that determine whether religion will or will not be present in a society, and what form it will take and how it will change over time in societies where it is present.

All religions reflect the cultural concerns of the societies they develop in. Other things being equal, gods of war are products of warlike societies; agricultural peoples worship fertility gods; and the gods of patriarchal societies are male. Monotheism is found in societies with three or more levels of hierarchical sovereignty (e.g., clan, city, empire); polytheism is found in societies dominated by classes; ancestor worship is a product of societies in which the extended family is a core institution; and reincarnation is associated with small village communities in which individuals experience intense face-to-face interaction.[1]

Most hunting and gathering peoples have no conception of a Supreme Creator. The belief in a Supreme Creator who is involved in and supportive of human morality is rare in hunting and gathering, simple horticultural (no plow), advanced horticultural (metal weapons and tools), and fishing societies, but common in agrarian and herding societies. In general, then, the sacred realm is a sort of map of the social geomorphology, and the correlations between types of societies and types of religions illustrate the relationship between technological and economic development on the one hand, and religious beliefs and institutions on the other.[2]

THE FUNCTIONS OF RELIGION

The common feature in all religious systems is a division of the world into sacred and profane realms. The profane world is that part of the world that can be dealt with in a practical, matter of fact way. The sacred realm, by contrast, has to be approached seriously, respectfully, and with careful preparations. Behavior in the sacred realm must be strictly controlled. Rituals accomplish this by stressing appropriate forms of behavior. One of the major functions of rituals and worship is to help ground and sustain the feelings and orientations necessary for group solidarity and for preserving the prevailing social structure. This idea is a key to the origins of religion. It was first discussed in sociological detail by Emile Durkheim in his study of the Australian aborigines.[3]

Among the Australian aborigines, clans are organized around and take their names from totems. A totem is generally a commonplace animal or plant. The symbol used to represent the totem is considered sacred. On the basis of his study of aborigine totemism, Durkheim concluded that, when people worship a totem or a more highly developed sacred object, they are really worshipping "society," their own group or community. Thus, there are referents for religious and spiritual beliefs, and they are real. Only they are not in some supernatural or transcendental realm but rather right here on earth in our own collective lives.

The earliest forms of religion have their roots in the periodic group activities of the earliest human societies. During these activities, individuals experienced a certain kind of excitement, not unlike the excitement we feel when we enter into the spirit of a rock concert crowd, or an intimate get-together with a small group of friends. The source of this feeling in early human societies was eventually located outside of the individual and outside the group. Some readily available object was chosen to symbolize or represent the activity or gathering (society) and the associated emotional response (religious feeling). Rituals were then developed which regularized and enhanced the solidarity generated by the gatherings. Rites are group activities oriented toward objects that symbolize the feelings or emotions generated by raw group activities. A cult is a collection of rites and associated myths and beliefs clustered around a group of sacred objects. A religion emerges when a set of cults becomes interrelated and rationalized.[4] The process of developing the complex religious systems already evident in the material remains of the earliest human societies we know about began in an unknown prehistory. And it took tens of thousands of years for the primordial generation of affect in group activities to develop into religious systems. One factor in this process was the human capacity for abstraction. This, combined with limited experience, helped to generate mistaken beliefs about referents for certain feelings and thoughts, and led to hypotheses about a supernatural realm.

Personal emotional experiences during collective rituals cannot by themselves explain the origin of beliefs about the supernatural and religion. Other important factors include the human capacity for generalization and abstraction, and the potential for reification that is characteristic of language use, especially in the process of naming experiences and objects. Imagination is another factor that should not be ignored.

An example of how such factors operate is the development of ideas about the gods in the Hindu tradition. In the ancient Hindu texts known as the Vedas, fire is considered a god, or at least a concrete god's body. Later on, the view develops that there is an eternal god who possesses and controls, or somehow incorporates, all individual fires. This idea is secured over time through the activities of a cult which identifies itself with the god.[5] The next stage, the development of a religion, is reached through the intellectual efforts of specialists who systematically organize ideas about the gods. Generalization, abstraction, symbolization, and reification are all at work throughout this development, side by side with organizational activities.

In societies where people have not yet been alienated from the basic rites that generate gods and religions, there may be some individuals who are aware at some level that the gods are created, sustained, nourished, and rejuvenated by the rites, that people literally manufacture the gods. But the concepts for consolidating that sort of awareness are unavailable at this stage of cultural development. By the time the concepts become available, their control has passed to classes of political, religious, and intellectual leaders. Some of them, especially in the intellectual classes, will develop and pass on the idea that religions and gods are social creations. For most people, however, religion will be so complicated and removed from any immediate relationship to social solidarity, and alienation will be so strong, that consciousness of projection will not have much of a chance to develop in any direct, experiential way.

Consciousness about the social meaning of religion may be greatest when a society or its political constitution is new, when people – even in complex societies – can recall that *they* designed the social order, and *they* created their gods as symbols of and in celebration of their new society. The fact that religions are active instruments in the creation of societies helps explain why creation is so central to religions. Religion is literally about creation; but it is not about the creation of the universe by gods; it is about the creation of social orders by men and women. Once the celebratory period has passed, religions become prescriptive frameworks for future generations.

An example of the creative, celebratory function of religion is provided by the history of the ancient Jews and Midianites. The Yahweh of the Old Testament was a god of the political organization they created, a celebratory symbol of federation, association, and alliance. The covenant represented a real contract binding the partners in a new social order.

Since societies, especially the more complex ones, are never totally unified, religion must ultimately construct rival gods, heretics, evil spirits, and devils. The symbolism of religion mirrors the simplicity or complexity of social worlds. Heaven, then, generally symbolizes the moral righteousness that makes you a member in good standing of the society or group. The security of knowing you belong is a reward for adhering to the moral standards of your group. Hell, by contrast, symbolizes the banishment of the deviant or heretic from the group. That is the social meaning of hell as a punishment for sinning against god – that is, deviating from the morality of your group.

Notions about right and wrong are intrinsically social; they regulate relationships among people. The very idea of morality implies a force beyond any individual. People adhere to moral precepts because the group demands it. People are taught – and most people learn – to want to belong. Some, of course, follow the moral guidelines of their society or group because they do not want to be punished or killed by the guardians of morality. In simpler societies, morality expresses the rules of behavior believed to be necessary (based on experience) for group survival. In more complex societies, morality is designed to sustain the reigning pattens of domination. If a person has multiple group memberships, if groups are in conflict, or if there is a pattern of joining and leaving groups then there will be multiple and often conflicting moralities.

THE TRANSCENDENTAL RELIGIONS

Transcendental religions emerged when the fashioning of early states into civilizations through urban and commercial revolutions gave rise to the social role of the priest and priestly organizations. These religions (including Christianity, Islam, Judaism, Confucianism, and Buddhism), sometimes referred to as "world religions," developed in cosmopolitan centers.

Priests and their organizations emerged in close alliance with military and political institutions, but with a certain degree of autonomy. This made possible the separation of "this worldly" and "other worldly" realms, transcendentalism, and new opportunities for salvation.

In traditional societies, people were considered to be in the good graces of the spirits if they were "prosperous, healthy, and victorious in war."[6] Bad luck was viewed as the result of "spiritual transgressions." In the transcendental religions, good and evil were separated from success in this world, and the possibility of salvation was separated from one's worldly fortunes.

Two basic pathways to salvation became possible with the emergence of the transcendental religions. Mystical salvation put the individual in direct contact with the "other" world. "This" world became more illusory or less important. For Christians and Moslems, the imbalances of this world were redressed in an after-life. The good who have suffered on earth are rewarded with everlasting life in heaven, and the evil who have prospered are punished at last and forever. The "ethical" religions such as Confucianism offered an alternative to salvation in a "real" heaven; the Confucians stressed "right behavior," behavior in tune with the basic principles of the everyday social world.

Religious specialists or virtuosos could, in the transcendental religions, devote themselves full-time to the project of achieving salvation. For everyone else, however, religion continued to serve social functions appropriate to their social classes. For the upper classes, it was a social activity intertwined with political ideologies and alliances, and a tool of oppression. For the lower classes, religion was a source of hope and release from the trials and uncertainties of everyday life. For the middle classes, it was the source of rules about appropriate demeanor and deference:

> For along with the more abstract accounts of the universe – the forces of Yin and Yang, the higher realms of Nirvana and the veils of illusion, the spiritual powers of an omnipotent and omniscient God presiding over the mundane world – came changes in the forms of deferential relationships and in the emotional tone of life.[7]

The demeanor emphasized in these religions reflected their ideal of eternal peace and quiet in the other world. It also represented a way of demarcating these religions from, and underlining their superiority to, traditional religions.

POLITICS AND RELIGION

Smaller, technologically less developed societies are, of necessity, relatively democratic. The centralization of power and the formation of states and ruling elites occur as societies increase in size, develop coalitions, and in particular develop surpluses of foodstuffs and other goods. The emergence of leaders under such conditions is based on the social positions and political skills of particular people. Given the appropriate material resources, the would-be ruler still has to fashion them into a basis for leadership. Relatively democratic small-scale societies do not get transformed into centralized states when access to the weapons of advanced societies makes war coalitions and "careers of conquest" possible.

> The leader of ... a coalition may wish to make himself a permanent king, but his followers are not likely to give him much

power if they can avoid it. The same applies to the more aristocratic forms of decentralization; a coalition of self-equipped
charioteers or mounted knights will put its weight on the side of
forms of weapons, supplies and division of labor that maintain
their feudal autonomies.[8]

A potential leader must thus create loyalty among his or her followers, especially in a way that allows him or her to use those followers to
enforce his or her commands upon themselves.[9] And he or she must
gain control of the distribution of supplies and the tax-collecting apparatus, preferably with the help of a non-military hierarchy of officials
reporting directly to him or her. These are all problems in religious
organization.

There has always been a close connection between politics and religion. Political and religious authority are usually vested in the same
person in societies up to the advanced horticultural level. Kings are
usually considered gods or the earthly ministers of gods. Organizing
military coalitions such as the Greek city states involved organizing
joint religio-political cults.

Religion and politics began to separate (institutionally) with the
emergence of agrarian, commercial, and cosmopolitan societies.
But crucial connections were, and continue to be, maintained. Religion
is drawn on by governments for ideological legitimation and administrative organization. And priests engage in political activity in order to
gain state support or theocratic (hierocratic) power. Gibbon, the historian of the decline and fall of the Roman Empire, noted that the people
of the Roman era considered the various religions that flourished in
their world equally true, the philosophers considered them equally
false, and the magistrates thought of them as equally useful.[10]

MAGICIANS, WONDERWORKERS, AND MESSIAHS

In social systems that are not characterized by a high or even moderate
degree of cultural diversity, identity crises are rare. This is the case for
the ancient world in which religion emerged. Boys and girls grew up to
be pretty much like their fathers and mothers. But it *was* possible to be
different. Individuals could be released from "routine succession to a
recognized role in life" by an "extraordinary endowment or event."[11]
Every society has labels for normal and abnormal social types or roles.
Some "normal" social types occur in a wide range of societies from

antiquity to the present, reflecting common social goals, functions, and activities tied to universal human needs and lifecycle events. Butchers, bakers, and farmers are such social types. But other "normal" social types are peculiar to given societies or historical periods. Such is the case, for example, for the tribunes and lectors of ancient Rome. "Abnormal" social types are also classified in similar and different ways depending on time and place:

> as we recognize hysterical, paranoid, and manic-depressive types, and psychiatrists and faith healers [the ancients] recognized demoniacs of various sorts, divine men, prophets and magicians. As we (depending on our sympathies) speak of "freedom fighters," "brothers," "communists," "rabble rousers," and so on [people] of [for example] first-century Palestine (depending on their sympathies) spoke of "messiahs," "prophets," "deceivers," "brigands," "charlatans."[12]

Jesus, for example, was variously viewed by contemporaries as a miracle worker, a messiah, a beggar, and a fugitive.

The lives of magicians, wonderworkers, and messiahs from Moses on (including Apollonius, Jesus, Simon Magus, Gregory the Wonderworker and, from our own time, Rasputin, Aleister Crowley, and Eduardo the Peruvian healer) are variations on a common theme. The stock legendary features of the magus' career are: the divine origin and miraculous birth, the annunciation and nativity portents, the menace to the future magus during infancy, the initiation, the trial of spiritual strength (temptation resisted after a long solitary fast), miracles, the sacrificial feast, trial and death (by crucifixion, for example), the disappearance of the body, and descent into hell, resurrection, and ascension.[13] There are parallels between this career pattern and the career pattern for mythic heroes (see box X).[14] And a similar pattern characterizes the transformation of outstanding personalities in ancient Greece into divinities. Seusippus, Plato's nephew, began the process of transforming the famous philosopher into a divine man when he delivered Plato's funeral oration; he referred to his dead uncle as the son of an alliance between his mother and Apollo.

CONCLUSION

The discovery that religion and the gods are social constructs has its origins in the works of some of the outstanding thinkers of the ancient

X THE CAREER OF THE MYTHIC HERO

1. The hero's mother is a royal virgin;
2. The father is a king and often a near relative of the hero's mother;
3. The circumstances of his birth are unusual;
4. The hero is reputed to be the son of god;
5. The life of the infant hero is threatened, usually by his father or maternal grandfather;
6. He is spirited away and raised by foster parents in a faraway country;
7. There is no information about the hero's childhood;
8. The hero reaches adulthood and returns or goes to his future kingdom;
9. He is victorious over a king, giant, or dragon;
10. He marries a princess (who is often the daughter of his predecessor);
11. He becomes king (at about age 35);
12. He reigns uneventfully, and prescribes laws;
13. He eventually loses favor with the gods and/or his subjects and is driven from the throne;
14. He meets with a mysterious death, often on a hilltop;
15. His children, if any, do not succeed him;
16. He is not buried, but nonetheless has one or more holy sepulchres

world. Credit for crystallizing and systematizing the discovery goes to a small number of the founders of modern sociological perspective, notably Max Weber, Emile Durkheim, Karl Marx, Michael Bukunin, Friedrich Nietzsche, and Oswald Spengler.[15] I have summarized some of their basic ideas on the origins, social functions, and political economy of religion, and on the social roles of the wonderworkers. The empirical evidence for this central discovery in the social sciences has been accumulating for centuries. Some efforts have been made to systematize that evidence and establish a firm empirical foundation for the theory of religion and the gods as constructions. For reasons mentioned earlier, this work has proceeded slowly, and has not been able to find its way easily into the worldviews of most contemporary social groups and classes. But as Marx pointed out, religion is not simply invented by scoundrel priests and rulers; it is also an expression of human suffering and the quest for comfort and security in an alien universe. He looked forward not to an atheist society, a society that needs to deny God, but rather to a society so transformed that the question of God will not exist.

Mathematics poses the same sort of problem for sociology that religion does. How can we make sense sociologically of phenomena that seem to be outside the arenas of everyday social interaction and experience? Mathematics seems to live a life of its own, in a world somehow outside of the flow of history, biography, and culture, very much like the heavenly referents for religion. Indeed, mathematics and religion are no strangers to one another; they are intimately linked in history. That they posed related challenges for the sociologist was recognized by Emile Durkheim when he concluded his study of the elementary forms of the religious life by speculating on the social nature of logical concepts.[16] Chapter 8 is an introduction to the sociology of mathematics.

NOTES

1 G. E. Swanson, *The Birth of The Gods* (Ann Arbor: University of Michigan Press, 1964).

2 D. L. O'Keefe, *Stolen Lightning: The Social Theory of Magic* (New York: Vintage Books, 1983), pp. 177–8; and G. Lenski and J. Lenski, *Human Societies*, 2nd edn (New York: McGraw-Hill, 1974), p. 134.

3 E. Durkheim, *The Elementary Forms of the Religious Life* (New York: Collier Books, 1961).

4 See the detailed discussion of this process in O'Keefe, 1983, pp. 187–191.

5 M. Weber, *The Sociology of Religion* (Boston: Beacon Press, 1964/1922), p. 10.

6 R. Collins, *Conflict Sociology* (New York: Academic Press, 1975), p. 180.

7 Collins, 1975, p. 181.

8 Collins, 1975, p. 65.

9 Collins, 1975, p. 365.

10 M. Harrington, *The Politics at God's Funeral* (New York: Penguin Books, 1983), p. 65.

11 M. Smith, *Jesus the Magician* (New York: Harper and Row, 1978), p. 19.

12 Smith, 1978, p. 19.

13 E. M. Butler, *The Myth of the Magus* (Cambridge: Cambridge University Press, 1979).

14 John Barth, *The Friday Book* (New York: Perigee Books, 1984), pp. 42–3.

15 For further reading: F. Nietzsche, *Twilight of the Idols/The Anti-Christ* (New York: Penguin Books, 1968/1889, 1895), M. Bakunin, *God and the State* (New York: Dover, 1970/1916). On the sociology and social history of Christianity see: W. F. Albright, *From the Stone Age to Christianity*, 2nd edn. (New York:

Doubleday Anchor Books, 1957); R. MacMullen, *Christianizing the Roman Empire* (New Haven: Yale University Press, 1984); G. Theissen, *Sociology of Early Palestinian Christianity* (Philadelphia: Fortress Press, 1978); H. C. Kee, *Miracle in the Early Christian World* (New Haven: Yale University Press, 1983); on some sociological aspects of the Eastern religions and mysticism, see S. Restivo, *The Social Relations of Physics, Mysticism, and Mathematics* (Dordrecht: D. Reidel, 1983), chapter 3. For general introductions to the social theory of religion, see J. Z. Smith, *Imagining Religion: From Babylon to Jonestown* (Chicago: University of Chicago Press, 1982), and B. Morris, *Anthropological Studies of Religion* (Cambridge: Cambridge University Press, 1987).

16 E. Durkheim *The Elementary Forms of the Religious Life* (New York: Collier Books, 1916), pp. 462–96.

8

The Social Construction of Mathematics

This chapter is an introduction to the sociology of mathematics. It illustrates one of the most interesting and difficult applications of the sociological way of looking at the world. It also shows how the findings and perspectives of sociology can be brought to bear on social issues, in this case the issue of mathematics education.

SOCIOLOGICAL TALK ABOUT MATHEMATICS

Mathematical talk can be technical talk about mathematics. This sort of talk is based on the assumption that the secret of mathematical power lies in the formal relations among symbols. But technical talk about mathematics cannot, by itself, provide a complete understanding of mathematics. It obscures and even denies the social dimension of technical talk. This dimension is highlighted in social talk about mathematics.

We can talk about mathematics using terms such as social power, social structure, social class, culture, and values. Whereas technical talk isolates mathematics from other social practices ("spiritualization of the technical"), social talk links mathematics to other social practices, and reveals the social nature of technical talk itself. Just as speech cannot be understood as "a parade of syntactic variations," and myths are not merely sets of "structural transformations," so mathematical objects are not simply "concatenations of pure form."[1] Thus, to study a mathematical form is to study a sensibility, a collective formation, a worldview. The foundations of mathematical forms – like the foundations of art, poetry, religion, and all other human activities and productions – are as wide and as deep as social existence.

I have adopted this way of talking about mathematics from Clifford Geertz's observations on "art as a cultural system." Talking about mathematics this way gives us the sociology of mathematics. In broader terms, following Geertz, we could speak of "the natural history of signs and symbols," "the ethnography of vehicles of meaning," or "the social history of the imagination." In order to engage in social talk about mathematics, we must study the social worlds in which mathematicians "look, name, listen, and make." Like the concept of "art worlds," the concept of "math worlds" draws us into a network of cooperating and conflicting human beings.[2] Mathematical objects embody math worlds. They are produced in and by math worlds. That is, we could say that math worlds, not individual mathematicians, manufacture mathematics.[3]

Mathematicians, like other workers, use tools, machines, techniques, and skills to transform raw materials into finished products. The products of mathematical work are mathematical *objects* (e.g., theorems, rational numbers, points, functions, the integers, numerals, etc.). There are two general classes of raw materials out of which mathematical objects can be fashioned. One is the class of all things in human experience which are outside mathematics but can be "mathematized." The second is the class of all mathematical objects. Understanding mathematics as a social fact depends in part on recognizing that the classes of mathematical objects, raw materials for mathematical work, and tools and machines for mathematical work overlap.

In broad terms, the sociology of mathematics is the study of mathematical work as a sociocultural activity and process, and the study of mathematics as a social construction and social product. In conjunction with other science studies specialties, the sociology of mathematics is generating arguments and perspectives that bear on our understanding of knowledge and science, and on issues and problems in science and technology policy.

THE SOCIOLOGY OF MATHEMATICS

Sociologists of science have traditionally been concerned with two basic problems: (1) how, and to what extent, is scientific activity facilitated or inhibited by external factors such as politics, economics, and religion; and (2) how does science operate as an autonomous social system, institution, or community? In both cases, sociologists assumed that scientific knowledge is not dependent on the peculiarities of human personalties, cultures, classes, or history. From this perspective, mathematics (along with, perhaps, logic) is the "purest" type of knowledge and thus the ultimate arbiter of the limits of the sociology of science. A little more than two decades ago, sociologists of science, many with academic and professional credentials in the physical sciences, began to challenge the assumption that scientific knowledge is "pure." Their studies of scientific knowledge helped to define a new interdisciplinary field known as science and technology studies (STS). One of the most important approaches in STS is the anthropology and ethnography of science, on-site research on scientific practice and scientific culture. Focusing on the social and cultural processes of knowledge production in the sciences (in historical as well as contemporary contexts) has helped to reveal or to underscore the human dimensions of science, and to identify the values and worldviews embodied in scientific knowledge. These developments in STS have contributed to a renewed and sustained interest in the sociology of mathematics among a small but growing number of sociologists and social historians.

Sociologists of mathematics have studied such things as the relationship between the development of the calculus and the emergence of capitalism, the influence of eugenics on the development of statistics in Great Britain, the role of negotiation in the development of logical and mathematical thought, and mathematical representations as cultural resources within and outside the mathematical community. These studies do not ignore the traditional focus on the social organization of science and the mutual influences between science and society. Rather, sociologists of mathematics (and science) now recognize that knowledge, the social organization of knowledge producers, and the cultural and historical contexts of knowledge production are all intimately interrelated.

My approach to the sociology of mathematics is based on two theses: (1) references to mental events, activities, and processes such as intuition and cognition are references to social phenomena; and (2) the activity or process of abstraction (the movement toward "purity") is grounded in the material world and in social processes such as specialization and professionalization (the process of extending, systematizing, and rationalizing the knowledge and training required in an occupation). The social structure of a field, discipline, or specialty is a causative sociological factor. There are indeed limits to the explanatory power of externalities in the analysis of mathematical and scientific knowledge. But there is more beyond those limits than pure thought. Not only is the inside social structure of a science a determinant of the form and substance of knowledge in that science; the scientist is also a social structure (according to the idea that the self is constructed out of social relationships). The idea that mathematical knowledge is a social construct does not necessarily lead to some sort of naive or radical relativism. But the avoidance of these forms of relativism depends on developing a complex and dynamic notion of objectivity as a social fact rather than a simple matter of coordinating "things in the world" and "terms that refer" (these terms are used by naive realists, who assume a straightforward relationship between objects in the world that are the referents for the words used to describe them; on this view, to put it crudely, nothing mediates between these two factors). A few examples will help to illustrate my perspective.

NUMBER FACTS

Number facts, statements, or expressions such as "1 + 1 = 2," "2 + 2 = 4," "1 + 1 = 1," and "2 + 2 = 5" (as well as more advanced theorems, equations, etc.) are cultural resources used to support, challenge, and symbolize interests and arguments inside and outside of mathematics. In *Notes From the Underground*, for example, Dostoevsky uses "2 + 2 = 4" to symbolize the taken-for-granted and often oppressive world of everyday life, and "2 + 2 = 5" to symbolize the anti-authoritarian and creative impulses in human beings.[4] Orwell uses these same symbols in *1984*. But for Orwell, "2 + 2 = 4" stands for everything that is true, beautiful, and liberating in society, and "2 + 2 = 5" stands for everything that is authoritarian, totalitarian, and oppressive.[5] Inside mathematics, number facts (even simple ones like "2 + 2 = 4" and "2 + 2 = 5") figure as resources in debates among formalists, logicists, and intuitionists, and in conflicts between "realists" and "relativists."

Terms such as "rigor," "truth," "proof," "false," "discovery," "pure," and "applied" are resources which are variously conceived and utilized to further interests. At the personal level, they can be useful in furthering day-to-day interests associated with making one's way in the world in a healthy, vital way; but they can also be pathologized, as Abraham Maslow pointed out.[6] Steiner has suggested that formalizing proofs may demand an obsessive-compulsive personality that is incapable of mathematical creativity.[7] And Silvan Tomkins has suggested that there are right-wing mathematicians who were attracted to mathematics as children by its certainty and discipline, by the possibility of knowing what the right answer was and whether they had attained it; and there are left-wing mathematicians who were attracted by its novelty and promise of excitement and its wild, unaccountable spaces.[8]

The relationship between the search for mathematical truth and various kinds of theological quests has not been studied in depth but provocative material is discussed by the historian of mathematics, Morris Kline. He argues that the "work of 16th, 17th, and most 18th century mathematicians was a religious quest."[9] The cases of Kepler, Newton, and other fashioners of the scientific revolution are well-known. So is the ancient connection between mathematics and religion in the works of Pythagoras and others. But even as late as the latter part of the nineteenth century, Georg Cantor was arguing that the transfinite numbers he had invented had religious significance. That the connection is not now an historical curiosity is indicated in the works of mathematicians such as Edward Nelson of Princeton University, who claims that his work on quantum fluctuations and other topics has religious implications, and G. C. Henry, Jr., author of *Logos: Mathematics and Christian Theology*. In the 1920s, Oswald Spengler (a mathematics teacher, and author of *The Decline of the West*) put the examples I have cited in a civilizational perspective in a pioneering analysis of the cultural bases of mathematics: "the greatest mathematical thinkers, the creative artists of the realm of numbers, have been brought to the decisive mathematical discoveries of their several Cultures by a deep religious intuition."[10] The connection between mathematics and religion is thus closer and deeper than most people, used to thinking about the warfare between science and religion, imagine.

PURE MATHEMATICS

"Pure mathematics" is grounded in, and constructed out of, social and material resources, and is not a product of some sort of unmediated cognitive process. For example, the attempt of the logician and mathematician George Boole (1815–1864) to discover the "laws of pure thought" failed because he did not recognize the social and material roots of categorical propositions. Such propositions are in fact high-level exercises in abstraction ultimately rooted in real world experi-ences and chains of inductive inferences. The self-evidence of such propositions arises not from their status as laws of thought but as generalizations based on generations of human experience. In the case of metamathematics, it is possible to show that problems, work, sym-bols, and meaning are not simple products of pure mentality or arbit-rary and playful creativity but rather elements of the highly refined professional culture of mathematics. Increasingly abstract ideas are generated as new generations take the products of older generations as the resources for their own productive activities.

G. H. Hardy's defense of pure mathematics – "I have never done anything 'useful'" – is less an argument for mathematics as a product of pure contemplation than a manifestation of his hatred for war and his opposition to applying mathematics to problems in ballistics and aerodynamics.[11] The perennial conflicts between pure and applied mathematics within and across university faculties reveal struggles both between competing value systems, and for scarce resources. The conflicts of the pure mathematician Giuseppe Peano (1858–1932) with Volterra and other applied mathematicians on the mathematics faculty at the University of Turin is one example from the early history of modern professionalized mathematics.[12]

Pure mathematics, as one instance of pure science or knowledge, can serve to demonstrate a society's capacity for research. It can demarcate and defend the pursuit of mathematics in the service of one as opposed to another set of social, political, military, and economic interests. Individuals can seize on it as a strategy for gaining control over a world that threatens to disintegrate into chaos at any moment, a world ruled by chance and fate. This strategy is readily combined with a search for god, beauty, truth, and all that is considered universal and eternal.

MATHEMATICS AS WORLDVIEW

Mathematics is a value system and worldview. Spengler, for example, argues that each culture has its own number-world. In classical (Greek) culture, the number-world is based on the Pythagorean conception of number as "magnitude," and on geometry as a visual exercise. In Western culture, the number-world transcends magnitudes and visual dimensions. Instead, numbers are images of pure thought (or, "desensualized understanding"); the focus is on relations and on function as the nexus of relations.[13] A more mundane, but no less dramatic, example is that summing a grocery bill "carries the non-neutral message that paying for food is natural, and that society should be organized in such a way that people must buy food from grocery stores."[14]

CONFLICT AND MATHEMATICS

Controversies in European mathematical work (for example, Tartaglia versus Cardano, Newton versus Leibniz, and Cantor versus Kronecker) are sociologically important for the following reasons: they suggest that mathematical (and scientific) changes are not basically the result of struggles between advocates and critics of an established paradigm but of struggles between rival innovators; and that controversies are important because they may reveal changes in organizational structures.[15] The Cardano/Tartaglia dispute in the 1540s over credit for the cubic equation solution marks the beginning of the breakdown of the patrimonial organization of intellectual property and interpersonal contests; and the secrecy of general methods and the publicity of particular problems and solutions begins to be superseded by a more abstract intellectual competition. The Newton/Leibniz priority controversy over the invention of the calculus (between 1670 and 1730) reveals a shift from traditional forms of patronage to more permanent government patronage through organized academies, and a related shift from an informal communication network held together by individuals who act as message centers to the more impersonal arena of scientific journals. Other controversies occur as the centralized form of institutional patronage is superseded by the research-oriented universities. And the late nineteenth century dispute between Georg Cantor, who invented transfinite numbers and defended extreme abstraction in mathematics, and Leopold Kronecker, who believed that only the positive integers exist, reveals a transition to a world-wide mathematical community of specialists, professionals, and bureaucrats.

This research does not lead to the conclusion that there are institutional stages that mathematics must go through. There is no reason to believe, for example, that secrecy can never again become normal behavior in mathematics (consider efforts today to classify mathematical advances related to cryptography).

PURE VERSUS APPLIED; THE LIMITS OF AUTONOMY

There is no such thing as pure mathematics in the sense of "pure contemplation." Nor is there such a thing as pure mathematics in the sense of a mathematics divorced from all social and individual interests. "Pure" is a label for mathematics in the service of the sorts of interests I described above. But it can also refer to mathematics carried out with reference to the internal organizational interests of a specialized or professional community of mathematicians. The very idea of purity is generated by the process of specialization. Specialization, professionalization, and bureaucratization have all been part of the organizational history of modern mathematics. These processes are not unknown in earlier periods; but their scope and scale in modern times is unparalleled. Their effect is to generate a certain degree of closure in social activities. As closure increases, the boundary separating a social activity from other social activities becomes more and more impermeable. Boundaries are thickened, for example, by developing increasingly specialized linguistic, symbolic, and notational systems.

As specialization proceeds, specialists (at least, a small sub-group within the specialty) take an increasingly active interest in promoting and protecting closure. This sort of process, in mathematics or elsewhere, generates increasingly abstract or general objects at the same time that it obscures the material and social origins of production. The idea that pure mental activity is the source of the objects produced becomes increasingly prominent and plausible. Workers forget their history and fail to reflect on the social aspects of production as sources of their thoughts. At the same time, certain specialists who are more aware of the social dimensions of their work set out deliberately to protect the sacred aspects of their work, as a way of gaining control over their specialty in opposition to external agents and agencies, and strengthening their competitive power relative to specialists in other fields in the struggle for scarce societal resources. This sort of battle can be repeated in its basic outlines within a specialty once it is large and complex enough to sustain sub-specialties.

The ultimate effect of this closure process is the creation of a closed system. This is an ideal state (in the theoretical not the normative sense), and impossible to achieve in the strictly technical sense. But any form of extreme closure and isolation in a social system is a sort of death warrant. At the very least, it inhibits social change; at worst, it causes the system to deteriorate. The advantages of closure – of specialization – must be balanced against the advantages of interaction with (exchange of information with) other systems.

Purity in the sense in which I have been using it here can affect both pure and applied mathematics; that is, we can have a "pure" pure mathematics and a "pure" applied mathematics in the sense of seeking to realize an unadulterated version of the given activity. In both cases, professional autonomy has its limits. The danger for pure mathematics is that it will be cut off from energizing external problems, and become increasingly self-generating; the result will be that pure mathematics will become less and less applicable to problems outside pure mathematics. The danger for applied mathematics is that it will not have enough autonomy to sustain its power as an institutionally independent generator of creative and innovative ideas and methods.

All communities reflect on themselves and generate folk sociologies. This occurs in the mathematical community too. Extreme closure protects folk sociologies from external sociologies (folk and professional), and thus lessens the likelihood that the community will develop a critical and flexible self-awareness. The implications of this converge with the implications of the purity analysis when we reflect on the potential for creative social change in a given community. Put simply, closed systems are less adaptable than open systems. Openness implies interaction across system boundaries. Ideally, there should be cycles of closing and opening in social (as in individual) systems. This serves to periodically reinforce the integrity of the system (closure cycle) and energize it through inputs and challenges from the outside (open cycle). Thus the interaction of insider and outsider sociologies of mathematics, the interaction between mathematical and non-mathematical systems, and the internal interaction between pure and applied fields are all aspects of the open cycle that can promote creative, innovative change in the mathematics community at the level of ideas and the organizational level.

CONCLUSION

Mathematics has, to varying degrees, been a tool of ruling elites and their political opponents from its development in the ancient civilizations until the present. In recent times, we have the examples of Napoleon I asserting that "The advancement and perfection of mathematics are intimately connected with the prosperity of the State;" and the slogan adopted in Mozambique in the 1970s, "Let us make mathematics a weapon in the building of socialism."[16] Mathematics, science, and knowledge in general are crucial resources in all societies. Systems of knowledge therefore tend to develop and change in ways that serve the interests of the most powerful groups in society. Once societies become stratified, the nature and transmission of knowledge begin to reflect social inequalities. Today, we see this principle illustrated in the mathematics curriculum: "it is the content and methodology of the mathematics curriculum that provides one of the most effective means for the rulers of our society to maintain class divisions."[17]

The mathematical curriculum, like curricula in general, is conditioned by the social function of education in a stratified society. Educational institutions in advanced industrial societies "foster types of personal development compatible with the relationships of dominance and subordinancy in the economic sphere:"[18]

> The rule orientation of the high school reflects the close supervision of low-level workers; the internalization of norms and freedom from continual supervision in elite colleges reflect the social relationships of upper-level white-collar work. Most state universities and community colleges, which fall in between, conform to the behavioral requisites of low-level technical, service, and supervisory personnel.

This form of political economy fosters low achievement expectations among teachers in inner-city schools, and allows children to be promoted on the basis of good conduct. In the wealthy districts, meanwhile, the schools "can offer up-to-date curricula, well-trained teachers, small classes, and computer education for every student...." In this context, the back to basics movement in mathematics (and other curricula) can be understood as a means for cutting funds for education and "freeing resources for an even greater military buildup;" and persuading "the poor, the minorities, and females to accept their inferior status in a capitalist society."[19] The same sort of situation is reproduced in the international system of stratification.[20]

The relationship between mathematics, class, and power in the everyday world is given deeper meaning by the sociology of mathematics I discussed earlier. The social construction perspective shows how deeply politics, education, and other social factors are implicated in mathematical work and mathematical knowledge. One important implication of the constructivist perspective is that mathematical reforms (or more radical changes) cannot be effectively carried out in isolation from broader issues of power, social structure, and values. If, on the other hand, we adopt conventional mathematical tools and ways of working to help solve social, personal, and environmental problems, we will fall short of our goals. As a social institution, modern mathematics is itself a social problem in modern society. It is therefore unreasonable to suppose that social reformers and revolutionaries could eliminate mathematics from society; and equally unreasonable to suppose that mathematical reformers or revolutionaries could force mathematics as we know it today into some alternative shape independently of broader social changes.

What, then, should be our approach to social change in mathematics and society? The constructivist perspective suggests that we should focus on transforming ways of living, social relationships, and values in society at large. As I have noted elsewhere: "A radical change in the nature of our social relationships will be reflected in radical changes in how we organize to do mathematics – and these changes will in turn affect how we think about and the content of our mathematics."[21]

There are a number of ways in which modern mathematics can be considered a social problem. It tends to serve ruling class interests; it can be a resource that allows a professional and elite group of mathematicians to pursue material rewards independently of concerns for social, personal, and environmental growth, development, and well-being; aesthetic goals in mathematics can be a sign of alienation or of false consciousness regarding the social role of mathematicians; and mathematical training and education may stress "puzzle-solving" (in Thomas Kuhn's sense) rather than "ingenuity, creativity, and insight."[22] Efforts to address these problems will fail if they are based on the view that mathematics is a set of statements, a body of knowledge, or a methodology. This view reflects the notion that technical talk about mathematics gives us a complete understanding of mathematics. If, on the other hand, we adopt the constructivist perspective that social talk about mathematics is the key to understanding mathematics (including mathematical knowledge), then our approach to solving the social problems of mathematics *and* the problem of mathematics as a social problem will necessarily focus on social roles and institutions.

New social circumstances and arrangements will give rise to new conceptions and forms of mathematics. We cannot anticipate these new conceptions and forms; to a large extent, we cannot even imagine them. The very notion of mathematics as we know it might disappear in a different social order. What we can imagine, and can do, is practising, teaching, producing, and using mathematics in new ways. This does not require attacking all social ills on all levels simultaneously; it does, at the very least, require that we approach revisions, reforms, and revolutions in mathematics always with an awareness of the web of roles, institutions, interests, and values mathematics is imbedded in and embodies.

It is more important, then, for people concerned with improving mathematical literacy and mathematical education in general in the interest of a more egalitarian and cooperative society to focus their attention on social arrangements rather than on matters of textbooks, curricula, problem-sets, and high-order pedagogy. Curricula, for example, can be changed without touching the basic social arrangements that ultimately give us our mathematical perspectives, products, and purposes. We have to think about social change in mathematics and society with the following sorts of questions in mind: what do mathematical workers produce; how do they produce it; what resources do they use and use up; what are the by-products and wastes of their work in human and environmental terms; what good is what they produce, and for whom; what is the relationship between mathematical workers and various publics; how do mathematical workers relate to each other, their families and friends, and their colleagues in mathematics and in other professions; what is their relationship, in the current setting, to the owners of the means of mathematical production?[23] In the end, we want to know what kinds of human beings mathematicians are and what kind of world they are helping to build.

The argument that concern for what kind of world mathematicians and the rest of us are building is a critical sociological problem is the focus of the next and last chapter.

NOTES

1   C. Geertz, *Local Knowledge* (New York: Basic Books, 1983), pp. 94–102.
2   H. Becker, *Art Worlds* (Berkeley: University of California Press, 1982).
3   Cf. L. Fleck, *Genesis and Development of a Scientific Fact* (Chicago: University of Chicago Press, 1979/1935).
4   F. Dostoevsky, "Notes from the Underground," pp. 107–240 in: *The Best Short Stories of Dostoevsky* (New York: Modern Library, n.d).
5   G. Orwell, *1984* (Harmondsworth: Penguin, 1954).
6   A. Maslow, *The Psychology of Science* (Chicago: Henry Regnery Co., 1966).
7   M. Steiner, *Mathematical Knowledge* (Ithaca: Cornell University Press, 1975).
8   S. Tomkins, "Left and Right – A Basic Dimension of Ideology and Perso-

nality," in R. W. White (ed.). *The Study of Lives* (New York: Atherton, 1963), p. 393.

9 M. Kline, *Mathematics: the Loss of Certainty* (New York: Oxford University Press, 1980), p. 34; and see O. Spengler, *The Decline of the West*, vol. I (New York: A. A. Knopf, 1926), p. 150.

10 Spengler, 1926, p. 66. On Cantor's work, see J. W. Dauben, *George Cantor: His Mathematics and Philosopohy of the Infinite* (Cambridge, Mass.: Harvard University Press, 1979); G. C. Henry, Jr's book, *LOGOS: Mathematics and Christian Theology* was published by Bucknell University Press in Lewisburg, PA, in 1976. Edward Nelson's views are sketched in a personal communication (Nelson is Professor of Mathematics at Princeton University).

11 G. H. Hardy, *A Mathematician's Apology* (Cambridge: Cambridge University Press, 1967), p. 150.

12 H. Kennedy, *Peano: Life and Works of Giuseppe Peano.* (Dordrecht: D. Reidel, 1980), p. 61.

13 Spengler, 1926, pp. 53–90.

14 M. Frankenstein, "Teaching Radical Math." *Science For the People* 15, 1 (1983) p. 12.

15 R. Collins and S. Restivo, "Robber Barons and Politicians in Mathematics: A Conflict Model of Science," *Canadian Journal of Sociology*, vol. 8, No. 2 (1983), pp. 199–227.

16 R. E. Moritz (ed.), *On Mathematics and Mathematicians* (New York: Dover, 1942/1914), p. 42; C. Zaslavsky, "Mathematics Education: The Fraud of 'Back to Basics' and the Socialist Counterexample," *Science and Nature* 4 (1981) p. 16.

17 Zaslavsky, 1981, p. 15.

18 S. Bowles and H. Gintis, *Schooling in Capitalist America: Educational Reform and the Contradiction of Economic Life* (New York: Basic Books, 1976) pp. 11–12.

19 Zaslavsky, 1981, pp. 20, 24.

20 U. D'Ambrosio, *Socio-cultural Bases of Mathematical Education* (Unicamp: Campinas, 1985).

21 S. Restivo, *The Social Relations of Physics, Mysticism, and Mathematics* (Dordrecht: D. Reidel, 1983), p. 266.

22 On "puzzle-solving" (normal) versus "revolutionary" science, see T. S. Kuhn, *The Structure of Scientific Revolutions*, 2nd edn (Chicago: University of Chicago Press, 1970); for a critique of Kuhn, see S. Restivo, "The Myth of the Kuhnian Revolution," pp. 293–305 in R. Collins (ed.), *Sociological Theory 1983* (San Francisco: Jossey-Bass, 1983); and see D'Ambrosio, 1985, p. 79.

23 S. Restivo, "Science, Secrecy, and Democracy," *Science, Technology and Values*, 11, 1 (Winter 1986) p. 83.

Part IV
Global Sociology

9

The Ecumene

The twentieth century has witnessed an increase in the scale of human activity and consciousness that has enveloped the world. This global system is now the arena of every human concern, interest, vision, and dream.[1] The theme of this chapter is the global context of development and change in self and society.

Regional increases in the scale of societies have occurred throughout history. In the fifteenth century BCE, for example, a cosmopolitan civilization emerged in the Middle East as changes in scale broke down geographical and cultural barriers.[2] Such developments have often been accompanied by ideas about world unity or one world.[3] The linguistic roots of the one world concept can be traced to the Cynic word, *kosmopolis*; the practical roots of the idea lie in actual or dreamed of increases in sociocultural scale. Some version of this idea is generally part of the ideological toolkit of conquerors, and is grounded in an expansionist, imperialistic, and dominating orientation to cultures outside the conqueror's current sphere of influence and control. Alexander, for example, conceived the goal of his conquests to be the establishment of *homonoia*, that is, of human concord among the nations he conquered. The idea of world order also occurs in the writings of philosophers and generally is grounded in an idealistic view of the basic unity of all human beings. For example, the Stoic, Zeno of Citium, a disciple of the Cynic Crates of Thebes, conceived of a world ruled by one divine and universal law. One needs to be careful in distinguishing the one world ideas of military adventurers and of philosophers; sometimes the philosophers (along with theologians) are responsible for providing an ideological or mythological defense of a conqueror's expansionist activities. The sociological perspective helps us to recognize that conquerors are not lone rangers who make and change history by themselves. They represent, and are used as representations of, particular social (including class) interests.

In China, the idea of *ta t'ung* (one world) originated in the pre-Confucian era and has survived into modern times.[4] In Islam, the universal society appears as *dar-al-Islam*, the abode of Islam.

World order is a central theme in Western intellectual history. In Dante's *De Monarchia*, the theme is manifested as the *respublica Christiana*. It is reflected in Francis Bacon's concept of global unification through the parallel growth of science and culture. And it appears in a variety of grand syntheses sketched by Comenius, Hegel, Marx, Comte, and others.

The remarkable quality of the twentieth century is an extraordinary change in sociocultural scale. Heilbroner describes this change as follows: "It is as if the familiar newsreel of history had given way to a gigantic Cinerama, as if the once dark wings of the theatre were now illumined by an immense extension of the screen on which history is projected to us."[5] This is not an illusion, he argues, based on our increasing distance from the past. The "unprecedented enlargement of human affairs" in the twentieth century may turn out to be one of the great watersheds in human history.

Unlike our predecessors, then, we can ground our ideas about a world society in the reality of world wide systems of transportation, communication, exchange, and a wide range of cooperative and conflictful relations among peoples and nations. The vocabulary of the world-minded reflects the challenges inherent in trying to comprehend the emerging future, and it conveys different visions: post-historic, post-modern, post-industrial, post-civilizational. Many modern visions of world order are informed by a Baconian notion of divine providence. Raymond Aron, for example, refers to industrialization and the unification of humankind as inevitable.[6] A divine teleology inspires the views of Teillard de Chardin and Karl Jaspers on evolutionary continuity and the inevitability of the emergence of cross-cultural consciousness.[7] For some observers, however, the future is less certain. Alongside the vision of one world, we find the vision of no world. Harrison Brown argues that of the alternative futures available to us, the one most likely to be realized is "a reversion to agrarian existence."[8] Brown's alternative industrial futures – collectivized and free – are personified in the conflict between Post-historic "Man," the bureaucrat-technocrat, and One World Person, who is oriented to enhancing the quality of human life on a global scale.[9]

There is, across the variety of world futures imagined, a pervasive Western and masculine bias, and a metaphysics of inevitability. This should not obscure the significance of the image of a world society. There is a need for practical responses to the obstacles preventing or slowing efforts to establish wider nets of cooperation among the world's peoples. There is also a need for a framework that can help us analyze and understand the realities of conflict and cooperation in today's world.[10] The idea of "ecumene" provides such a framework.[11]

THE ECUMENE

The idea of the ecumene as a level of sociocultural and organizational evolution and development was introduced by the anthropologist Gordon Hewes. Hewes defines an ecumene or ecumenical system as:

> a set of functionally interconnected civilizations, linked by actual roads, sea-routes, and other channels of transport and communication, over which move agents of commerce, diplomacy and warfare, and religion, such that constituent civilizations tend toward a common and advancing technological base, come to share various styles, scientific, philosophical, and religious ideas, political forms, and so on.[12]

Ecumenes tend to be expansive. New areas and people are incorporated through trade, conquest, colonization, and missionary activities. Ecumenical affiliation may also be attractive for the leaders of societies outside the ecumene. The long-distance transportation and communication networks within the Ecumene are also a basis for reaching out to areas beyond the ecumenical boundaries.

The process of ecumenization is imagined to begin in an historical era characterized by the isolation of nuclear civilizations. The ecumene emerges when communication, transportation, and exchange linkages across these and secondary civilizational centers produce a certain level of effective interaction. Our own century, Hewes observes, has seen the emergence of ecumenes. In some of these systems, a high degree of cultural similarity is associated with political disunity, as in Latin America or Western Europe.[13]

Hewes' conceptualization defines the process of ecumenization as the unilinear development and diffusion of Western culture. His perspective carries with it a clear intimation of inevitability. Nonetheless, his analysis can be applied, with modifications, to a study of increase in scale at the sociocultural level. The earth can be considered a geophysical, biospherical environment upon which sociocultural history unfolds. A global ecumene of sorts is now in existence as a consequence of the development of links between, among, and across subsystems on the same order as those Hewes describes within the Old World ecumene: local primary communities, local or regional sociopolitical units, and civilizations. In addition to the Old World ecumene, it is possible to identify two other major ecumenical systems, one in the Chinese culture-area, and another on the Indian sub-continent. Smaller scale ecumenical systems can be identified in the Middle East, South America, and Africa. In these terms, the global ecumene is viewed as emerging out of the development of linkages between and among major and minor ecumenical systems. The process of ecumenization, whether the frame of reference is the Old World, China, or the globe, depends on the movement of persons engaged in such prosaic activities as foreign trade, diplomacy, missionary work, translation, science, journalism, and tourism.[14] It is important to keep in mind that there is a dark side to ecumenization. The unification of regions, independent states, and diverse cultures has often been the work of conquerors such as Alexander and Napoleon. They pave the way for the prosaic activities that actually create new sociocultural systems. The fact that ecumenization can occur without conquest does not necessarily mean that the process is completely free of military or quasi-military forces. The role of multinational corporations and other economic interests in provoking the development of the Common Market in Europe, for example, is not a role free of vestiges of militarism. Today, some pirates wear three-piece business suits, and they "deal" rather than engage in swordplay.

It is not difficult to understand why a comprehensive study of the historical unfolding of the increase in scale of human activities has led to the creation of ecumenical theories which are sustained by the idea of progress. The commitment to the idea of progress, however, is an example of what might be called "the fallacy of chronological causality," described by Durkheim: "The stages that humanity successively traverses do not engender one another ... All that we can observe experimentally in the species is a series of changes among which a causal bond does not exist."[15] I do not interpret this to deny the validity of searching for laws of social change (for example, invariant sequences), which are theoretical and therefore conditional statements. In studying the increase in scale of human activities, our objective should be to construct theories which specify relevant variables, and the conditions for ecumenization *and* de-ecumenization.

The emergence of the modern world ecumene has made it necessary for social scientists to develop concepts for describing and interpreting the emergence and development of collectivities possessing some form of cultural boundary, but not the usual political and geographical boundaries.

John and Ruth Hill Useem use the term "third-culture" to refer to the cultural patterns created, shared, and learned by people from different cultures as they interact in conflicting and cooperative relationships.[16] The term "third-culture" has some drawbacks. It has entered the literature of the sociology of science in an entirely different sense through S. A. Lakoff's critique of C. P. Snow's "two cultures" idea.[17] The term also reflects its roots in bi-national studies. The Useems have, however, broadened the empirical referent for "third-culture" to include international and multinational linkages.

B. W. Aginsky's concept of "lateralization" is also designed to capture human activities that cut across conventional sociocultural boundaries.[18] A lateralization is composed of:

individuals who are interrelated and participate in varying degrees sometimes as an organized group and sometimes with little structured organization, with relatively little interference or control from the plural "governments" under which they, as individuals, live that portion of their lives. There are present varying degrees of similarity in, for example, activities and skills, material objects, ideas, and goals, which means some degree of cultural similarity.

Aginsky stresses the fact that a lateralization is person to person contact. It involves segments of the societies involved, and is maintained over time through the interaction of people with similar cultural orientations, and systems of communication and control. Such systems make possible a continuing process of reciprocal diffusion.[19] While Aginsky's concept is an important contribution to the conceptualization of the prosaic activities in ecumenization, it remains (in spite of refinements) tied to his early work among native Americans of the Far West. His conceptualization does not encompass the complex inter- and intra-national dynamics of, for example, scientific activities. Science is, in fact, widely considered to be the best example of a third-culture or lateralization. I would therefore like to examine science from this perspective with three objectives in mind. The first is to reveal the nature of science as a third-culture, lateralization, or, in Boulding's terms, a "superculture."[20] Second, I want to explore the potential of the social network vocabulary for solving some of the conceptual difficulties noted about third-culture and lateralization. Finally, I want to return to the theme of a new worldview of science and say something about the promise for creating a viable world, and what such a world might look like.

There are many human activities which are important in the struggle to create a viable world. The struggles between world order and world disorder forces are being carried out in virtually every institutional sphere. On the political level, there are global activities that range from the work of the United Nations to such activities as the internationalization of black and minority power, the feminist movement, and the world citizen movement. In religion, narrow sectarianism seems to find an opposition in ecclesiastical ecumenization. In economics, nationalistic trade policies vie with common markets, an emerging international monetary system, multinational corporate activities that challenge conventional political and economic boundaries, and theories of international political economy. In education, the struggle is between training for vocations and professions, education for wisdom, and in some cases a specific orientation to education for the world society of the future.

Important linkages are being established among the peoples of the world through the activities of scientists. Using the Useems' vocabulary, the third-culture of science is the cultural (including intrascientific) patterns created, shared, and learned by scientists of different societies who are in the process of relating their societies (or sections of them) to each other. The concept of a scientific third-culture links the cross-societal activities of scientists to the development of an international scientific community, and the development of cross-societal linkages which ideally foster increasing communication and cooperation among the world's peoples.[21] To the extent that the scientific process and the general increase in cross-societal movement of scientists and other persons is unimpeded, we can expect the transactions between scientists and the "reality" they study to generate a dynamic system of values, norms, and beliefs (concomitant with the growth of scientific knowledge) which will challenge conventional cultural boundaries.

Scientific inquiry, as J. R. Ravetz has argued in an important contribution to the study of science and its social problems, is delicate and vulnerable, "conditioned by its social and cultural environment, and subject to cycles of growth and decline."[22] Industrialization, a process which, for Ravetz, encompasses the challenges to scientific progress raised by professionalization, bureaucratization, and ideology, poses problems for scientific inquiry which are not "merely accidental difficulties to be removed by exhortation or by administrative devices."

Ravetz suggests that the counterprocess of "critical-science," emerging out of the ideas and activities of Barry Commoner and his colleagues and of other groups of scientific workers who exhibit a sense of social responsibility, can help solve the social problems of industrialized science.[23] Another source may be the "radical caucuses" such as those that were a regular and often unpredictable feature of professional scientific meetings some years ago and which can stimulate counterestablishment activities, organizations, and publications. Critical, radical, and feminist science have a variable and precarious potential for generating new forms of scientific inquiry in response to the dysfunctions of professionalization, bureaucratization, and ideology. A third-culture of science emerging out of these counter-processes on the foundation of a disappearing and older scientific tradition may indeed finally affirm the vision of science as a microcosm of and stimulus for a world community. In any case, science is a model third-culture and can serve as a focus for developing a sociological vocabulary for third-cultures in general.

THE THIRD-CULTURE OF SCIENCE

Science is neither homogeneous nor static; nor is its sociological reality captured by such notions as "scientific community" or "invisible colleges." It would help to have a vocabulary with which to describe and comprehend the heterogeneity and dynamism of scientific activities. One promising possibility is the vocabulary of social networks and social sets.

A social network is distinguished from a social group as follows:

A group is a bounded unit. A network, on the other hand, ramifies in every direction, and, for all practical purposes, stretches out indefinitely.

Networks can be either close-knit or loose knit. . . . The chain of relations emanating from a person may either lead back to him, or it may not. . . . in the limiting case, a close-knit network becomes a group (or a category).[24]

It is possible, with a vocabulary built on this definition, to conceive worldwide scientific activities as a relational system constituted of categories, networks, formal and complex organizations, and identifiable core groups, cliques, factions, seminars, and caucuses. This entire system is stratified at individual, group, organizational, national, and regional levels. The advantage of the social network vocabulary is that it is ideally self-contained; the necessary concepts are logically related to one another. Let me illustrate the type of scheme that might emerge from a careful study and application of this vocabulary.

There is a set of human beings who have the attributes associated with the position, role, and status of scientist; they constitute a social category. "Scientist" is a variable; individuals are more of less scientists, depending on their experience, qualifications, and the ideas accepted by scientists themselves and outsiders about who is and who is not a scientist.

Scientists are located in all parts of the world, but their activities, persons, products, organizations, and technologies emanate from, feedback to, and converge on major centers which are relatively stationary geographically. Centers can be defined regionally, institutionally, in terms of nations, or in terms of organizations. Transcenters (following, with modifications, Aginsky) are defined as the convergence points of activities, persons, products, organizations, and technologies around goals which manifest a consciousness and desire among scientists to develop, maintain, and diffuse in perpetuity transnational systems of transportation, communication, and exchange in science.[25] The distinction between centers and transcenters is not always clear cut; but, for example, the American Physical Society is more like a center, and the International Conference on Weights and Measures more like a transcenter.

There are rules for combining the elements of the set of scientists; for example, norms, values, belief-systems, paradigms, and interests direct predictable associations of certain types of scientists with certain specifiable types of relationships. This usage of set and rule is a crude variation on the logical, mathematical, and informational sense of these terms; but it is interesting to note that in the latter sense, a group is defined as "a collection of entities that possess the . . . property of *self-closure*. This is a way of saying that if we have a set of numbers, sequences, operations, or symbols and a rule for combining any two of them, the set becomes a group, if the result of their combination is an entity also belonging to the set."[26] Correspondingly, we can conceive the collectivity of scientists as a set, and norms, values, interests and so on as rules for combining elements of the set, that is, bases for group formation. Such combinations would be groups. The combinatory rules must, obviously, be science-related. Thus, if several scientists discover that they have a common interest in ring theory and arrange to work together, they become a scientific group; if several scientists combine around a common interest in fishing, they do not form a scientific group. The concept of self-closure is interesting because it suggests the development of bonds between and among scientists in the set according to rules which can be specified.

Viewed in global perspective, the number and types of scientists undergo changes. New elements are added, and old ones shifted in position, status, and role. Scientists are constantly leaving the system in different ways, by changing profession, semi-retiring, retiring, or dying. At any one time, we can identify different subsets (e.g., social groups, cliques, factions) which are more or less enduring. Under such conditions, changes in the social system of science are certain to occur.

One source for such changes may be grounded in two types of temporary groups, the international seminar, and the caucus. The caucus in particular seems to provide a flexible form of organization for persons who must deal on a day-to-day basis with enormous increments in information and in general scientific activity. Such disciplinary caucuses may be counter-processes in response to problems generated directly and/or indirectly by professionalization and bureaucratization. Associational caucuses, such as radical caucuses, Black caucuses, and women's caucuses, at professional scientific meetings are usually counter-processes to professionalization and bureaucratization. Sometimes, however, they are the work of people trying to create alternative professional and bureaucratic arenas. But the caucus can be a counter-process for generating new developmental sequences, and organizational forms resistant to self-aggrandizement.

The view of the social organization of science I have sketched is an example of how we might be able to capture the complexity of third-cultures in sociological terms. This is a prerequisite for understanding third-cultures as facilitators of and obstructions to the development of some form of world order.

THE SEARCH FOR WORLD ORDER

The contemporary search for world order is being pursued along a number of different lines, from Buckminster Fuller's World Game approach to Jay Forrester's computer simulations of world dynamics. The different lines reflect different values; there are many possible future world orders. The basic stimulus for world order thinking is simple. We are increasingly encountering problems that transcend conventional neighborhood, community, and societal boundaries. Food and energy production and distribution, the threat of nuclear destruction, and environmental crises are global problems. Having recognized social organization as a mode of human problem-solving at the sociocultural level, it should be evident that global problems can only be solved by organizing on a global level. This awareness underlies the comprehensive approach outlined by one of the foremost world order activists, Richard Falk. Falk, working from the distinction common in futures research among probable, possible, and preferred futures, proposes a model of a preferred world. He begins by identifying four central values associated with his preferred world model: (1) minimizing large-scale collective violence, (2) maximizing social and economic well-being, (3) realizing human rights and political justice, and (4) rehabilitating and maintaining environmental quality.[27] The most important condition for world order, Falk stresses, is making progress toward "diminishing the role of the war system in international life and toward dismantling the national security apparatus in the major states of the world." Falk underscores the fallacy of mutual deterrence. In the first place, if the deterrence system fails, the result could be a catastrophic nuclear war. Secondly, mutual deterrence is inherently unstable. The deterrence situation can deteriorate as a consequence of technological innovations, arsenal buildups, and changes in the personnel or orientations of governments. Other factors that create instability include the uncertainties associated with secrecy and intelligence estimates, the vested interests of arms organizations, and the concept of preparing for the worst possible situation, thus stimulating a spiraling arms race.[28]

Progress toward maximizing social and economic well-being depends on eliminating poverty, reducing inter- and intra-national disparities in per capita income, reducing economic exploitation and dependence, and reducing waste, while increasing the proportion of resources allocated for bettering the human condition.

The principal dimensions of the human rights/political justice value orientation are (1) the prevention of genocide, (2) the elimination of colonial regimes, (3) the drastic modification of racist regimes, (4) the elimination of all forms of torture and cruelty, (5) progress toward equality of treatment for different races, sexes, ages, religions, tribes, and political groups, (6) providing for the realization of rights of self-expression and meaningful political participation.

Falk identifies the following types of ecological problems:

Type A   Sudden, dramatic ecological disasters
Type B   Gradual deterioration by cumulative processes
Type C   Risks and injuries associated with ultrahazardous materials
Type D   Deliberate or negligent policies dealing with preservation and conservation
Type E   Failures to conserve scarce resources for the future or to satisfy requisites of development in the power areas of the world
Type F   Wasteful and destructive use of scarce resources
Type G   Control of environmental warfare and a ban on ecocidal activities
Type H   Control of weather modification activities

In addition to the four central values introduced earlier, Falk lists eight secondary values:

1   Securing the conditions of social life in each society that promote harmony, joy, and creativity
2   Eliminating coercive and manipulative approaches to the exercise of governmental authority at any level of social organization
3   Planning the physical milieu of human existence to reflect a concern with beauty and the maintenance of privacy and personal dignity
4   Conserving the diversity of nature and conceiving of ethics and politics as embracing the relations between men-and-nature as well as between men-and-men
5   Experimenting with different [ways of] organizing human activities
6   Affirming the diversity of lifestyles, political organizations, belief systems, and economic arrangements, provided only that their espousal and practice reflect a general pattern of adherence to the four [primary] values and a general orientation of humanistic toleration of others
7   Assuring a better appreciation of differences in male and female

value perspectives and of their beneficial embodiment in various social circumstances

8 Assuring that advances in science and technology (for instance, genetic engineering and computer technology) are used for purposes consistent with the realization of primary and secondary values

Falk's program for the transition from the present to his preferred world order system has the following features:

1 identifying agencies receptive to world order change
2 mobilizing them to support transition to the preferred world order
3 creating public support for global reform
4 strengthening the present world by promoting transnational co-operation, and developing more cooperative approaches to international problems.

In schematic form, Falk's program is as follows: an emphasis on political consciousness and the domestic imperative in the first stage; political mobilization and the transnational imperative in the second stage; and political transformation and the global imperative in the third stage.

Falk concludes that the prospects for creating the preferred world order he outlines are bleak. His postscript is an appeal to his readers "to join with us in this grave but exhilarating struggle to achieve global reform at the eleventh hour of the human race." He ends with a line from Walt Whitman: "Even for the treatment of the universal, in politics, metaphysics, or anything, sooner or later we come down to one single, solitary soul."

One way to begin to engage the world in this Falkian way is to examine the opportunities for democratic participation in your own terms, at a local, regional, or international level. Ask yourself how democratic your organizational life is. Here are some basic queries to help you; they are posed as questions about society as a whole, but can be modified and applied to other levels of social reality, including the family, or international political economy.

First, to what extent can people from various walks of life, social classes, and so on participate in the political and economic decisions which affect them? Do they have equal access to the information they need to participate in such decisions? Do they all enjoy equal protection on matters of life and death? Do they all enjoy equality before the law, and equality with the institutions of law enforcement (to ensure that everyone's person is safeguarded equally, and equally protected from interference by others, including the government)? Are the resources necessary for health and well-being, leisure, recreation, and growth and development equally distributed? Is there equal access to education, knowledge, and training (so that people can achieve as much of their potential as possible, and enlarge that potential as much as possible)? Does everyone have equal access to freedom of expression on all issues, and the freedom to communicate with other people, no matter where they reside? To what extent does the society protect individuality and privacy in personal life, intimate and sexual relationships, family relationships; does everyone enjoy the right to privacy? Is the society organized to minimize regulation? That is, does the culture encourage the level of cooperation and friendship necessary to sustain the conditions of freedom and equality? Finally, do members of the society have the right, the opportunity, and the resources to protest and disobey laws in order to protect, recover, and restore democratic forms that are threatened from within the system?[29]

THE SOCIOLOGY OF THE WORLD

Falk's program succeeds where so many others fail by providing political guidelines for the transition from the present to the preferred future. But his program would not satisfy all proponents of a new world order. Some political radicals might argue, for example, that even though Falk is not a gradualist, he stresses reform rather than revolution. In Falk's perspective, world order emerges out of the activities of a world order third-culture or lateralization. It is important, however, not to ignore value differences among nations and cultures, and the significance of these differences for world order, revolution and evolution. In this respect, many observers believe that China is undergoing a crucial series of experiments in values for survival and evolution. Sahlins and Service, for example, suggested some years ago that China was a likely center for the next stage in sociocultural evolution.[30] They applied the principles of phylogenetic and local discontinuity, and the law of evolutionary potential to the contemporary world system. This led to the conclusion that China, less adapted to "the present and soon-to-be-outmoded industrial complex of coal and oil energy," had a greater potential for moving into a new stage of industrial development based on new energy sources. They quoted Mao Tse-tung on China's "evolutionary potential:"

> Apart from other characteristics, our people of over 600 million souls is characterized by poverty and by a vacuity which is like that of a sheet of blank paper. This may seem to be a bad thing, whereas in reality it is a good one.... Nothing is written on a sheet of paper which is still blank, but it lends itself admirably to receive the latest and most beautiful words and the latest and most beautiful pictures.

Sahlins and Service concluded that because the Chinese did not have a commitment to existing or earlier forms of economic and energy systems, they would have less difficulty accepting and incorporating new forms. The implication of this viewpoint is that the center of civilization could shift to China. In any case, our individual and collective lives – no matter where on earth we live – have become global in a literal way. The problems of survival, development, and evolution we confront are global. Since our basic problem-solving tools are social organization and culture (including values), we are faced with the problem of designing and experimenting with forms of social organization and culture that reflect the various global imperatives. There is no guarantee that we will be able to create a viable world, or even one in which all of us survive at some basic level day to day. That we live in a global village, however, is beyond dispute. For the foreseeable future, the sociology of the world will be about the pushes and pulls of local and global imperatives, and the likelihood of achieving one or another future – or no future at all.

The fact that the possibility of realizing Falk's agenda is bleak should not deter us from envisioning, experimenting with, and struggling to achieve a new world order. Sociologists have helped us to understand the nature of the iron cages we have built around ourselves and others. They have helped to uncover the dark side of human affairs. And they have helped to reveal the material nature and limits of our individual and collective lives. But they have also helped us to understand some of the ways in which we might be able to free ourselves from our iron cages, not by suspending the laws or necessities of social life but by understanding and utilizing them. We do not suspend the laws of gravity when we fly in airplanes. Thus, even as we become more aware of the constraints that bind us to a life of conflict, violence, pain, oppression, uncertainty, and death we become more aware of the cooperative imperative that is the very basis of our existence, and the most important tool in our efforts to survive and prosper.

It is impossible to achieve and sustain self-actualization in a world of mass populations, nation-states with the power to destroy the planet, and spreading urban-industrial wastelands. If we are going to create a liveable world, it is going to have to be rooted in revitalized communities that bring back a human scale to social life. This has been recognized in every reasoned effort to propose new directions for humanity. The ascendance of the cooperative principle and the community unit as conditions for human survival, sanity, and wise, high quality living has been recognized in the watchwords of those world order advocates concerned with lifting the yokes of oppression, social control, and authority from humanity: participatory democracy and direct action, mutual aid, and self-management. They have argued for experiments in community that foster and develop norms of reciprocity, short-circuit the state through direct political participation in community matters, and stimulate and even require less specialized interpersonal relationships. Theodore Roszak's blueprint for such a world society is a "visionary commonwealth," a "confederated community of communities."[31] There are other blueprints, some more, some less, mystical or spiritual than the one sketched by Roszak, some based on secular rather than religious bonds.

World order blueprints tend, in general, to converge on a vision of a global village of villages. The alternative society envisioned in those proposals is based on achieving a proper balance of handicraft activities, intermediate and alternative technologies, and heavy industry; self-determination in the workplace (workplace democracy); the regionalization of transportation and communication networks (in conjunction with a global network that links communities); a resurrection of the local economy based on labor-gift and barter exchange; user-developed and user-administered community services; neighborhood courts; and other social changes that stress personal and local control. But these are more than mere imaginings. We know that human beings have, to varying degrees and in different times and places, lived in small, cooperative, egalitarian communities. We know of people in our own time who have created more or less viable communities ranging from utopian experiments and the *kibbutzim* to neighborhood associations, cooperatives, and collectives.

None of these experiments has been free of baser values and motives; none has erased the dark side of humanity. And none has been able to insure that it would not be overrun by brutality from within or without, or by the forces of nature. And if we want to feed our pessimism, we can probably do so as easily in examining human efforts in peaceful, cooperative living as we can in looking at superpowers in action. Nonetheless, it is abundantly clear that our ability to bring some sort of visionary commonwealth into existence is a necessary condition for stemming and reversing the deterioration of lives, environments, and human and cultural potentials that is now in progress. The form of social organization needed to deal with the problems of basic survival and human and cultural development in a global village is some form of world order built upon the foundation of a system of more or less independent but interrelated communities. Such communities would be home to 2,000 to perhaps 10,000 to 20,000 people.

It is impossible to predict whether a global ecumene that respects the integrity, dignity, and creative potential of the individual can in fact be constructed *and* sustained, even in a grossly imperfect form. There is no assurance that a world educated to secular realities will be able to construct meanings and values sufficiently strong to sustain and motivate people even under the most comfortable and rewarding conditions. What is predictable is that if we continue on the paths we are now following, life will become more brutish, dangerous, and alienating even as technology and science march forward to greater and greater heights; and that the probability of worldwide social and ecological disasters will increase.

We need to be cautious about evaluating the significance of the so-called democracy movements in Eastern Europe, *perestroika* and *glasnost*, and the new European economic system that goes into effect in 1992. Not enough attention has been paid to the extent to which these developments reflect (directly and indirectly) the activities and interests of multinational corporations and other economic interests intent on expanding, creating, and stabilizing markets. On the other hand, there has not been enough recognition given to the role of the European nuclear disarmament movement and other peace and freedom activities in the 1980s and earlier in fashioning contemporary events in Eastern Europe and in promoting new relationships between the superpowers. And just as we must look for the social classes and interests and historical forces behind the individuals who take and get credit for societal changes, we must look for those same collective and structural causes when the heroes are masses of people rather than generals, presidents, and kings.[32]

The high tradition in sociology and in the world of learning in general has always been directed simultaneously to learning about the world and making it more liveable. In the face of the more recalcitrant and brutal facts of life, those of us who carry on in the high tradition can not be satisfied with pointing out and documenting all the details of the iron cages around us. Nor can we let down our guard in the face of superpower *détentes* and the seemingly overnight and relatively peaceful overthrow of totalitarian governments. We are bound to try to break out of the iron cages of political authority, religious dogmas, and the disinformation constructed in the media and in our schools.

CONCLUSION

We are faced with a global crisis in sociological terms and an interrelated species-level crisis in bio-ecological terms that transcends the cycles of crisis-mongering that have punctuated human history. These are real crises that reflect the emergence of ecological and evolutionary challenges that are new in type and scale. New forms of social organization and new values are necessary if we are to have a chance at surviving in ways that enhance our individual and collective lives. We are more likely to behave in ways that promote individual liberty, enrich community life, and cultivate healthy environments in social formations that are diversified, cooperative, egalitarian, and participatory.

There is no hope of evading the endemic conflicts, tensions, and contradictions of the human condition. Nor can we avoid the problems that will arise as more and more of the world becomes secularized and is forced to generate meaning out of the finite aspects of human life in an infinite universe. How we will respond, especially in the long run, is unknown. But to encounter the tensions between evolutionary and devolutionary forces at work in our world without care and passion for one's self and one's community, to meet them technocratically and scientistically, to sit back and rely on divine providence, or to ignore or remain unaware of them can only court disaster. Sociology cannot insure that we will find appropriate solutions to our problems or participate indefinitely in some sort of social and cultural evolution. It can, however, provide us with a better sense of what has to be done, and what (in terms of available resources) can be done. It can help us identify conditions of evolution and devolution, progress and regress. It can help us shed illusions about ourselves and our social worlds. This can be an illuminating and exciting adventure. It can also be a dangerous one insofar, for example, as it undermines traditional sources of comfort, motivation, and meaning. But only our participation in this process of uncertainties can determine whether wisdom, sanity, and liberty can take root in our lives.

NOTES

1 Raymond Aron, *The Dawn of Universal History* (Praeger: N.Y., 1961); J. J. Honigmann, *The World of Man* (Harper and Brothers: N.Y., 1959).

2 W. H. McNeill, *The Rise of the West* (New American Library: N.Y., 1965), pp. 127. In addition to McNeill's descriptions of "increase in scale," see also Gideon Sjoberg, *The Pre-Industrial City* (The Free Press: N.Y., 1960) for a comparable history of increase in scale based on economic change and industrialization.

3 This discussion follows W. W. Wagar, *The City of Man* (Penguin Books: Baltimore, Md., 1967).

4 K'ang Yu-Wei, *Ta T'ung Shu: The One World Philosophy of K'ang Yu-Wei*, edited by L. G. Thompson (Allen & Unwin: London, 1958). The original and complete work was published in 1902.

5 R. L. Heilbroner, *The Great Ascent* (Harper Torchbooks: N.Y., 1963), p. 7.

6 Aron, 1961: pp. 44–5.

7 Karl Jaspers, "The Unity of History," in H. Meyerhoff (ed.), *The Philosophy of History in Our Time* (Doubleday-Anchor: Garden City, N.Y., 1959), p. 340. T. de Chardin, *The Divine Milieu* (Harper and Row: New York, 1960.) See also John Useen, "The Community of Man: A Study in the Third-Culture," *Centennial Review* 7 (Fall, 1963), p. 481; and A. Toynbee, *A Study of History*, abridgement of vols I–VI by D.C. Somerwell (Oxford University Press: N.Y., 1949), p. 207.

8 H. Brown, *The Challenge of Man's Future* (Viking Press: N.Y., 1954), pp. 264. See also his more recent book, *The Human Future Revisited* (Norton: New York, 1978).

9 See, for example, Lewis Mumford, *The Transformation of Man* (Collier Books: N.Y., 1956), p. 180; P. Drucker, *Landmarks of Tomorrow* (Harper Colophon Books: N.Y., 1959), pp. 246; McNeill, 1965: pp. 867–78; K. Boulding, "The Place of the Image in the Dynamics of Society," in G. K. Zollschan and W. Hirsch (eds), *Explorations in Social Change* (Houghton Mifflin: Boston, 1964), p. 347.

10 Julian Steward, *Theory of Culture Change* (University of Illinois Press: Urbana, Ill., 1955), p. 44.

11 A. L. Kroeber, "The Ancient Oikoumene as a Historic Culture Aggregate," *Journal of the Royal Anthropological Institute*, vol. 75 (1964), pp. 9–20.

12 G. H. Hewes, "The Ecumene as a Civilizational Multiplier System," *Kroeber Anthropological Society Papers*, vol. 25 (Fall, 1965), pp. 74–75.

13 Hewes, 1965: pp. 74–5, 103.

14 Hewes, 1965: p. 81.

15 E. Durkheim, *The Rules of Sociological Method*, 8th edn, trans. by S. A. Solovay and J. H. Mueller (The Free Press: N.Y., 1964), pp. 117–18. Originally published in French in 1895.

16 John and Ruth Useem, "Interfaces of a Binational Third-Culture: A Study of the American Community in India," *The Journal of Social Issues*, vol. 23 (January, 1967), p. 130.

17 S. A. Lakoff, "The Third-Culture of Science: Science in Social Thought," pp. 1–61 in S. A. Lakoff (ed.), *Knowledge and Power* (The Free Press: N.Y., 1966).

18 B. W. Aginsky, "Lateralization Among American Indians," mimeographed, 1958, p. 5.

19 Aginsky, 1958: p. 13.

20 K. Boulding, "The Emerging Superculture," pp. 336–50 in K. Baier and N. Rescher (eds), *Values and the Future* (The Free Press: N.Y., 1969).

21 The following discussion draws on S. P. Restivo and C. K. Vanderpool, "The Third-Culture of Science," pp. 461–73 in S. P. Restivo and C. K. Vanderpool (eds), *Comparative Studies in Science and Society* (Charles E. Merrill: Columbus, Ohio, 1974). Most of the references which appear in the original text have been deleted, but the major references consulted in preparing the sections on pre-institutionalized and institutionalized third-culture science are reproduced here: W. F. Albright, *From the Stone Age to Christianity* (Doubleday-Anchor: N.Y., 1957); A. S. Altekar, *Education in Ancient India* (Kishore: Benares, 1948); G. Basalla, W. Coleman, and R. Karger (eds), *Victorian Science* (Doubleday-Anchor: N.Y., 1970); S. Dedyer, " 'Early' Migration," pp. 9–28 in W. Adams (ed.), *The Brain Drain* (Macmillan: N.Y., 1968); H. S. Galt, *A History of Chinese Educational Institutions*, vol. I (Probsthaim: London, 1951); T. Haarhof, *Schools of Gaul* (Oxford University Press: London, 1920); W. Martin, *The Lore of Cathay* (F. H. Revell; N.Y., 1901); R. K. Moskerji, *Ancient Indian Education* (Macmillan: London, 1947); J. Needham, *Science and International Relations* (Blackwell Scientific Publications: Oxford, 1949).

22 J. Ravetz, *Scientific Knowledge and its Social Problems* (Clarendon Press: Oxford, 1971), pp. 408–9.

23 Ravetz, 1971: pp. 422–36.

24 M. N. Srinivas and Andre Beteille, "Networks in Indian Social Structure," *Man* (November-December, 1964), p. 166.

25 B. W. Aginsky (ed.), *A Methodology for the Comparative Study of Population, Culture, Language* (Institute for World Understanding of Peoples, Cultures and Languages: LaJolla, Calif., 1966), pp. 1–18.

26 J. Singh, *Great Ideas in Information Theory, Language, and Cybernetics* (Dover Press: N.Y., 1966), p. 55.

27 R. Falk, *A Study of Future Worlds* (The Free Press: N.Y., 1975), p. 11.

28   Falk, 1975: p. 13; further references for this section are pp. 23–31, 278–83, and 494.
29   R. A. Goldwin (ed.), *How Democratic is America?* (Rand McNally: Chicago, 1971).
30   M. D. Sahlins and Elmer Service (eds), *Evolution and Culture* (University of Michigan Press: Ann Arbor, 1960), pp. 109–10.
31   T. Roszak, *Where the Wasteland Ends* (Doubleday-Anchor: New York, 1972).
32   For interpretations of these events that reflect a critical sociological perspective, see the contributions of E. P. Thompson, Daniel Singer, and Noam Chomsky on "The Revolution of 1989: What it Means," *The Nation* 250: 4 (January 29, 1990), pp. 117–33.

Bibliographical Epilogue

A number of works have come to my attention too late to be incorporated or mentioned in my text or notes, and some that I did not cite for other reasons. They may help to clarify, support, advance, or provide a critical grounding for the point of view I defend. My first concern is that because of the enormous influence sociological thinking has had on my view of myself, others, and the world, I may have overlooked or not made explicit enough the extent to which the very idea of sociology, like the idea of science, embodies the prejudices (including masculine biases) of modern Western culture. I therefore want to encourage readers to explore some of the recent feminist literature on sociology and on science.

R. A. Sydie's *Natural Women/Cultured Men* (Methuen: London, 1987) illustrates the extent to which the founders of mainstream sociology took for granted a sexual dichotomy between "natural" women and "cultured," "rational" men. Sydie focuses on how this dichotomy and the hierarchy of sex relations provide the foundation for classical sociological theory. She does not dismiss classical theory; but she argues that it has been Marx, Engels, and Freud rather than Weber and Durkheim who have been important for feminist critique and theory. The reason is that the works of the former theorists are more clearly prescriptive. For a more advanced discussion of and antidote to the silence of women in sociological discourse, see Dorothy Smith, *The Everyday World as Problematic: A Feminist Sociology* (Northeastern University Press: Boston, 1987). Smith echoes, it seems to me, Harriet Martineau's call for a sociology that starts from the standpoint of women, but without the burden of Martineau's Comtean positivism. Marxism plays a key role in Smith's analysis as the only viable basis for an ontology grounded in the everyday activities of real human beings.

At the same time, she argues, the standpoint of women can anchor Marxism as a method of thinking and inquiry.

The feminist critique and understanding of modern science as a masculine project has produced an enormous literature in the past decade. See, for example, Carolyn Merchant, *The Death of Nature* (Harper and Row: New York, 1980), Evelyn Fox Keller, *Reflections on Gender and Science* (Yale University Press: New Haven, 1985), and the essays by Elizabeth Fee, including "Women's Nature and Scientific Objectivity," pp. 9–27 in Marian Lowe and Ruth Hubbard (eds), *Women's Nature* (Pergamon Press: New York, 1983). Other recent critical discussions of modern science include Stanley Aronowitz, *Science as Power* (University of Minnesota Press: Minneapolis, 1988), and Ashis Nandy (ed.), *Science, Hegemony, & Violence* (Oxford University Press: Delhi, 1988). I also recommend Sharon Traweek's *Beamtimes and Lifetimes: The World of High Energy Physicists* (Harvard University Press: Cambridge, MA: 1988). This is the most detailed and extensive ethnography/anthropology of science published so far, and includes interesting material on gendered science.

Chapter 5 on the self and chapter 8 on mathematics introduce some of the conceptual resources needed for developing a sociological theory of mind and consciousness. It will, I think, eventually turn out that consciousness as something localized in the individual is an illusion, and consciousness is grounded in a more profound way than we can appreciate at this time in social relationships. See the interesting paper by Randall Collins, "Toward a Neo-Meadian Sociology of Mind," *Symbolic Interaction* 12: 1 (1989), pp. 1–32. A sociology of mind and consciousness is a necessary precondition for resolving the continuing debates about artificial intelligence. These debates are hampered by impoverished views of culture, language, and social relations, especially in terms of how they bear on our understanding of the nature of thinking. On the other hand, the debates are also hampered by oversimplified views of what computers are capable of and sociologically naive views of computers as asocial or nonsocial constructions. Obviously, a sociology of mind would also contribute to resolving the perennial mind-body problem.

A more advanced discussion of love and evolution (chapter 6) would be carried out in terms of a theory of erotics. The relevant literature is a growth industry at this time. But readers might find Jessica Benjamin's *The Bonds of Love: Psychoanalysis, Feminism and the Problem of Domination* (Pantheon: New York, 1988) of special interest. Benjamin argues that the "splitting" and gendered opposition characteristic of patriarchal society is not inevitable. Her argument for an alternative way of becoming human is grounded in the assumption that the personal and the social are interconnected. See also John Schumacher, *Human Posture: The Nature of Inquiry* (SUNY Press: New York, 1989), for a profound interpretation of social life. My discussions with Schumacher helped me to recognize that the triad rather than the dyad might be the fundamental unit of sociological analysis. Language and communication may be impossible without the role of the third person.

Some caution is required in thinking about the theme of sociocultural evolution that runs throughout this book. The continuing study of evolution has shown that it is a complex interplay of forces, a process of turns and twists, growth and decay, development and extinction. The writings of Stephen Jay Gould are a good source of up-to-date critical thinking about evolution, and about the pitfalls of drawing analogies between biological evolution and sociocultural history. See, for example, his *Ever Since Darwin* (Norton: New York, 1977), and *The Mismeasure of Man* (Norton: New York, 1981).

Two intriguing books by Alfred W. Crosby, Jr. add an interesting dimension to the global sociology I outline in chapter 9: *The Columbian Exchange: Biological and Cultural Consequences of 1492* (Greenwood: Westport, CT 1972), and *Ecological Imperialism: The Biological Expansion of Europe 900–1900* (Cambridge University Press: Cambridge, 1986). In the first book, Crosby shows the disruptive impact of the post-Columbus exchange of native life forms on the global ecosystem. In the second book, the same general thesis appears in the form of an ecological explanation for European conquests in the Americas.

For a general introduction to the sociology of mathematics, see the early chapters of Part II of my *The Social Relations of Physics, Mysticism, and Mathematics* (D. Reidel: Dordrecht, 1983; Pallas paperback, 1985). On the sociology of science in general see R. K. Merton, *The Sociology of Science* (University of Chicago Press: Chicago, 1973) for the traditional paradigm; and for an overview of developments in the past two decades, see Michael Mulkay, *Science and the Sociology of Knowledge* (George Allen and Unwin: London, 1979), and D. Chubin and E. Chu (eds), *Science Off the Pedestal: Social Perspectives on Science and Technology* (Wadsworth: Belmont, CA 1989). For more advanced essays, see S. L. Goldman (ed.), *Science, Technology, and Social Progress* (Lehigh University Press: Bethelem, PA 1989).

Finally, I have over the course of my career found one writer especially important in curbing any tendencies I might have to exaggerate the importance and the claims of sociology and of inquiry in general, even though he is somewhat naive sociologically and in important ways a conservative defender of the science many scholars think of him as criticizing outrageously: Paul Feyerabend. See *Farewell to Reason* (Verso: London, 1987), *Science in a Free Society* (Verso: London, 1978), and the classic *Against Method: Outline of an Anarchistic Theory of Knowledge* (Verso: London, 1978).

Index

134–5, 137–8, 141, 189; genital 131;
intercourse 140; and law 140;
marketplace for 127; and power 140;
as a social construction 139–40
sexually transmitted diseases 131
shame 105
Shapiro, J. 71
Simmel, G. 39–42, 57
Sivin, N. 72
skepticism 68
Snow, C. P. 181
social action, Weberian concept of 36
social change 52, 66, 79–80, 86, 101,
105, 131, 138, 149, 192; and closure
168; laws of 180; in mathematics
171–2; and open systems theory
169; in science 185
social classes 49, 52, 154, 163, 170,
178, 192
social conflict 49, 64, 85, 89, 92, 102,
153, 190
social contract 19
social control 191
social facts 31–3
social interaction 105
social isolation 106
social learning, metaphor 86;
principles of 88
social movements 132
social networks 182; and social sets
183–5
social organization 83, 89, 92, 102,
129, 132–4, 138, 141, 151–2, 155,
163, 167–9, 183–6, 190; caucus 185;
international seminar 185; among
vertebrates 133
social problems 65, 95, 171
social processes 89
social relationships 42, 100, 106, 114,
135, 171; Weberian concept of 36
social responsibility 70; in science 183
social role 33, 89, 105, 155–6; of
mathematician 171; of scientist
184

social stratification 149, 170, 184;
cultural and political 38
social structure 52, 55, 63, 100, 104,
150, 163–4, 171
socialism 41, 63, 70
socialization 104
sociation 40, 132
society, as adaptive mechanism 133;
agrarian 155; bourgeois 65;
commercial 155; concept of 25;
cosmopolitan 155; high synergy
129–35; horticultural 155; increases
in scale of 177; low synergy 129;
modern 130–1, 137; as organism 44;
systemic contradictions 81; theory
of 91
sociobiology 136
sociocultural change 99, 102
sociocultural evolution 87, 92, 94, 132;
theory of 90
sociocultural potential 94
sociocultural system 83, 93, 95, 133,
137–8, 162, 177, 180–1
sociologism 29, 33–4
sociology: Black 66; bourgeois 63,
conflict theories 15; definitions of
57–9; folk 169; humanistic 73;
Marxist 64–5; radical 62–3, 66–7,
73; reflexive 66–7, 69; socialist 65;
varieties of 57
sociology of knowledge *see*
knowledge
sociology of science *see* science
sociology of religion 5
Socrates 119, 131; and Diotima of
Mantinea 118–19
Sorokin, P. 131, 138
soul 99, 103
specialization 163, 167–9
speech 161
Spencer, H. 43–6
Spender, D. 23
Spengler, O. 157, 165–6; on
mathematics 2